The Philosophy of Improvisation

Gary Peters

The University of Chicago Press :: Chicago and London

Gary Peters is chair of critical and cultural theory at York St. John University and the author of *Irony and Singularity: Aesthetic Education from Kant to Levinas*.

The University of Chicago Press, Chicago 60637
The University of Chicago Press, Ltd., London
© 2009 by The University of Chicago
All rights reserved. Published 2009
Printed in the United States of America

18 17 16 15 14 13 12 11 10 09   1 2 3 4 5

ISBN-13: 978-0-226-66278-7 (cloth)

ISBN-10: 0-226-66278-0 (cloth)

Library of Congress Cataloging-in-Publication Data

Peters, Gary, 1952–
    The philosophy of improvisation / Gary Peters.
       p. cm.
    Includes bibliographical references and index.
    ISBN-13: 978-0-226-66278-7 (cloth : alk. paper)
    ISBN-10: 0-226-66278-0 (cloth : alk. paper)
       1. Improvisation (Music) 2. Music—Philosophy and aesthetics. I. Title.
ML3877.P47 2009
781.3'6—dc22

                                                    2008033642

Contents

Acknowledgments

As an improvisor my natural inclination is to try something
else if things don't seem to be working. And if that something else fails, then to give up altogether and start again.
Left to my own devices, then, this book would never have
found its way into print. So, first and foremost I must express
my gratitude to Elizabeth Branch Dyson for the support, encouragement, advice, and faith in the project throughout,
without which I would have undoubtedly have given up
long ago. May I also thank her colleague Emilie Sandoz and
freelancer John Raymond for their helpfulness and profes-
sionalism during the preparation of the manuscript.

During the writing of the book I carried with me, as
silent but constant companions, many of my old friends
with whom I improvised way back in the '70s and '80s.
I know they don't need a "philosophy of improvisation"
to help them along (well, that's what they think!), but I
would like to thank them, belatedly, for opening up a new
world to me. So, thanks to Veryan Weston, Simon Picard,
Dan Brown, Cliff Venner, Dave Storey, and Lol Coxhill.

Being an improvisor within an academic institution is
not, perhaps, the most sensible career path, but I think the
students have enjoyed it over the years and their response
to my teaching has often sustained me when little else did,
so thanks are due to all who have responded so positively
to my efforts.

Among my colleagues and friends, it is Mary Modeen and Iain Biggs who have offered me invaluable encouragement as well as opportunities to develop and propagate my work in interesting and unexpected ways: thanks.

As always, I must mention Greg Bright, whose very careful reading of an early draft of the text coupled with his usual rigorous critique helped me enormously in developing my ideas and finding a better way of articulating them. No doubt his dismay at my punctuation is shared by all at the University of Chicago Press!

I would like to dedicate this book to my wife, Fiona, and to my children, Isabelle and Francis, in the knowledge that children are not in the least bit impressed by an improvising father—they prefer things to work!

Gary Peters
Bristol, UK

Introduction: The Sense of a Beginning

Improvisation has always already happened. The decisiveness of a beginning, the marking of an unmarked space, always comes after a multitude of false starts, erasures, and abortive attempts to get things going: this book being no exception. Such an invisible or silent process of fixing and unfixing *prior* to the fixity (and fixation) of the work is essentially improvisatory, thus introducing into the apparent solidity of the work a contingency that can either be ignored or acknowledged, concealed or unconcealed.

Much of what follows is situated on this edge between the absence and the presence of the work, not, it should be emphasized, in order to take up residence in the *now*, the "being in the moment" so celebrated by improvisors, but as a way of bringing into view the prehistory of the work, thought in terms of its origin and the aesthetic process of origination. Inevitably this results in a certain emphasis being placed upon the old rather than the new, something of a departure for a book on improvisation, but this should not be misunderstood. Perhaps above all else the overriding ambition here is to demonstrate the deep-rooted entwinement and entanglement of the old and the new, which is often obscured by the desires and claims of improvisors themselves, heirs to a modernist aesthetic (or ideology) of innovation and novelty that is often at odds with the real predicament of the artist at work.

The initial chapter is of an introductory nature, an initial sketch that is mainly occupied with identifying some of the central themes to be addressed throughout the book. Chief among these is the dialectic (Walter Benjamin) or co-presence (Martin Heidegger) of preservation and destruction regarding the past understood as tradition. The importance of this for the discussion as a whole cannot be overestimated, not least because the entwinement of preservation and destruction invites us to make a transition from a closed conception of the past to one that rethinks it as an endlessly ongoing event or occurrence whereby tradition is re-originated (Benjamin) or re-opened (Heidegger). Using, somewhat lightheartedly, the genre of scrap yard game shows for illustrative purposes, the objective at the outset is to begin the consideration of a rather different model of improvisation, one that is not intended to counter so much as augment the existing accounts of improvisation that privilege the new. In particular, it is the manner in which such games demand a form of improvisation from the competing teams—within the strictly delimited material universe of the scrap yard—that brings into view the productive interpenetration of origination and re-novation as the new and the old are engaged with simultaneously. In a sense the *Angelus Novus* of Benjamin's famous vision of Paul Klee's painting of that name—facing backwards into the future—hovers above and is ever present in the tragic predicament of the improvisor as described throughout this book.

The discussion proper begins in chapter 2 with an extended account of free-improvisation. Presented and promoted throughout as an exemplary form, free-improvisation is approached via two different but interlinked conceptual routes: freedom and origin (the beginning). In the first instance the task is to liberate the concept of freedom from the discourses of emancipation that have been dominant since Schiller and his positing of a "play-drive." Instead of situating freedom in a future yet to be attained, the discussion follows Immanuel Kant in tracing the origin of freedom to the *prior* play of the cognitive faculties, a sense common to all (*sensus communis*) and one that the artwork helps us *remember*. This strategy is crucial because it allows for a rethinking of freedom in terms of memory rather than hope while also introducing into the past a freedom that, once remembered, must be preserved in the artwork. In other words, the prioritization of the past is able to be conceived in conservationist rather than conservative terms: the conservation of freedom understood as the infinite opening of the artwork.

It is by thinking freedom as the *beginning* rather than the end of the artwork that the link between freedom and origination is established. Thought in this light, free-improvisation is no longer presented as a radically autonomous art, outstripping the past and the present in transcendent acts of innovation pure and immaculate, but as a predicament within which the artist performer is saddled with the "tragic" task of preserving the beginning of art without destroying the freedom of this origin through the creation of an artwork conceived as an *end*.

As a consequence of the above relocation of freedom and the subsequent reorientation of free-improvisation a number of key assumptions evident in much of the literature are brought forward for reassessment. Chief among these is the (universally celebrated) role of dialogue and empathy within improvisatory practice, both of which form an important part of the humanistic politico-ethical *Weltanshauung* that figures so large here. By shifting attention away from the communicative communion that can emerge within the now of an improvised performance toward instead the silent (or silenced) origin of the artwork outside of or "alongside" (Franz Rosenzweig) the intersubjective world, the emphasis throughout is on mounting a resistance to all dialogics that would reduce improvisation to a glorified love-in dressed up as art. In short, the fundamental relationship is here understood to be between improvisor and improvisation, not between improvisor and improvisor. It is such coldness that allows the figure of the ironist to play such an important role in this and subsequent chapters, not least because it is the knowingness of the ironist that exemplifies the "hyperawareness" necessary for effective improvisation to take place. And again, this is not an awareness of the other but of the inevitable situatedness of the improvisor in a work, the contingency of that work, and of the agility necessary to avoid becoming trapped in the communicative community created by it.

Where chapter 2 attempts to make a strong case for free-improvisation by claiming that it is exemplary in its enactment of the beginning of art, thus bringing into view the tragedy secreted beneath the immaculate surfaces of "finished" works, chapter 3 begins by considering a range of anti-improvisatory positions as traced across the comments of such artists and writers as Theodor Adorno, Pierre Boulez, Luciano Berio, Antonin Artaud, and others. Notwithstanding this initial move, however, the chapter is not primarily concerned with either recounting or rebutting such critical perspectives; it is, rather, more interested in integrating such antagonism into a *richer* model of improvisation, one that does greater justice to the many forms of improvisation that often go unrecognized. So when, for example, Adorno draws attention to the "pseudo-individualization" and "standardization" of jazz improvisation by contrasting it (fleetingly) to "actual improvisation" or "real improvisation," it is the affirmation of the latter rather than the negation of the former that is of interest in this discussion. Similarly, when Berio and Boulez comment (critically) on the gestural nature of improvisation, its predictability and clichéd obviousness, this too is read against the grain and incorporated into a model of improvisation that has no problem whatsoever with the cliché and the gesture once they are properly understood.

Behind the above dismissals lies what is in essence a more deeply seated critique of *re*-presentation, *re*-production, and mimesis, all of which are claimed to be transcended in the pure productivity of improvised art, a claim denied by its critics. But, as seen, the approach presented here is that, given the *a-priority* of freedom, *all* improvisation labors to represent or reproduce the memory of this originary opening of art. It is not a question of denying the representational aspect of improvisation so much as explaining in more detail the complexity of representation itself, and in particular demonstrating the productive dimension of representation and reproduction. This is attempted by bringing together Benjamin, Adorno, and, perhaps unexpectedly, Artaud as a way of drawing out the underlying representational dynamic of mimesis and the "mimetic faculty" (Benjamin). Far from being the passive rehashing of the given, here mimesis concerns the re-production not of the given but of the *transition* from the marked to the unmarked that constitutes the originary gesture of art: the imitation of a *movement* that, as Benjamin affirms, "interrupts" the given and produces difference. It is this reproductive movement, the movement of *"espacement,"* as described by Jacques Derrida, that offers up a different way of thinking improvisation. And the rationale behind including Artaud in this discussion is that, quite apart from his own critique of improvisation (a secondary issue), it is the intensity of his engagement with the "cruel" fixing of the unfixed that draws to the surface the originary movement from the unmarked to the marked space and the contingency of the fixing process. It is this consciousness of the fixing of "fixed improvisation" (Richard Wagner) that necessitates once again the introduction of irony as the mode of thought and action that is most aware of the artist's predicament.

In another attempt to save improvisation from the charge that it merely rehashes the given, chapter 4 embarks upon a reading of Heidegger, Emmanuel Levinas, Friedrich Nietzsche, and Gilles Deleuze with a view to demonstrating that what is *given* is by no means identical with what is *there*, a claim that is crucial to the conceptualization of a re-novative model of improvisation. At the heart of this discussion is the fundamental distinction made between the Levinasian *il y a* (there is) and the Heideggerian *es gibt* (it gives), with a view to showing that the *there* and the *given* are not identical but separated by the "generosity" of the latter and the *difference* the giving of the *there* produces. Thought thus, the improvisatory exigency is no longer to outstrip the dead weight of what is there but to give it again and again as if for the first time. It is this, the discovery of difference within the same by "hearkening" (Heidegger) to a certain "calling" within the *there*, that is rendered more dynamic and productive by linking it to Nietzsche's concatenation of the eternal recurrence and the will-to-power. By so doing, the giving of what is there is thought as the willing of a future that is worthy of becoming a past that returns eternally. One consequence of this regarding improvisation is that instead of "being in the moment" the creative act is here thought in terms of a willed future past—flying backwards into the future—one that draws the artist away from the presence of the dialogical other within the present toward the "essential solitude" (Maurice Blanchot) of an art practice stretched across time.

The underlying problem here for the formation of a re-novative model of improvisation is that Nietzsche famously speaks of the eternal recurrence of the *same*, whereas what is at stake here is the conceptualization of a mode of return—re-*production*—that contains difference: without which improvisation would collapse back into the same sameness of the standardized and the pseudo. In order to draw out the difference within the same, Deleuze's distinction between diversity and difference is cited in an attempt to show that the former represents the mere appearance of difference playing across an underlying sameness—pseudo-improvisation—whereas the latter describes the *same* eternally recurring willing of difference. That is to say, the *same* interruption of continuous time in the name of an origination of a future past that is always new: the same difference rather than a different sameness (diversity).

The final chapter begins by considering the nature of an ending, one that, in keeping with the thrust of the book as a whole, might also be thought of as a beginning. In the first instance this is presented in relation to the philosophical project of creating a concept of improvisation. Following Deleuze's definition of philosophy as the act of creating concepts, and also tying this to his own philosophy of becoming, creating a concept of improvisation is here understood as itself an improvisatory process that, like Deleuze's *ritornello*, both marks and produces the space or territory simultaneously. It is this sense of infinite becoming that separates a philosophy of improvisation from a theory of improvisation, which in turn leads to a further distinction being made between a philosophical *method* and a theoretical *methodology*.

Following René Descartes, as well as Blanchot's gloss on Descartes, method is here considered not as a systematic path to knowledge available to all, but as a singular mode of progressing tied, as the former expresses it, to an individual life. What is more, unlike a methodology in which rigorousness is measured against the organization of thought around a têlos that allows the fullness of this thought to fulfil itself as truth, method delays the attainment of truth through a movement that both Heidegger and Blanchot describe as erring: a rigorous error always maintaining a distance from truth and its allure.

All of the above is by way of a preliminary to the central concern of this chapter, which is to begin the task of forging not only a philosophy of improvisation but of identifying what might be described as the improvisation of philosophy: the end of this book but the beginning of another. The outlines of this are drawn here from the singular movement of Heidegger's writing with its own methods of delay, its unique performative and rhetorical agility coupled with a mode of ontological, hermeneutical, phenomenological *espacement* that exemplifies a manner of improvisation that is pursued throughout.

It would be misleading to suggest that this book manages to arrive at a concept of improvisation any more that it is able to provide a methodology for the budding improvisor. Perhaps a certain *becoming* of such a concept is in evidence, one that, hopefully, can be sensed in the movement rather than in the substance of this book. In many ways it has to be admitted that this movement is away from, if not the practice of improvisors, then certainly their apparent self-understanding of such practice as witnessed in the majority of the discourses that have emerged thus far. But, to reiterate, this is not intended as a critique of other views on the nature of improvisation but simply as the affirmation of something different. However, one consequence of this pursuit of difference (not for its own sake of course) is the difficulty in finding supporting voices that might also affirm at least some of the same ideas. Thus the "names" appealed to throughout—Kant, Friedrich Schlegel, Nietzsche, Heidegger, Rosenzweig, Adorno, Benjamin, Deleuze, Blanchot, Derrida—may not be the most obvious choice of participants in this attempt at a reconceptualization of improvisation, but their presence should not be misinterpreted. This book is not and was never intended to be a commentary on those thinkers that grace its pages: this is not a secondary text. Although there are, no doubt, many occasions in the following where a more detailed and comprehensive commentary on one particular idea or another would have satisfied the demands of the different experts and their chosen philosophers, this would have resulted in a different book, a book much more like all the other books. This book was and is intended to be different and the names appearing on the page are perhaps violated to the extent that they are forced to serve this difference; but they are also celebrated as the originary inspiration that set this work in motion.

1

Scrap Yard Challenge—Junkyard Wars

The improvisor has to be like a man walking backwards. He sees where he has been, but he pays no attention to the future.   **Keith Johnstone**

The storm irresistibly propels him into the future to which his back is turned, while the pile of debris before him grows skyward. This storm is what we call progress.   **Walter Benjamin**

: : :

There are surprisingly few books on improvisation in print and most of those available are eager at the outset to make a clear distinction between the art of the improvisor proper and that which merely passes as improvisation in common parlance: the makeshift, the cobbled together, the temporary solutions to problems that remain unsolved. As the British composer, performer, and writer Neil Sorrell expresses it:

> The word [improvisation] itself poses all kinds of problems, not only because of its extensive and vague applications to music, but also because of its usage in everyday speech, conveying something that is insufficiently prepared and of no lasting value (for example "an improvised shelter").[1]

The desire to legitimate improvisation in the face of a perceived derogation that would reduce it to little more than a form of tinkering is understandable but unfortunate in that it too often results in celebratory accounts that overlook or obscure the real situation of the improvisor and the ontological significance of improvisation. An emphasis on the power rather than the predicament of the improvisor, the dynamics of creative strategy rather than the problematics of a specific (often brute) aesthetic situation, leaves its mark on the literature as a vibrant positivity that is as infectious as it is partial. One of the aims of this book will be to offer an account of improvisation that, while positive, returns it to its originary and originating predicament.

At the time of writing it is precisely the pejorative overtones associated with improvisation that are entertaining television audiences across the United States and the United Kingdom thanks to a spate of programs that rely on the construction of given predicaments that specifically demand the improvisatory skills of muddling through, quick fixes, and make-do solutions. A number of these programs are set in scrap yards where contestants (competing teams) are required to produce, within a set time limit and using only materials found on location, such things as working submarines, off-road vehicles, self-propelling railway carriages, deadly weapons, instruments of torture, and other useful household items.[2] Amusing though the results often are it is the improvisatory process itself, the chronicling of a series of decisions, insights, confusions, successes, and failures that is so engaging. Such programs have none of the elevated inspiration so often associated with improvisation as promoted within legitimate and legitimating cultural practices; on the contrary, they are crude and messy, they speak of fallibility, error and erring, and triumphs that are fragile, temporary, and often dubious. In fact, everything that is human-all-too-human—hence the ratings! But on a more serious note, the antics of such media scrap improvisers should not blind us to the fact that some fundamental principles of creative practice are here in evidence, principles that do not always sit comfortably with the blithe voluntarism so often on display in the discourses spun around fully fledged improvisatory art.

The Demands of the Work

To begin with, consideration might first be given to the manner in which scrap yard improvisation gains its urgency not from the dynamism of collective autonomy but, on the contrary, through the founding principles of demand and delimitation: the heteronomous. The demand is for a work, produced within a restricted time frame, within a delimited productive space with delimited resources. Whether thought inside or outside of the fabricated televisual spectacle, the demand for a work is in truth the demand *of* the work, both the material demands of a work that carries within itself the history of its own developing resources, and the demands of the work to *be* a work, to become itself once it is under way.

In common with our television contestants, all improvisers must face the demand for a work from within the confines of a limited material universe. Although it is true that the scrap yard imposes an absolute material limit (crashed and rotting cars, for example), one that is, no doubt, necessary for the desired audience engagement, our main concern will be with what Adorno calls the "inherent tendency" of aesthetic material. Here it is not a question of the availability or not of actual technical resources so much as the inherent *possibilities* of material at any particular historical moment as part of an inherent temporal unfolding that is largely unresponsive to the whims of the individual subject. It is not a question of how much material the improviser has available but in what ways all material contains, sedimented within it, historical patterns of human engagement and creativity that impose limits on what can and cannot be done on the occasion of the material's subsequent reworking, whether improvised or not. It is this intertwining of matter and creativity, thought as the historical objectivization of subjective spirit in artworks, that sensitizes Adorno to the complex interplay of autonomy and heteronomy within aesthetic practice and, thus, to the predicament of the artist in his or her struggle with the work: to its demand.

> The demands made upon the subject by the material are conditioned much more by the fact that the "material" is itself the crystallization of the creative impulse, an element socially predetermined through the consciousness of man. As a previous subjectivity—now forgetful of itself—such an objectified impulse of the material has its own kinetic laws. That which seems to be the mere self-locomotion of the material is of the same origin as the social process, by whose traces it is continually permeated.[3]

The price paid for such insight however is, in the case of Adorno, a deep-rooted antagonism to any aesthetic models, including improvisatory models such as those to be found in jazz, which rest upon naïve conceptions of subjective autonomy. Interestingly though, it is precisely Adorno's insistence on the material demands of the work that allows him to dialectically demonstrate the very conditions for the "disobedience," "independence," and "spontaneity" that are necessary for any improvisation worthy of the name. Needless to say, Adorno can only think this through an analysis of the rigors of composition, but the principle remains that this same dialectic can be identified within what will be called a re-novative model of improvisation:

> But at this point the picture of the composer is transformed. He loses that freedom on a grand scale which idealist aesthetics is accustomed to grant the artist. He is no longer a creator. It is not that the times and society impose external restrictions upon him; it is rather the rigid demand for compositional accuracy made upon him by his structure which limits him. . . . [W]ith every measure technique as a whole demands of him that he do it justice and that he give the single correct answer permitted by a technique at any given moment. . . . His efforts find fulfilment in the execution of that which his music objectively demands of him. But such obedience demands of the composer all possible disobedience, independence and spontaneity. This is the dialectical nature revealed in the unfolding of musical material.[4]

To introduce here the vocabulary to be used later, one might say that while everything is *there* for the artist as brute matter, it is the "crystallization" of "previous subjectivity" that transforms matter into aesthetic material, thus allowing specific and delimited patterns or structures of human endeavour to be *given* at any one time. In short, the *there* and the *given* are not identical but, rather, a shifting dialectical or differential relation (depending on your philosophical loyalties) that, precisely because of its interminable mobility, demands both obedience and disobedience to ensure one never collapses into the other (the *there* into the *given*): the death of improvisation.

Marking the Unmarked

Turning now to the work's becoming or emergence, the initiation of a work requires the marking of an unmarked space,[5] although it is important to recognize that the marked and the unmarked are qualitatively different. The absence of art (the unmarked) does not demand art whereas the presence of art (the mark) demands a continuation that is governed by the available mark-making resources, thought both materially and as a history of mimetic patterns. What will be at issue throughout the following is not only the *manner* in which the artwork demands to be worked within its material or mimetic possibilities but also the prior emergence of the artist and the work within what Heidegger describes as the "lighted realm" of art itself.[6] Here the demand of the artwork on the artist is, in truth, the demand of art that must itself be answerable to the demands of Being as that which must be unconcealed. Heidegger famously describes this conjunction as follows:

> On the usual view, the work arises out of and by means of the activity of the artist. But by what and whence is the artist what he is? By the work; for to say that the work does credit to the master means that it is the work that first lets the artist emerge as a master of his art. The artist is the origin of the work. The work is the origin of the artist. Neither is without the other. Nevertheless, neither is the sole support of the other. In themselves and in their interrelations artist and work *are* each of them by virtue of a third thing which is prior to both, namely that which also gives artist and work of art their names—art.[7]

In spite of the "thingly" nature of the work of art, insisted upon throughout Heidegger's essay, in his hands such a notion has little if anything to do with materiality as understood by Adorno. The artwork as thing is only significant for Heidegger to the extent that it points toward thingness itself, something prior to both artworks and things in general. His real concern as far as art is concerned is to identify a means of tracing the emergence of beings out of Being, figured here as the triangulation of artist, artwork, and art. For our purposes it is this, the mutual support of art, artwork, and artist, understood in the first instance existentially rather than ontologically, that will enjoy primacy in this discussion as it relates to the construction of the more inclusive model of improvisation intended here. Placing on one side, then, the more essential question of Being, the issue to be addressed initially must be the more straightforward existential demands of the artwork on the specific existential acts and experiences of the improviser.

The marking of a space—the tumbling contact of dancing bodies, a cluster of notes, the figuration of a page or a canvas—sets in train a movement, an emergence or occurrence that, while producing an artwork, is also the originary and originating gesture of the artist too. To repeat: "The artist is the origin of the work. The work is the origin of the artist." Thought thus, the demand of the artwork above and beyond the legislation of its materiality to simply *be* an artwork cannot be separated from the analogous task for the artist to *be* an artist. This, the existential interdependence of the artist and the artwork, ensures that the marking of an unmarked space is not a singular, momentary act but the initiation of a process that ties the artist not to this or that work, each with their own beginnings and endings, but to the *working* of the work that produces both the artwork and the artist.

Recognition

This way of thinking echoes Georg Wilhelm Friedrich Hegel's aesthetics where art is conceived as one subsidiary but necessary stage of Spirit's self-actualization. Traced through what he calls its symbolic, classical, and romantic forms, his central concern is with the dialectic of "recognition" that is played out within the aesthetic realm as witnessed in the shifting interrelationship between meaning and configuration. It is from within this phenomenological predicament that the artist emerges, dependent upon configured meaning as the aesthetic road to self-recognition:

> Man brings before himself by practical activity, since he has the impulse, in whatever is directly given to him externally, to produce himself and therein equally to recognize himself. . . . The universal need for art . . . is man's rational need to lift the inner and outer world into his spiritual consciousness as an object in which he recognizes again his own self.[8]

The value of this conception of art is that, in shifting the emphasis away from the prevailing (then and now) reception aesthetics of subjective taste, it foregrounds not only the all-important but largely ignored productive dimension of art (ultimately thought, by Hegel, as the production of Spirit) but it also helps explain the aesthetic demand that concerns us here. The demand of the work to become itself, to persist, to attain completion, is here understood as a demand made in conjunction with the artist who similarly strives for continuation and completion. In other words, the marking of an unmarked space sets in train a dialectic of "recognition" that introduces into art practice an urgency that has nothing to do with either questions of aesthetic taste or, indeed, expressivity in spite of its rise to prominence in post-Hegelian aesthetics. Art does not express the self, it meaningfully configures it. Where autonomy aesthetics (popular among improvisors) has a tendency to *assume* the self that, within the aesthetic realm at least, is free to act, both the Hegelian and the Heideggerian models understand art as a situation, a predicament, a "clearing," within which the self approaches itself from out of the darkness of misrecognition into the "lighted space" of recognition. This understanding of art refuses Kant's injunction that art be purposeless and disinterested, recognizing instead that, at the point of production, the purposiveness of art is not without purpose, the purpose being its own becoming as a work. Similarly, the artist cannot remain disinterested in a work that meaningfully configures the very subjectivity that is sought and "recognized" in that which emerges. From the point of view of the producer all art is self-interested, that is to say, the interest of the self to be a self.

The Open

Within Hegel's world-historical phenomenology aesthetic self-recognition is achieved, thus constituting one moment of Spirit's self-actualization: self-conscious externality. This, however, results in a death sentence being passed on art as the self-substantiation of Spirit moves on from the aesthetic into the philosophical and religious, leaving art as the plaything of an ironic artistic consciousness that knowingly embraces misrecognition in the face of the philosophical demand. One encouraging sign is that the trajectory of Hegel's thought from the aesthetic to the philosophical is, on the face of it, reversed by Heidegger who famously "turns" from the philosophical to the poetic in his later work, thus very much raising the stakes regarding the role of the artist and the demands of the artwork. Instead of allowing art to be overrun by the philosophical, Heidegger proposes a model of "recognition" (to retain Hegel's terminology) that goes beyond the self without necessitating the sublation of the aesthetic. He achieves this by turning his attention away from the dialectic of meaning and configuration toward what he describes as the increasing solitude of the artwork, intended as a reminder that the emergence of the artist and the artwork has less significance as an identity-bestowing relation than it does as a break with the human and the opening of Being. The creation of the work and the simultaneous self-creation of the artist here give way to what Heidegger describes as the "thrust" of the work into the inhuman solitude of the "Open," a movement that returns us to our initial concern with the interest or demand of the work to *be*:

> The more essentially this thrust comes into the Open, the stronger and more solitary the work becomes. In the bringing forth of the work there lies the offering "that it be." . . . The more solitarily the work, fixed in the figure, stands on its own and the more cleanly it seems to cut all ties to human beings, the more simply does the thrust come into the Open that such a work *is*.[9]

This passage is a useful reminder that the co-origination of the artist and the artwork, while bringing a degree of existential urgency to art practice, is nevertheless ontologically secondary to the recognition that prior to what Heidegger calls the "createdness" of the artwork there is art which, to recall, gives both the artist and the artwork their names. There are then two different demands that play upon the artist and, as will be emphasized throughout, both have an impact on improvisatory practice. The essential issue here concerns the relationship between and the interpenetration of creation and preservation, the latter bringing us back to the scrap yard.

The scrap yard challenge for the improvisor is to create something new within the decaying site of the old. The demand of the work, forever playing upon the improvisor, concerns not only the self-creation of the artist and the artwork but also what Heidegger describes as the "self transcendence which exposes itself to the openness of beings as it is set into the work."[10] Once again it is the "Open" that is the primary concern here, or more precisely the relationship between an existential openness of beings and an ontological openness of Being where the former is necessary for the preservation of the latter. As he makes clear, Heidegger has no interest in the "sphere of familiarity and connoisseurship" where preservation "no longer reach[es] the work's own being, but only a recollection of it."[11] It is not the thing but the "Open" that demands preservation, and it is only by "standing-within" and willing the openness of the work that this can be achieved:

> Preserving the work means: standing within the openness of beings that happens in the work. This "standing-within" of preservation, however, is a knowing. Yet knowing does not consist in mere information and notions about something. He, who truly knows what is, knows what he wills to do in the midst of what is.[12]

Improvisors pride themselves on their openness to the other: this is at the heart of the collaborative practices that dominate the improvisatory field, particularly in music, dance, and theater. But the humanity of one being opening him- or herself to another within an aesthetic space created by improvisation only touches upon one aspect of the work of the artwork: its createdness. But our scrap yard improvisors are doing something different. Certainly, there is collaboration (they are in teams) but the human interaction that provides the dramatic tension necessary in the world of entertainment should not be allowed to obscure the fact that it is the knowledge and will of the individual participants "in the midst of what is" and their preparedness to use this will to preserve the openness of the wreckage that is piled up before them that ultimately determines the success or failure of the improvised response to their predicament. It is not so much working together to make something new out of the old but, rather, the more solitary act of "standing-within" the old, occupying it in such a way that its own opening onto being or "thrust into the Open" is preserved. If there is a collaborative dimension to improvisation it is not empathic but closer to what Heidegger describes as the "*unsociability*" of "Being-with."[13] This should remind us again of the antihumanism of Heidegger's thought and his intention to strip the artwork of its human-all-too-human accoutrements and the intersubjective social relations that feed on these. Instead we find him in pursuit of a relation or "affiliation" that is collaborative but not intersubjective, human but not humanistic, closer than might have been expected to Adorno's conception of materiality as the objectivized impulse of man "now forgetful of itself." Heidegger writes:

> Preserving the work does not reduce people to their private experiences, but brings them into affiliation with the truth happening in the work. Thus it grounds being for and with one another as the historical standing-out of human existence in reference to unconcealedness.[14]

There is also perceptible here a bridge to Adorno's friend Walter Benjamin, one that will allow us to reach the end of this chapter.

Scrap

The scrap yard challenge offers one final insight into improvisation that is easy to overlook: it concerns the nature of scrap itself. The artist, like our contestants, is thrown into a situation piled high with the discarded waste products of cultural history. These are the defunct, clapped-out, disintegrating remnants of past times on the edge of an oblivion that promise, at best, a faint but continuing resonance as nostalgia and the cliché or, at worst, as universal forgetfulness. Improvisation, in the celebratory sense, conceives of itself as transcending these outmoded structures and threadbare pathways through acts of spontaneity that inhabit the moment, the instant, the pure futurity of the "now," without history's "spirit of gravity" (Nietzsche) weighing upon the shoulders of the creative artist. Improvisation in the pejorative sense, however, is bogged right down in the mangled or decaying debris that constitutes both its temporal and spatial horizon. Success for the scrap yard improvisors does not depend upon the transcendence of or liberation from the dead weight and waste of history but, rather, on the ability to find new and novel ways of inhabiting the old and revivifying dead forms through a productive process of reappropriation that promotes improvisation more as a means of salvation and redemption than of creation: re-novation. Such a view recollects Walter Benjamin's late philosophy of history and most memorably his famous reflections on Klee's *Angelus Novus*. Too often quoted, to be sure, but here is the passage yet again:

> His face is turned towards the past. Where we perceive a chain of events, he sees one single catastrophe which keeps piling wreckage upon wreckage and hurls it in front of his feet. The angel would like to stay, awaken the dead, and make whole what has been smashed. But a storm is blowing from Paradise; it has got caught in his wings with such violence that the angel can no longer close them. The storm irresistibly propels him into the future to which his back is turned, while the pile of debris before him grows skyward. This storm is what we call progress.[15]

In this view of history it is precisely flight, transcendence, and the lure of the future that prevents the necessary engagement not only with actuality but with the potentiality of the given, forever piling up before our eyes but beyond our grasp. Just in case this is considered somewhat fanciful, the British writer and director Keith Johnstone's famously down-to-earth vision of the improvisor has much in common with this engaging image:

> The improvisor has to be like a man walking backwards. He sees where he has been, but he pays no attention to the future. His story can take him anywhere, but he must still "balance" it, and give it shape, by remembering incidents that have been shelved and reincorporating them. Very often an audience will applaud when earlier material is brought back into the story. . . . They admire the improvisor's grasp, since he not only generates new material, but remembers and makes use of earlier events that the audience itself may have forgotten.[16]

Thought in terms of our two models of improvisation perhaps it is not so absurd to think of the lowliest forms of improvisation as engaged in something not unrelated to Benjamin's own scrap yard artist, discovered in the writings of Baudelaire: the "ragpicker." Here the former quotes the latter:

> Here we have a man who has to gather the day's refuse in the capital city. Everything that the big city threw away, everything it lost, everything it despised, everything it crushed underfoot, he catalogues and collects. He collates the annals of intemperance, the stockpile of waste. He sorts things out and makes a wise choice; he collects, like a miser guarding a treasure, the refuse which will assume the shape of the useful or gratifying objects between the jaws of the goddess of industry.[17]

Here the derogation of improvisation as a base art devoid of the aesthetic nobility necessary for aesthetic production worthy of the name finds its source, but to continue to ignore what has been ignored in all books on improvisation hitherto leaves a gap in the account of improvisation that is just too large to be acceptable. One of the central aims of the current book is to at least make a start in filling in this gap, not least as an acknowledgement of the many improvisors out there who have yet to be recognized as such.

2

Freedom, Origination, and Irony

The act of engaging in free-improvisation will become a liberator, and emancipator, for many people to touch into their emotional lives in a non-verbal and non-judgmental way. We must introduce this healthy way of life.

LaDonna Smith

: : :

Discourses of emancipation are usually in a major key, positive, sometimes celebratory, even joyous, always engaged and committed, rarely if ever ironic. Such writings, however, for all their positivity, harbor within them a deep-seated negativity that should remind us of freedom's own questionable duality. One would do well to remember this—the aporia of freedom—when considering the claims made for improvisation by the improvisor. Something of an exception, the improvisor Anthony Braxton is clearly alert to the problem in the following passage:

> One of the problems with collective improvisation, as far as I'm concerned, is that people who use anarchy or collective improvisation will interpret that to mean "Now I can kill you"; and I'm saying, wait a minute. . . . So-called freedom has not helped us as a family. . . . So the notion

of freedom that was being perpetrated in the sixties might not have been the healthiest notion.[1]

This is an interesting statement coming, as it does, from an African American musician who one would have expected to identify with an aesthetic that emerged out of the civil rights movement of the 1960s.[2] To speak on behalf of a putative "family" demonstrates a continuing commitment to a collectivity, thought both politically and aesthetically, but Braxton's problematization of freedom ("so-called freedom") bespeaks a certain skepticism regarding the utopianism of much liberatory politics that suggests an awareness of the perceived dangers accompanying the always difficult transition from negative to positive freedom. As Isaiah Berlin expresses it in his *Two Concepts of Liberty*:

> "Negative liberty" . . . seems to me a truer and more humane ideal than the goals of those who seek in the great, disciplined, authoritarian structures the ideal of "positive" self mastery. . . . It is true, because it recognizes the fact that human goals are many, not all of them commensurable, and in perpetual rivalry with one another.[3]

Braxton's concerns echo these same sentiments. In common with most collective improvisors his primary concern is actualizing a series of overlapping negative freedoms, in his running through the desired freedom-from racism, intimidation, and exclusion; the freedom-from a capitalist superstructure that commercially rewards artistic conformity and obedience to rigid stylistic codes while freezing out the alterity of genuine innovation. And also, to return to Braxton's problem with "so-called freedom," the freedom-from freedom *itself*: the freedom-from the freedom-to. Berlin identifies precisely this aporia as it unfurls in the increasingly conflictual history of liberty:

> The freedom which consists in being one's own master [positive/freedom-to], and the freedom which consists in not being prevented from choosing as I do by other men [negative/freedom-from], may, on the face of it, seem concepts at no logical distance from each other—no more than negative and positive ways of saying the same thing. Yet the "positive" and "negative" notions of freedom developed in divergent directions until, in the end, they came into direct conflict with each other.[4]

As Berlin demonstrates, in essence negative freedom is a collective ideal. It protects the collective by establishing a regime of noninterference that, in breaking with "men's constant tendency to conformity," allows the individual the scope and the space for "spontaneity, originality, genius [and] mental energy,"[5] all of which figure large in the world of improvisation. Positive freedom, on the other hand, is an ideal of singularity, and it has a rather more worrying vocabulary, one inescapably intertwined with a notion of mastery that has not worn well during the modern period:

> The "positive" sense of the word "liberty" derives from the wish on the part of the individual to be his own master. I wish my life and decisions to depend on myself, not on external forces of whatever kind. I wish to be the instrument of my own . . . acts of will . . . I wish to be somebody, not nobody; a doer.[6]

Standing alongside Braxton again, the "doer" who wants to be somebody becomes the anarchist who would "kill you" as a means to this end, the master who would rather enslave you than go unrecognized as a nobody. So we end up with a situation where it is the *singularity* of the master that threatens the diversity, spontaneity, and originality seen by the vast majority as essential to improvisation, while the *collective* consciousness of the group acts as guarantor for these self-same concepts by pitting the "family" (Godfather-fashion) against its individual members. What Roger Dean, in his discussion of Braxton, sees as the latter's "ambivalence toward free-improvisation,"[7] is, in fact more than a matter of personal preference; it is, rather, a function of the conflictual history of freedom that emerges here as the complicating factor. As a consequence of this, it is not the ambivalence of Anthony Braxton or anyone else that is the issue but the ambivalence of improvisation *itself* as the aesthetic space wherein the aporia of liberty is enacted and reenacted. If freedom as perpetrated in the 1960s is not the "healthiest notion," this, perhaps, has less to do with the era and more to do with the notion. However, one could be forgiven for thinking it somewhat ironic that jazz, of all genres of improvised music, implicated as it is in a whole history of drug- and drink-related excess, should give birth to a cultural movement dominated by the desire for the realization of an "aesthetic dimension" that has liberated freedom from its own imperfection, cleaned it up and purified it, but that is exactly what has happened.

Improvisation is now a form of health, an exercise in healthy living. The cultural turn toward the spirituality of the East, the self-sufficiency of the land, the concern for peaceful coexistence with the Other "man," the concern for the ecosystem, the concern for the downtrodden and silenced, all of this has left its indelible mark on the dominant discourses of improvisation as they can be found today. Gone are all traces of the brash and virtuosic exhibitionism that excited performers and audiences alike before the 1960s, the competitiveness and one-upmanship that was everywhere in evidence, the arrogance, callousness, and cruelty that gave so much performance its edge. For the last four decades the discourses of improvisation have become increasingly submerged in a collective language of care and enabling, of dialogue and participation, a pure, aesthetically cleansed language of communal love. However, while the more strident political proclamations typical of an earlier, more "militant" time may have subsided, there remains a no less engaged but gentler activism that, rather than challenging our dominant institutions head-on, constructs instead what might be described as microcosmic aesthetic communities that live out or act out the utopian potentiality that has remained a constant since those more exuberant days, now (it would seem) past.

Although largely of historical interest only nowadays, Herbert Marcuse, writing at exactly the right moment for what might be called the first wave of militant improvisors, inspired a generation of artists and activists by tracing the radical dimension of art practice back to its own liberal bourgeois origins, that is to say to the aesthetics of Kant and Schiller, to the *Critique of Judgement* and *On the Aesthetic Education of Man*, respectively. Particularly influential was the politicization and radicalization of Schiller's notion of the "play-drive" in an attempt to integrate Marxism and psychoanalysis in *Eros and Civilization*. Regardless of the strengths and weaknesses of this book, it was the suggestion that the artwork allowed an aesthetic substantiation of political ideas *in advance of* the socioeconomic conditions for their actual realization that resonated with those in search of an agency of political change within a conformist mass society. In a "one-dimensional" culture of positivism and technological reason, of the "performance principle" and status seeking, the very purposelessness of play was seen as a slap in the face for the unsmiling means/ends bureaucrats that constituted the power elite. Passages such as the following give a flavor of the way in which German aesthetics came to American radicals of the '60s:

> The quest is for the solution of a "political" problem: the liberation of man from inhuman existential conditions. Schiller states that in order to solve the political problem, "one must pass

> through the aesthetic, since it is beauty that leads to freedom."
> The play-drive is the vehicle of this liberation. . . . These ideas
> represent one of the most advanced positions of thought. . . . the
> reality that "loses its seriousness" is the inhumane reality of want
> and need, and it loses its seriousness when wants and needs can
> be satisfied without alienated labor. Then man is free to "play"
> with his faculties and potentialities and with those of nature, and
> only by "playing" with them is he free.[8]

The charge of aestheticism that has always haunted Schillerian aesthetics
and which, no doubt, motivates Marcuse's projection of art's substance
onto a political problem yet to be solved, is perhaps of less concern to
those artists who have experienced the onset of postmodernism in the
'80s, '90s, and onwards. Perhaps the degree to which culture in general
and cultural politics in particular have become aestheticized has rendered the notion of aestheticism increasingly redundant. Be that as it
may, the real intention here is to try and direct this discussion away from
the political perspective that characterizes so many discussions of Schiller's thought back into the aesthetic: the reaestheticization of the aesthetic. The thinking behind this reorientation is the hope that, while the
continuing relevance of Schiller's particular appropriation of Kantian
aesthetics and, indeed Kant's own aesthetics might be open to debate,
they nevertheless offer some important insights into the nature of improvisation that can be pursued here.

Freedom and Play

To begin with, it might be useful to take an initial step back or backward from Schiller's notion of the "play-drive" to consider first the role
of "play" within Kant's aesthetics, one that will prove helpful in understanding better the model of collectivity informing much group improvisation. The following passage from the *Critique of Judgement* will be a
good starting point:

> The cognitive powers brought into play by this [aesthetic] rep-
> resentation are engaged in a free play, since no definite concept
> restricts them to a particular rule of cognition. Hence the mental
> state in this representation must be one of a feeling of the free
> play of the powers of representation. . . . This state of *free play*
> of the cognitive faculties attending a representation by which an
> object is given must admit of universal communication.[9]

There are a number of things here that need to be highlighted at the out-set, primarily that the conjunction of freedom and play is, for Kant, sim-ply a statement of aesthetic fact and not a political gesture. His notion of free play describes a positive rather than a negative freedom, something that distinguishes it from Schiller's "play-drive" and latter-day radical-ized versions of the same. The hallmark of the aesthetic free play is its freedom from the restrictions of determinate concepts, but play does not *free itself from* concepts, it is *prior* to them, thus so is the aesthetic. Just to make the point, section 9 of book 1 of the third *Critique* is entitled "Investigation of the question of the relative *priority* in a judgement of taste of the feeling of pleasure and the estimating of the object." The free play of the imagination and the understanding prior to the determina-tion of concepts might here be thought alongside the aforementioned use of the distinction marked/unmarked space. Free improvisors want to mark an unmarked space; their ideal is a pure virgin territory within which to commune with the other. LaDonna Smith, in her somewhat ecstatic "Improvisation as Prayer . . . ," positions herself on the edge of a virgin silence about to be shattered. She begins thus: "Beginning in si-lence, holding only an instrument, listening within, observing a point for departure into the inner world of sudden creative expression, tapping the well to draw out a first sound in musical exploration." The dramati-zation of the instant prior to making the first sound, indeed, the dramati-zation of risk and contingency as associated with the transition from the unmarked to the marked, articulates a freedom that is, in fact, doubly negative. The art of improvisation is the art of making something hap-pen and, as such, a liberation-from the absence of the work. Silence, still-ness, blankness are all valorized as originary aesthetic essences only to be cancelled by sound, movement, or figuration. The problem, however, is that once at play within the marked space, the improvisor or improvisors risk being enticed or indeed forced into the given structures of gameplay, thus posing a threat to the positive freedom desired and demanding, in turn, a liberation-from the game. Squeezed from both sides, from the unmarked and the marked respectively, free-improvisation must either compromise and fall back on certain identifiable rules of gameplay or, conversely, devise strategies that allow a vestigial productivity on the very edge of self-negation. As the saxophonist Evan Parker remembers his duo with drummer John Stevens: "The moments of interaction got shorter and shorter, you couldn't go any further than that."[10] But you can, as the British writer and improvisor David Toop reminds us in his consideration of "lowercase" improvisation:

Experiencing the work for the first time, I experienced a sense of disconnectedness. . . . Sounds tend to be brief—the kind of short, harsh, messy sound that happens when dust is brushed off the stylus of a record turntable, or a plug is inserted into an amplifier socket when the volume is turned up. These sounds don't feel aggressive, however, and in fact, references to emotional states such as aggression seem irrelevant. . . . Sometimes there are long, high tones, which introduce smoother lines into the broken impact sounds and crackles. Nothing lasts long enough to become intense, or reveal a conscious method. There is a stillness, without the progressive resolution we call development. . . . The initial impression is disconcerting, because this seems to be extreme minimalism without the ideology of Minimalism, or its self-conscious dedication to process. I can imagine it would be possible to listen to this . . . and not hear it as music, or any kind of significant event at all, other than a faint disturbance of the atmosphere.[11]

If this is free play then it is a form of play that, having liberated itself from the game, arrives at a mode of improvisation that might be better approached in Kantian terms.

Reception and Memory

Notwithstanding the extraordinarily productive dimension of his aesthetic thought,[12] Kant, in common with the majority of philosophers, speaks from the place of aesthetic reception as is evident in his concentration on, to repeat, the "free play of the cognitive faculties *attending a representation by which an object is given.*" In this form the artwork must already be in place *before* the subject of aesthetic experience and judgment can be broached. For Kant, in other words, aesthetic experience can only take place as a moment of reception within a marked space, while the issue under consideration here is the nature of a freedom conceived as a moment of production, the positive force of a beginning. What relevance then could Kant's reception aesthetics possibly have for the improvisor in that moment (if such exists) of silence or stillness prior to the marking of space? One way of answering this would be to recall that although, for Kant, the pleasure experienced during the reception of a work of art "attends" rather than produces that work, this feeling can in fact be traced back to an anteriority that, while no longer strictly aesthetic, might offer some clues as to the nature of productivity, particularly as it figures within the context of improvisation. As such, the artwork is not the origin of aesthetic pleasure but rather the manner in which we are reminded of a freedom that is prior not only to conceptual determination but to the aesthetic itself, a "memorial"[13] aesthetic as Jay Bernstein describes it when responding to passages such as the following from the *Critique of Judgement*:

> It is true we no longer notice any decided pleasure in the comprehensibility of nature. . . . Still it is certain that the pleasure appeared in due course, and only by reason of the most ordinary experience being impossible without it, has become gradually fused with simple cognition, and no longer arrests particular attention.[14]

By drawing this pleasure to the surface, the artwork does not, as with Schiller and Marcuse, signal a liberatory or liberated future yet to come but an existing (if forgotten) freedom to be affirmed—an affirmation and confirmation of the present rather than its negation. The moment of stillness prior to the initial improvisatory gesture of the work is not an aesthetic vanishing point where both absence and presence between them threaten to erase art but, rather, the space/time where a shared freedom can be recognized and reaffirmed. More than this, by grounding aesthetic pleasure in the prior attunement of our mental faculties with nature, Kant is able to claim a universality for aesthetic judgment that dramatically broadens the scope of the communicative community assumed by the domain of collective improvisation. By installing free play into the very heart of human understanding he is able to offer a model of "common sense" (*sensus communis*) that assumes rather than strives for individual liberty, albeit as an *idea* necessitating an aesthetic demand rather than (as with Schiller and Schillerians) an *ideal* fueling an aesthetic utopia. The result is an image of human intersubjectivity and communication that in some respects undoubtedly resonates well with many models of collective improvisation but which also, in its sensitivity to the counterposition of singularity and universality, raises some fundamental issues regarding the limits of communicative communication and the dialogical models that have subsequently come to dominate so many of the texts. Here is how Kant introduces the notion of a *sensus communis* into the third *Critique*:

> [Judgments of taste] must have a subjective principle, and one which determines what pleases or displeases, by means of feel-

> ing only and not through concepts, but yet with universal valid-
> ity. Such a principle, however, could only be regarded as a *com-
> mon sense*. This differs essentially from common understanding,
> which is also sometimes called common sense (*sensus commu-
> nis*): from the judgements of the latter is not one by feeling, but
> always one by concepts. . . . The judgement of taste, therefore,
> depends on our presupposing the existence of a common sense.
> (But this is not to be taken to mean some external sense, but
> the effect arising from the free play of our powers of cognition.)
> Only under the presupposition, I repeat, of such a common
> sense, are we able to lay down a judgement of taste.[15]

Thought receptively, the judgment of taste is made in the presence of a
representation that formally triggers the feeling of pleasure that is at the
root of aesthetic experience. But thought productively, is the judgment
of taste laid down before or after the marking of the unmarked space?
Or to pose the question that will be addressed throughout the next chapter: How does the artwork begin? What determines the initiating sound,
mark, or movement of an improvisation? In those performance arts particularly prone to improvisation, where the aim is to combine freedom
with irreversibility and the accompanying impossibility of correction or
erasure, these are critical questions.

   The shift from reception to production raises the issue of a felt pleasure that precedes the artwork or, put another way, is part of the prior
work of the artwork. One question that immediately arises is that if it
is the pleasure we take in the artwork that reminds us of our cognitive
freedom within the conceptually undetermined aesthetic realm, as Kant
claims, by what means can we attain an awareness of this freedom prior
to the work itself? Outside of performance art this may or may not be
such an important issue, but within the context of group improvisation
the collective acknowledgment or assumption of a prior freedom represents a crucial aspect of its self-legitimation and consequent allure as an
aesthetic strategy. Certainly, within the fraternity of collective improvisors there is what might be called an acute awareness of awareness. The
dancer Susan Leigh Foster, writing on improvisation, speaks of "a kind
of hyperawareness of the relation between immediate action and overall
shape, between that which is about to take place and that which has and
will take place."[16] For her, however, this "hyperawareness of relationali-
ties," while bound up with what she calls the "playful labor" of improvisation, is restricted to the space/time of the dance itself rather than being
directed toward the origin of the work prior to the artist and the artwork:

toward art. Foster's account assumes from the outset that the improvisor enters the "relational" space as an agent already free and ready to play, armed with an awareness that is ultrasensitive to any imminent threat to this productive freedom and its ongoing work. Such a view, however, does not pay sufficient attention to the "hyperawareness" that is necessary to both recognize and to render aesthetically productive the singular feeling of pleasure attending not the artwork but the play of the cognitive faculties and the certainty that such pleasure in play can be universally communicated, underwritten by the *sensus communis*. Moving attention to the anteriority of the work in this way is not intended to disable the aforementioned vocabulary of free-improvisation; on the contrary, it can now be redeployed more effectively and certainly with more ontological weight. The language of wholeness, dialogue, participation, sharing, oneness, community, and communion, stripped of its dubious actuality in improvisatory works, returns here to register the promise and possibility of a collective work that is rooted in the memory and potentiality of an unworked freedom. This returns the discussion to Bernstein's notion of a "memorial aesthetics," which can now be reviewed more carefully:

> Judgements of beauty are memorial: in making aesthetic judgements we judge things "as if" from the perspective of our lost common sense. . . . This "remembered" common sense is, as Kant has it throughout the third *Critique*, both presupposed in the judgement of taste and yet to be obtained. It is present by virtue of its absence. . . . Common sense is the communicability of feeling, and not the demand for such. But such a common sense does not exist, or exists only as a memory, but in so far as "we" remember it (in virtue of serious participation in aesthetic discourse and practice), judge through it, it does exist. In its existing it binds us, not as a constraint but as ties of affection (and disaffection) do.[17]

As a reading of Kant's third *Critique* and, in particular, as an alternative to the more anticipatory politicizations of the aesthetic forever cast out into the future this certainly gives pause for thought, but for all its resonance the above passage continues to make "participation in aesthetic discourse and practice" a condition of the "we" being able to feel itself emerge out of its originary source: *sensus communis*. It would seem that for Bernstein it is only *within* the marked space of the artwork and the aesthetic discourses spun around it that *common sense* comes into being as an existent absence: outside or prior to the work it is forgotten.

So the question remains: Is it possible to think beyond the memorializing continuum of existing artworks? Is it possible to imagine an aesthetic memory that is not only prior to the artwork but gives birth to it, is its *beginning*?

Reception, Production, and Mourning

Jay Bernstein speaks primarily from the point of aesthetic reception and seems less comfortable when negotiating the issue of aesthetic production. Correctly identifying Kant's discussion of genius as the place in the third *Critique* where production is foregrounded, Bernstein is both engaged but also unsettled by the "hyperbolic" claim that the work of genius, far from being "memorial," is in fact a work of forgetting that itself must be forgotten in subsequent work. Exemplary works of genius, as Kant describes them, are models of autonomous aesthetic production that can only be followed by being themselves abandoned in the name of that very autonomy. This "exaggerated severity"[18] that demands the infinite beginning of art out of nothing through the successive interruption of one genius by another results, to Bernstein, in a "frenzied autonomy"[19] that only begins to make sense within the context of the (Nietzschean) "active forgetfulness" of modernism. Kant expresses this in his far from hyperbolic style as follows:

> The product of genius . . . is an example, not for imitation (for that would mean the loss of the element of genius, which constitutes the very soul of the work), but to be followed by another genius—one whom it arouses to a sense of his own originality in putting freedom from the constraint of rules so into force in his art, that for art itself a new rule is won—which is what shows a talent to be exemplary.[20]

Bernstein grafts this onto the aesthetic discourses and practice of modernism in the following way:

> While Kant's autonomy requirement sounds utterly hyperbolic, its urging of novelty and originality coheres, with unnerving accuracy, with at least that dominant stretch of modernist art that restlessly searches after the "new."[21]

One final citation from Bernstein will allow these thoughts to arc back to the earlier discussion of "preservation":

An exemplary work begins a new movement of history, and will act as a constraining provocation to a later genius. Further, as Kant's genius-to-genius argument suggests, the audience of genius must itself respond "autonomously"; this form of response will be akin to the manner of Heideggerian preservers as opposed to connoisseurs or aesthetes.[22]

We will not on this occasion follow Bernstein back down the well-trodden path to modernism but will, instead, respond to his ideas in a manner that will allow us to take up again the question of the freedom of free-improvisation and the existential predicament of the new rather than its inscription in a received tradition of the modern. One last remark before doing so: Bernstein understands the prehistory of modernism as what he calls "the collective labour of mourning,"[23] where "we (re)experience in painful pleasure our lost common sense; [where] we mourn the death of nature and community."[24] Of interest here is the way in which this thought points back to the earlier discussion of Heidegger and Benjamin where, in Howard Caygill's reading, the catastrophe of history is staged in two ways, either as tragedy (Heidegger) or as mourning (Benjamin). At stake in this distinction is the place and the efficacy of the subject in the face of this perceived destruction and the extent to which the domain of singular human action is, can, or indeed should be the arena in which this drama of loss is played out. This is how Caygill presents the issue:

> The differences over origin and tradition extend repeatedly into the two theories of art. In Benjamin tradition is ruination—barbarism—it destroys what it hands over; yet without this destruction nothing would be handed over. The work of art is a ruin, a site of mourning where the destruction of tradition can be acknowledged. For Heidegger tradition may gather what it would hand over, deliver it into the light, and for him the work of art is a temple which presents this gathering. Heidegger celebrates tragedy as a place of witness to this handing over, while Benjamin discounts tragedy in favour of *Trauerspiel* [mourning play] as a communal lament for ruin.[25]

What draws this difference out even more clearly is the contrast between the melancholic perspective of Benjamin's communal lament and the singular suffering of the tragic artist to be found in (early) Heidegger. Caygill continues:

> By introducing the dialectical logic of subjectivity . . . [Heidegger] transforms the paradox of tradition into the agonal and tragic struggle of the subject. The resolute subject struggles with tradition in the guise of fate and destiny, and in the struggle finds freedom. . . . The struggle clears the space for a moment of decision, one in which the past and future may be gathered and granted significance in the present.[26]

As with Bernstein, Caygill's primary concern here is the continuation of Benjamin's avowed project: the "politicization of the aesthetic." And also like Bernstein he finds the promotion of a hyperbolic subjectivism deeply problematical as a politico-aesthetic response to the scrap yard of history. While he acknowledges with approval that Heidegger ultimately turns away from the reflexive subject toward the working of the work and the site of its occurrence, and while it is also interesting to note that it is precisely this removal of the subject that receives Bernstein's disapproval, they both feel able to articulate their politico-aesthetic concerns through the dark melancholia of Benjamin's mourning play, where fulfillment can only be awaited as the messianic rupturing of lived time outside of time. Caygill perfectly captures this lamentable predicament here:

> For Trauerspiel the world was empty, a place of "never-ending repetition" with no possibility of ever becoming genuine or authentic: "For those who looked deeper saw the scene of their existence as a rubbish heap of partial, inauthentic actions." The world handed down to us by tradition is uncanny, undecipherable, always other.[27]

But who makes up this community of mourners? Who laments? The suggestion throughout the above is that philosophers and artists are together engaged in the labor of mourning, that it is, to recall Bernstein's words again, "participation in aesthetic discourse and practice" that forges the links between those left grief stricken in the face of an indecipherable alterity. So the philosopher would have it, but for all its undeniable philosophical resonance is it really credible to conceive of postromantic art practice as a work of mourning when one considers the productive aesthetic action taken by artists within time as distinguished from the inert futility and resignation that locks mourning into a melancholia that, like all mourning, is therapeutic at best, a road to productivity perhaps, but never productive itself? In a telling remark Caygill admits that "when the question is asked what the new configurations of tradition might be, what shape the new gathering of the past, present and future might take, Benjamin is almost silent."[28] It is Paul Klee who paints *Angelus Novus*, not Walter Benjamin—Benjamin mourns, Klee paints. Benjamin *receives* the artwork as the inauthentic repetition of the same, Klee *produces* the artwork as the authentic repetition of difference. As far as the "gathering" of a dislocated history into the now of an aesthetic beginning is concerned, the artist speaks while the philosopher looks on in silence and despair. It is for this reason, and notwithstanding Caygill's philosophical reservations, that we will often in what follows take Heidegger's tragic vision as the point of reference on returning repeatedly to the existential predicament of the artist rather than the ontological essence of art.

By taking up again here the specific predicament of the free improvisor it is hoped that the complex of themes introduced thus far might be brought together in such a way that the existential drama of improvisation can be better understood. If, as suggested, the notion of freedom operative in free-improvisation at the level of aesthetic discourse seems to be hamstrung by both the negativity that runs through it—freedom-from—as well as the apparent inability to think freedom outside of the work where it is assumed, respected, and protected by myriad forms of "hyperawareness," this should not prevent us from trying to retrace some of our steps here in an attempt to reconnect these discourses with that which, at the level of practice, remains outside of them.

Returning to Kant, it is the free play of the cognitive faculties that grounds the *sensus communis*, the loss of which Bernstein identifies as the aesthetic "death" that gives rise to the "mourning" of modernist art. But if this were the case no art would ever be produced. In this regard, *at the level of practice* the *sensus communis* is never lost as the origin of the artwork. This is not to say, of course, that it is not lost, forgotten, destroyed during the course of the work's unfolding—it is (the tragedy)—but that is a different matter that concerns the reception of the work (by its creator or creators), not its production. If, as may be the case, an artwork is merely imitative, part of a continuum of reception without beginning or end, then it is of no interest to us here. No doubt a great deal of what passes for art is of this nature, but by no means all, a fact that should be apparent to anyone who is genuinely engaged with art practice, but which is somewhat obscured by Kant in his welding together of aesthetic production and genius. But, far from advocating a "frenzied autonomy," the model of aesthetic production proposed by Kant is not at all remote from the actuality and ingenuity of much aesthetic practice. Certainly, the idea that works of genius radically break with the continuum of cultural history, confronting us with unprecedented aesthetic acts that are both exemplary and inimitable would appear to set the bar ludicrously high, but given that, for Kant, *all* fine art requires genius, can this really be his intention? The truth is that any art worthy of the name will contain within it unwonted moments of originality, interruptions of the given and exemplary acts of ingenuity, often lodged within a mimeticism that, in reality, can by no means be crudely opposed to origination and originality. This, the "repetition of difference," is a vital dimension of all "idiomatic" improvisation, as the late avant-garde British guitarist Derek Bailey calls it, and will be discussed in due course, but at this stage it will suffice to note the active and productive dimension of imitation as noted here by Paul Ricouer in very Kantian language:

> Whether we say "imitation" or "representation" . . . what has to be understood is the mimetic activity, the active process of imitating or representing something. Imitation or representation therefore must be understood in the dynamic sense of making a representation, of a transposition into representative works.[29]

This should alert us to the highly complex relationship to be found in Kant's aesthetics between presentation and representation, production and reproduction, and, to reintroduce Heidegger, creation and preservation. Indeed, it is Heidegger who, in his attempt to ground the whole Kantian project in the productive imagination, identifies the profound interrelationship between production and reproduction or spontaneity and receptivity as he describes it here in his *Kant and the Problem of Metaphysics*:

> We must point out that spontaneity constitutes but one moment of the transcendental power of imagination and that, accordingly, while thinking indeed has a relationship with the power of the imagination, this is never indicative of a full coinciding of their essences. For the power of the imagination is also and precisely a faculty of intuition, i.e., of receptivity. And it is receptive, moreover, not just apart from its spontaneity. Rather, it is the original unity of receptivity and spontaneity.[30]

This statement will reverberate through much that will follow, but for the moment it is the introduction of the *imagination* that adds one crucial component to the Kantian framework within which we are working at the moment.

To summarize, the singular feeling of pleasure that grounds the aesthetic judgment of taste attains its universal communicability by being itself grounded in the free play of human cognition, which is common to all (*sensus communis*). Although this offers an explanation of the pleasure (both singular and shared) we have in the reception of the artwork, it leaves out of account the manner in which the same free play actually produces that work *prior* to the judgment of taste. Kant's response to this is to introduce the exemplary figure of the genius who, as the incarnation of the productive imagination, appears able to spontaneously originate artworks untarnished by the history of representation sustained by the mimetic activity of the reproductive imagination outlined above. The intermingling of the productive and the reproductive imagination, however, as illuminated by Heidegger, complicates the picture further in a manner that will deepen and enrich our understanding of improvisation while, at the same time, configuring the ground upon which the tragedy of the self-reflexive artist is played out: free-improvisation being the purest form of this drama.

The Beginning of the Work

Think of the above not as an aesthetic space constructed by a philosopher but as the existential predicament of a free improvisor situated within a *practice*. This practice has to begin and the dramatization of this beginning is achieved by introducing freedom into the silence prior to the work—will or won't it begin? But this is disingenuous: nothing could be *more* certain than that such work will begin. An infinite multitude of artworks never manage to mark the unmarked space from which they are intended to be liberated-from, but freely improvised performances *have* to begin precisely because that is their primary role within the aesthetic: to make the distinction between nothing and something. The aesthetic discourses underpinning improvisatory practice will tell us that the absence prior to the work, so important for the self-understanding and self-dramatization of the improvisor, concerns the absence of planning, the risk taking associated with an unguided journey into the unknown where "anything can happen." Future plans are of course based on past successes, so the removal of all planning does raise the specter of failure, which is always entertaining. But there is a deeper issue here, one that concerns neither the future nor the past but, rather, the now that gathers each into the originary moment where the birth of the work is copresent with the "death" of the subject, a different absence necessary for improvisation to begin, if Derrida is to be believed:

> It is not easy to improvise, it's the most difficult thing to do . . .
> [but] I believe in improvisation, and I fight for improvisation,
> but with the belief that it is impossible. But there, where there is
> improvisation, I am not able to see myself, I am blind to myself.
> And it is what I will see, no, I won't see it, it is for others to see.
> The one who has improvised here, no I won't ever see him.[31]

On the face of it this seems like an odd statement but it touches upon a
crucial aspect of aesthetic production, one that free-improvisation more
than any other form brings into view.

At issue here is not just the aforementioned transition from absence
to presence constitutive of the artwork but also the position and status
of the artist whose productive freedom is also dependent upon the liberation of the reflexive subject from the subjection to subjectivity, which
is necessary for the artist to attain presence within the artwork. It is the
sacrifice of this originary positive freedom to the negative freedom of the
work's unfolding that introduces tragedy into the aesthetic experience of
the artist, as we shall see, but for the moment it is the manner in which
Kant can offer up some clues to an understanding of the above scenario
that will be of interest, especially given the charge of subjectivism that
continues to hang over his aesthetics.

For Kant, genius is the power of origination in the artist, a power that
can be "followed" by another artist but not imitated. In other words, the
marks of the marked space can be imitated but the transition from the
unmarked to the marked can only be followed by an-other transition.
Clearly, all spaces are in reality marked by the presence of other works,
not least the artist's own, which implies that the ingenuity of origination
must find ways to erase or forget the presence of the given in order to
both avoid imitation (including self-imitation, perhaps the most common
form) and open up the path to be followed, the "Open" that Heidegger
believes is created and preserved by art. As an ideal-type in this regard
free-improvisation is able to achieve, or at least strive to achieve, a prior
degree of aesthetic erasure beyond the reach of other art forms precisely
because its primary aim is *not* to produce works. Its primary aim is to
produce *beginnings*. As Eddie Prevost affirms:

> Now, nothing is more dead than yesterday's improvisation. What's
> happening to a listener exposed to a repeated (recorded) impro-
> visation? What's happening to the music? As [Cornelius] Cardew
> noted, at least one feature of an improvisation is absent in a record-
> ing: that is, its *transience*. . . . A recorded improvisation is forever

fixed, its routes to be *learnt and remembered*. This is exactly not
the case with the playing and listening situation at the moment an
improvisation *begins*.[32]

This is confirmed by Derek Bailey and Stephen Hicks in conversation:

> BAILEY: Most of the time... I think an improvisation should be
> played and then forgotten.
> HICKS: It's appropriate or not and that's it?
> BAILEY: It's either good or bad but if you listen to an improvisa-
> tion over and over again it just gets worse....
> HICKS: But it's of the nature of improvisation, I would have
> thought, that you don't listen to it over and over again. With-
> out recording you couldn't, could you?
> BAILEY: No, you couldn't, and I don't think you should. It's
> something that should be heard, enjoyed or otherwise, and
> then completely forgotten.

> It may be that opponents and supporters of improvisation are
> defined by their attitude towards the fact that improvisation em-
> braces, even celebrates, music's essentially ephemeral nature.
> For many of the people involved in it, one of the enduring attrac-
> tions of improvisation is its momentary existence: the absence of
> a residual document.[33]

Prevost, Bailey, and Hicks here speak for many improvisors, most of
whom are much more interested in finding and doing work than they are
in fixing the working of the work in documents that clog up the aesthetic
space with ever more marks that will only need to be erased before the
work can begin again. The transience Cornelius Cardew speaks of here
concerns the gathering of past and future time in the now of the work
that must begin again at every moment if its negative and positive freedom are to be maintained. By transforming this labor into a work, ready
and available for reception, the futurity of the improvisation is removed
as is also the engagement and negotiation with the past, which during
the work is riddled with a compelling uncertainty, now lost. But what
would the past of a free-improvisation be if *per impossible* the space
was cleared of all other works, thus enabling the work to truly *begin*?
From where would the work draw the originary force necessary for it to
become a work? Improvisor Susan Leigh Foster speaks of a "suspense-
filled plenitude of the not-quite-known,"[34] which is certainly evocative

but lacks definition regarding the substance of this plenitude. Staying with Kant's account of genius might suggest some possibilities here.

If all works are removed/forgotten, and with them the temptation to imitate, the artist is only left with the figure of the genius to follow. But if the genius is not a figure but, rather, a creative act, an originary transition from absence to presence, then the artist as follower must begin by similarly erasing all traces of self-configuration in order to gain access to the same creative force. The genius-to-genius model of creativity promoted by Kant speaks of a "sense" of originality being "aroused" in the follower such that the transition to the work becomes a possibility. Kant speaks elsewhere of the "mutual quickening" of the productive imagination and the understanding, a cognitive intensification that is responsible not only for the feeling of pleasure associated with the reception of the work but also for the *production* of the work out of (what appears to be) nowhere. But the question remains, how can one come to a sense of one's own creativity? A Kantian answer to this might be framed as follows: within the third *Critique* Kant asserts that aesthetic judgment is grounded in a singular feeling but is, nonetheless, a "*public sense*," thus encapsulating the dialectic of singularity and universality that runs through his aesthetics as a whole. Clearly, although Kant is primarily concerned with the judgment of taste as it relates to the reception of existing artworks, judgment is also needed for a work to begin, an originary "yes!" Gerhard Richter writes that "the making of pictures consists of a large number of yes and no decisions and a yes decision at the end,"[35] which is, no doubt, true for the painter (and much improvisation) but not for the free-improvisor whose work is never intended as an end but as a beginning. Thus, the free-improvisor can only say "yes" if the working of the work is to be sustained beyond the instant of its origination. Keith Johnstone captures the tone in his *Impro for Storytellers* where his notion of a "Group-Yes" produces the following:

> When I arrived at class I asked the students to say "Yes!" to any suggestion, explaining that the suggestion should come from everyone—that there were to be no leaders: "If you can't respond with genuine enthusiasm, please leave the group and sit quietly at the side. We'll time how long the group can sustain itself, so don't fake it! Is that agreed?"
> "*Yess!*"
> "You promise not to say 'Yes!' to any suggestion unless you really mean it?"
> "*Yess!*"

"You accept these conditions?"

"*Yess!*"

"You want to begin?"

"*Yess!*" . . .

If you want to accelerate the stories for entertainment purposes switch to *Yes! And . . .*

—Let's explore the forest!

—*Yes! And . . .*

—Let's go into the deepest part of the forest!

—*Yes! And . . .*

—Let's discover an old castle surrounded by thorn bushes!

—*Yes! And . . .*

—Let's make our way through the thorns!

—*Yes! And . . .*

—Let's explore the castle!

—*Yes!* And . . .

—Let's find a sleeping princess!

—*Yes! And . . .*[36]

The positivity of an originary "yes," the affirmation that brings the artwork into being and then sustains it, is not thought in isolation by Kant but as part of a reflective process that places aesthetic judgment between the realms of determination and freedom, thus casting art in the role of a transitional moment between the two. To illustrate this Kant introduces into the third *Critique* the "maxims of common human understanding" taken from the *Critique of Pure Reason*, which, as he admits, do not properly belong in a critique of taste. Kant introduces them in the following way:

> They are these: (1) to think for oneself; (2) to think from the standpoint of everyone else; (3) always to think consistently. The first is the maxim of *unprejudiced* thought, the second that of *enlarged* thought, the third that of *consistent* thought.[37]

The first adjustment to be made here, one proper to Kant's aesthetics, will be to replace the word "think" with "feel." Kant speaks of the first maxim in terms of a "never-passive reason" that avoids prejudice through action, the positive freeing or "emancipation" of thought from the heteronomy of the other. Within the context of our discussion this might be rethought in terms of the necessary erasure of past work to allow an unmarked opening for the new work to begin. The feeling necessary for the first "yes" of the work to be delivered should not only be singular but also, as Kant insists, be independent and thus intolerant of interference or indeed contradiction by any external authority. In other words, the initial and initiating aesthetic judgment must itself be unjudged. The singularity of feeling necessary for a universally valid judgment of taste is not itself sufficient to produce a work, however. For that the other is needed, not the authority figure of the other but a sense of the other, a presence that can come to inhabit our feelings without prejudicing them. This, for Kant, is the crucial difference between the merely agreeable and the aesthetic, between the private and the singular. Privacy, for all its apparent freedom-from external influence is, in its attachment to "subjective personal conditions," both "cramped and narrow,"[38] whereas singularity and universality can be thought together thanks to Kant's second maxim that encourages the singular self to always aim to think from the standpoint of the other. What is particularly interesting here is the way in which Kant suggests that accounting for the other allows the individual to become not only "of enlarged mind" but also *intense*:

> As to the second maxim belonging to our habits of thought, we have quite got into the way of calling a man narrow (*narrow*, as opposed to being *of enlarged mind*) whose talents fall short of what is required for employment upon any work of any magnitude (especially that involving intensity).[39]

The all-important transition from private feeling to public sense is not only necessary for the validation of judgment, it is, speaking now from the standpoint of the producer, necessary for the artwork to come into being. Feeling, alone, is not productive; the pleasure we might take in an emergent consciousness of cognitive freedom is not sufficient to transform us into artists. For this we need a sense of an audience, not the actual audience so important for improvised performance but the sense of a possible audience ready to validate a work that has yet to arrive. The audience must await the work, but for the artist the sensed audience is not only a têlos but also, as we have seen, an origin that, following Bernstein, is remembered. However, it is not the (mourned) absence of the *sensus communis* but its presence as a sensed intensity or, better, an intensification of sense that transforms the possibility of a work into an actuality. In other words, the "enlarged mind" of Kant's second maxim has nothing to do with a broadening of knowledge through empathetic and dialogical understanding. Rather, the "standpoint of the other" is not a position or perspective to be understood but an intensity that is sensed as a double demand: the demand that the artwork be universally communicable, coupled with the demand that, given Kant's ingenuity aesthetics and the emancipatory nature of his first maxim, the artist follow an exemplary rule rather than imitate a given model. In this regard, the productivity of genius (or of any artist) is not a fact of nature, as Kant sometimes seems to think, but the aesthetic response to an audience that requires endless works to confirm the commonality of its common sense while at the same time demanding a productivity capable of introducing alterity into this commonality, thus protecting it from the commonness (in the bad sense) of common sense. This, perhaps, is where a "memorial aesthetics" would go astray. By treating common sense as a fact that can be lost and mourned, rather than as a work that must be worked and reworked, it fails to do justice to the tragic predicament of the artist who must gather together these originary demands in a work that must not only break with the past in the moment of its beginning but also be sustained into the future. That is, the intensity necessary for the artwork to begin must be carried over into the work itself. This leads us to Kant's third maxim of consistency.

The consistency of thought inherited from the first *Critique* will here be reconsidered in terms of feeling and sense, but first a reminder of Kant's understanding of the third maxim:

> The third maxim—that, namely, of *consistent* thought—is the hardest of attainment, and is only attainable by the union of both the former, and after constant attention to them, has made one at home in their observance.[40]

We might here think of the artwork in these terms and say that it is the transition from the singularity of feeling to the universality of sense that provides the intensity necessary for the possibility of a work, but that its actualization requires more than an infinite transition or oscillation between the polarities of singularity and universality if it is to attain any substantial presence. The duality of meaning evident here, that is to say, consistency thought in terms of logic, and consistency thought as material density, is problematic for the artist who must find ways of ensuring that the intensity of the work's beginning is not sacrificed to the density of the work's being. Put another way, to be logically consistent the artwork (and particularly the freely improvised work) should rehearse the intense interpenetration of singularity and universality through an incessant self-interruption that constantly opens the work up to another beginning, and another, thus protecting the homelessness of the productive imagination from the conceptual structures that would limit its play. At the same time, however, Kant recognizes that the substantiation of consistency requires us precisely to feel at home within the accord of self and other, conceived aesthetically as consensus. The artwork must become a dwelling place, a gathering together not only of past, present, and future, but also of the one and the many. If the third maxim is, for Kant, "the hardest of attainment" within the context of the first *Critique*, then the same could be said here in the third: How can the disruption that is production, its spontaneity, surprise, its originary interruption of the repetition of the same take on the consistency or density of a work without sacrificing or betraying the logic of its production? Notwithstanding Kant's famous injunction that aesthetic judgments should always be cast without the determining concept of an end, for the artist there will always be an end: the work. This is the problem—the predicament of the improvisor—how to bring into accord a beginning and an end. What is philosophically problematical within the confines of an aesthetic discourse becomes tragic when played out existentially within the lives and practices of actual artists and it is in the dramatization of the above predicament that free-improvisation excels.

An attempt has been made to establish that the freedom of free-improvisation is neither something to be unproblematically assumed within the collective, participatory, and dialogical play of the hyperaware work itself, nor does it have to be cast out Schiller-fashion into a utopian future that would see play liberate the artist from the contradictory claims of the work's formal logic and brute materiality. Instead, the artwork and the artist are understood here to *originate* in freedom, a freedom that is always already there cognitively but only given aesthetically to those who develop a feel for this freedom and who gain a sense of its universality. In order to gain some purchase on the event of the artwork as an originary marking of an unmarked space we have strayed somewhat during the course of the discussion from the receptive orientation of Kant, which places the judge in front of the work rather than prior to it. Prior to the work, it is not a question of assuming a *sensus communis* in order thus to validate the aesthetic judgment that would, in turn, validate the work, but, rather, attaining a feel for feeling and a sense of sense. It is one thing to claim that the aesthetic is grounded in an attunement of the faculties that is common to all, it is quite another to *sense* this common sense as an intensity that is aesthetically productive. The *sensus communis* is, one might say, a common sense that is by no means commonly sensed, hence the rarity of artists and the peculiarity of art.

Improvisation and Fear

Perhaps free-improvisors are the rarest and most peculiar artists of all, but what is clear is that such improvising brings to the surface in a very pure way not only the energy, passion, spontaneity, and extraordinary inventiveness upon which it stakes its reputation but also the contingency, fragility, and alterity of the aesthetic project. Derek Bailey claims that free-improvisation is the most natural thing in the world, being perhaps the most ancient mode of art practice: "Historically, it pre-dates any other music—mankind's first musical performance couldn't have been anything other than free improvisation."[41] This may well be true but it does not change the fact that the world of free-improvisation remains a strange place, strange because it is not really a place but more an edge between spaces, between times. This might explain the widespread fear of free-improvisation, both among audiences who tend to avoid it and performers who apparently are terrified by it. This is not an exaggeration: whenever and wherever improvisation figures in performance art, fear management becomes the central problem and task. So many improvisation workbooks are rooted in terror. Virtually every exercise, game, or "sport" to be found in such manuals has been designed to ward off the fear of the unmarked space, of the unknown and unplanned, of failure and ridicule, and above all of the fear of nothingness—that nothing will happen and the work will fail to begin. As Johnstone admits, almost all the games in *Impro for Storytellers* were created to allow "improvisors to defend themselves against imaginary dangers as if these dangers were real."[42] Of course, the strategies devised to manage and overcome such fears, so important for developing improvisational confidence and inducing performers into the community of improvisors are, for all of their value, nevertheless in danger of obscuring the fact that fear is not something that needs to be overcome so much as rerendered as aesthetically productive. Certainly the fear *of* improvising needs to be dealt with at the outset (so the books have some value), but this should be carefully distinguished from the fear *for* the improvisation, for the work of improvisation. This would be closer to the fear for one's child, closer, that is, to what Heidegger would call "care,"[43] a primary concern for the existence and continuance of the improvisation that is too often forgotten in the discourses of care and enabling that surround improvisation but which are directed toward improvisors rather than the improvisations.

The peculiarity of free-improvisation is that it does not produce works. To echo Kant's description of art as "purposiveness without a purpose," it is a working without a work; indeed, in certain respects it might be considered a working to *avoid* works. The absence of works, of "master-pieces," might partly explain the small fan base for free-improvisation, fandom normally being driven by the promotion and consumption of "great works," but, one suspects, it is the radical defamiliarization of the artwork enacted in such performances that is most alienating to audiences who have been weaned on a diet of set pieces and wall-to-wall favorites. Instead of art simply being there, improvisation renders it questionable, insecure, contingent, and endangered. Representing, along with the performers, the "standpoint of the other" necessary for an improvisation to attain the intensity necessary to begin, the audience is here denied the all-too-familiar pleasures of the known and forced instead to witness close up not only the contingency of the artwork's occurrence but also the uncertainty of its continuance, the contestation of its identity, and its eventual destruction at the hands of the improvisors. Part of the strangeness for the audience is the fact that they are expected to make aesthetic judgments during the course of the work's production rather than as a moment in the work's reception. Or, to be clearer, the audience's judgment is based on the reception of production rather than the reception of the finished work. Although many improvisors allude to this in their valorization of audience participation, Keith Johnstone actually integrates judgment into his performances through the nomination of "judges" who determine the "success" or "failure" of the improvisations as they unfold. Here is a typical passage from his *Impro for Storytellers*:

> In the early days we were so protective of the players' feelings that a team kept possession of the stage until the third warning, and all warnings had to be unanimous. Then we threw teams off after the second warning. Finally, after much heart-searching, we decided that justice was less important than getting dead scenes off the stage, and we said that any Judge could end any scene at any time (without consultation), but even then dreary scenes were sometimes allowed to continue while the bored judges toyed with their rescue horns but were reluctant to "do the deed."
>
> These days the so-called Hell-Judges (improvisors who are sitting at the rear of the audience) can press a button when they're bored. This flashes a red "Hell-light" at the Judges' feet, and in the lighting booth. The official Judges can ignore this, but it's likely to shake them out of their apathy.[44]

Johnstone makes a serious point here, one that distinguishes his very fine book from the plethora of touchy-feely discourses that honor the audience as "the most revered member of the theater" (Viola Spolin) while, at the same time, denying it any judgmental potency for fear of terrorizing the poor improvisor. Spolin writes:

> Exhibitionism withers away when the student-actor begins to see members of the audience *not as judges* or censors . . . but as a group with whom an experience is being shared. When the audience is understood to be an organic part of the theatre experience, the student actor is immediately given a host's sense of responsibility toward them which has in it no nervous tension.[45]

The removal of an improvisor's nervous tension, fear, and dread can never justify the removal of judgment from either the audience or other improvisors, regardless of the damaging effect this might have on the familiar (but dubious) organicism that underlies such aspirations. If a case can be made for free-improvisation as an exemplar in the Kantian sense, then the centrality of judgment must be insisted upon if such a claim is to have any credibility. Undetermined by concepts, aesthetic judgments do not have the power to verify or falsify an artwork, but as a demand made from the standpoint of one judge to another such judgments set in motion a reflective process that, while assuming a consensual ground (*sensus communis*), is in practice contestational and intolerant. Here are two passages from Kant to illustrate the point:

> In all judgements by which we describe anything as beautiful *we tolerate no one else being of a different opinion*, and in taking up this position we do not rest our judgement upon concepts, but only on our feeling.[46]

> *I stop my ears: I do not want to hear any reasons or any arguments about the matter.* I would prefer to suppose that those rules of the critics were at fault, or at least have no application, than to allow my judgement to be determined by *a priori* proofs.[47]

As Kant himself accepts, the *sensus communis* is an "ideal norm" that drives an "ought" rather than describing an "is" and, as such, acts as a benchmark by which to measure the failure of judgments to achieve universality or consensus. Indeed, the crucial difference between the merely "agreeable" rooted in private sense and the aesthetic rooted in public sense is that the latter will *always* fail to reach agreement because, unlike the former, it disallows an agreement to disagree. To resist this, as does

Spolin and LaDonna Smith (at the top of this chapter) in the name of nonjudgmentality is to return art to the realms of the "agreeable." Aesthetic judgment is not open to discussion, suggesting that the notion of a *sensus communis* does not and cannot give birth to the communicative communities and dialogical models of intersubjectivity assumed and celebrated by so many improvisors. Not only that, in a fascinating passage Kant recognizes that the failure or refusal to enter into dialogue may not only lead to open conflict and the collapse of the aesthetic relation but to a culture of dissemblance and (to follow the logic) the ironization of art, a possibility that was raised in passing earlier and will be returned to again below. First the passage from Kant:

> Hence it is that a youthful poet refuses to allow himself to be dissuaded from the conviction that his poem is beautiful, either by the judgement of the public or his friends. And even if he lends them an ear, he does so, not because he has now come to a different judgement, but because, though the whole public, at least as far as his work is concerned, should have false taste, he still, in his desire for recognition, finds good reason to accommodate himself to the popular error (even against his own judgement).[48]

It will be remembered that the choice of tragedy or mourning was offered by Caygill, and that, along with Bernstein, he chose mourning. Considering the latter choice to be aesthetically unproductive, this book is attempting to pursue a different course, one that is concerned to engage with the tragic predicament and practice of the artist working in the face of a forever failed commonality. But while continuing with this theme we might introduce here the concept of irony as an additional choice for the artist or improvisor. This will allow us to revisit an earlier quotation and, on this occasion, offer two overlapping readings of it, both of which will inform the subsequent discussion. This is the passage again:

> For Trauerspiel the world was empty, a place of "never-ending repetition" with no possibility of ever becoming genuine or authentic: "For those who looked deeper saw the scene of their existence as a rubbish heap of partial, inauthentic actions." The world handed down to us by tradition is uncanny, undecipherable, always other.[49]

The fundamental problem for Benjamin and Heidegger (and Caygill and Bernstein) is that the destruction of tradition and the breaking asunder of an originary commonality that cannot be remade is a catastrophe brought upon art by the creators and preservers of art itself. It is this complicity that encourages Benjamin's departure from this catastrophic history into the time outside of time he reserves for mourning. Improvisors too rush forward into the future with their faces turned to the rubbish heap of the past, but the difference—the existential tragedy—is that they feel compelled to gather up this past and carry it into the future as a work of art. Free-improvisation gathers the past as an otherness not to be imitated but as the originary site of an aesthetic freedom to be sensed and followed. Weighed down by the scrap heap of history, by dead styles and wrecked idioms, free-improvisors are happy to contribute to this ongoing destruction through an active forgetfulness that clears the site for the beginning of new work out of nowhere. But then again, it is not out of nowhere because, as Søren Kierkegaard and Nietzsche agree, in order to forget you must find something to remember: "Try to forget it! That indeed is a hollow mockery . . . try to get something else to remember, and then it will succeed."[50] Free-improvisation forgets in order to remember the new obscured by the old, the beginning concealed by the end. So here destruction and construction go hand in hand through acts of aesthetic redemption that, as a moment of clearing, allows the work of destruction to begin. As Heidegger and Benjamin agree, tradition is destroyed by becoming a tradition. The raw performativity of free-improvisation is exemplary in the manner in which it dramatizes this aesthetic self-destruction in full view of a judicial audience that at best returns an inconclusive verdict and at worst is damning. More than any other form free-improvisation turns self-destruction into a spectacle. A microcosmic fragment of tradition, the work is destroyed by becoming a work. It is destroyed by the improvisors, by the audience, by all modes of preservation and documentation, and, not least, by the aesthetic discourses (including this one) that would construct arguments to hold the work together even as it unravels before our eyes.

Once the work is in play, and contrary to the claims of Schiller and radical Schillerians alike, the possibility of freedom and commonality are progressively lost as continuity once again takes precedence over the discontinuity of origination. This loss is the tragedy of the work enacted by the performers and audience alike. Rather than being helplessly and hopelessly witnessed through the paralysis of mourning, the shattering of tradition is here localized within the individual work and the existential predicament of the artist who is made to suffer the contentiousness of the reflective judgmental process that, notwithstanding its ideals, forever fails to meet its own demands. This, it should be emphasized, is not the failure of art or of the aesthetic, and certainly not of free-improvisation; it is, rather, the failure of idealism. The aesthetic does not fail, it succeeds. Or at least it succeeds to the extent that it allows an articulation and configuration of what might be viewed as an ontological failure but one that is nonetheless successful *as art*. Taking a Kantian view, the artwork would lack all intensity if it did *not* fail to realize the ideality that inhabits it. For him, there can be no aesthetic ideal—something that is confined to the merely "agreeable" (hence the "Ideal Home Exhibition")—which should remind us that the *sensus communis* as "ideal norm," while introducing intensity into the artwork in the form of the "standpoint of the other," is not itself aesthetic, which might help explain the intensity. It is not aesthetic but, unlike the "agreeable," which locks the subject into a private sensibility that makes no demands on the other, common-sense has an enormous impact *on* the aesthetic and on the nature of art practice, not only because the sense of or feel for common-sense is an essential prerequisite of the originary gesture of the artwork but because the aesthetic judgments necessary for the work to unfold beyond the instant of its origination would lack all validity if the universality of sense could not be imported into the contingency of the work. It is this, the introduction of the cognitive into the aesthetic, the ideal attunement of the senses into the real dissonance of sensibility, that results not only in the intensity of the artwork but also in the tragic predicament that must be lived by the artist. But the art world is dominated by works that, as Norman Bryson has argued in relation to the aesthetic "gaze,"[51] have removed the working from the work, the temporality and physicality of this working that speaks of a singular life and an existential predicament that is thus rendered invisible. Of course, some artists may try to bring this working of the work back into view through a performativity that brings it closer to free-improvisation as can be seen in following statement by the artist Keith Haring:

> One of the things I have been most interested in is the role of chance in situations—letting things happen by themselves. . . . This openness to "chance" situations necessitates a level of performance in the artist. The artist, if he is a vessel, is also a performer. I find the most interesting situation for me is when there is no turning back. Many times I have put myself in situations where I am drawing in public. Whatever marks I make are immediately recorded and immediately on view. There are no "mistakes" because nothing can be erased. . . . The expression exists only in the moment. The artist's performance is supreme.[52]

By drawing much closer to performance art Haring exposes the radical contingency of art practice, an unsettling fact that is suppressed or repressed in the "finished" work (of the "gaze"), presented to an audience once the work necessary to disguise this contingency has been completed. Working alone, Haring has to make his own decisions about how chance events are managed and how mistakes are integrated into the unfolding work. For collective improvisors, however, things are not quite so straightforward partly because the openness to chance and error so celebrated by improvisors is seriously compromised by the play of aesthetic judgment both on the work (from the audience) and within it (from the performers, not uninfluenced by the audience). There is an idealism in improvisation that is heart-warming but misguided. The terminology that inhabits and informs the hegemonic dialogical language of care, enabling, sharing, and participation is only aesthetically productive to the extent that it confronts the far from ideal reality of the work, where the necessity of singularity plays havoc with any dreams of universal consensus. In this regard Kant, in his discussion of the "young poet," is quite right to draw attention to a certain delay in the consentaneity of judgment, recognizing that it is only over time ("in aftertime")[53] that the intolerance of contradiction, perhaps necessary for authentic work, comes to be tempered by the judgments of others. But again, as with Haring, this is the situation of the individual artist producing a finished work that can be considered and reconsidered at will rather than that of the collective improvisor who must make judgments *now* in a performance with no aftertime in which to resolve the differences between one singularity and another. As the dancer David Gere writes:

> Choices . . . cannot be arrived at with the leisure of the studio, over the period of hours or days, months or years. These decisions must be made now. This moment. While it is true that virtually all artmaking demands decisiveness, in improvisation choices must be arrived at without creative blocks or procrastination. There is not time for delay in improvisational performances. There is simply no time.[54]

Again, one can see how free-improvisation brings to the surface and plays out as spectacle the contingency and contentiousness of the artwork before it has a chance either to disappear (return to the unmarked) or re-present itself as a work (the marked).

Competition

What would a successful improvisation be? The claim being made here is that success should not be measured against a consensual goal or *têlos* that drives the work ever urgently toward a communicative conclusion. On the contrary, an imputed consensus is the *origin* of the work, but one that is destroyed by the working of that work. Indeed, one could go further and suggest that the primary aim of free-improvisation is to ensure that this ongoing and endless destruction is not short-circuited by the finished artwork or by any spurious community promoting an ideology of oneness. The care for the work, one that overrides the more trivial concerns of intersubjectivity, is a care for the work's beginning, not its end; as such, it will be ever ready to destroy the work in an attempt to preserve what Heidegger describes as the openness of that beginning. The result is a mode of performance that is much more combative and competitive than the majority of discourses on improvisation are willing to admit. Indeed, and the two are not unrelated, just as Spolin moves against judgment in improvisation so she also takes a dim view of competitiveness as damaging to the harmonious "total environment." Contest, on the other hand, is permitted and encouraged:

> A highly competitive atmosphere creates artificial tensions, and when competition replaces participation, compulsive action is the result. . . . Should competition be mistaken for a teaching pool, the whole meaning of playing and games is distorted. Playing allows a person to respond with his or her "total organism within a total environment." Imposed competition makes this harmony impossible, for it destroys the basic nature of playing by occluding the self and by separating player from player. . . . Contest and extension, on the other hand, is an organic part of every group activity and gives both tension and release in such a way as to keep the player intact while playing.[55]

Spolin is certainly working with a very fine distinction indeed here, and it is difficult to imagine what an uncompetitive contest would be like, but one suspects it would be extraordinarily dreary. The idea that competition occludes the self, while opening the way for an organicism uncontaminated by individual desire, loses sight of the fact that such a model of collective participation is in danger of sucking the improvisor into what we might call, following Emmanuel Levinas, a "rhythm" of "totality" where the "I" is sacrificed to the "we" and where consensus is fatally confused with anonymity. In his essay "Reality and Its Shadow" Levinas describes the situation in the following way:

> Closed wholes whose elements call for one another like the syllables of a verse . . . *impose themselves on us without our assuming them.* Or rather, our consenting to them is inverted into participation. Their entry into us is one with our entry into them. Rhythm represents a unique situation where we cannot speak of consent, assumption, initiative, or freedom, because the subject is caught up and carried away by it. The subject is part of its own representation. It is so even despite itself, for in rhythm there is no longer a oneself, but rather a sort of passage from oneself to anonymity.[56]

This, unhappily, shows the dark side of all organically conceived participatory cultures: in an effort to save the artwork from destruction at the hands of the competitive artist, the artist is destroyed instead, leaving nothing. For good or ill, free-improvisation, like all improvisation, is riddled with competitiveness and, as Ben Watson in his book on the history of free-improvisation puts it, "the idea that the ego can be transcended is obviously a convenient ideology for collectives. The problem is that, in a highly competitive scene, it's invariably absolute humbug."[57] Whether or not competition is perceived as a problem will depend on the understanding of the improvisational project and the place and nature of subjectivity within that project. Certainly anyone familiar with improvisation either as a spectator or participant could not fail to be aware of the fact that free-improvisation is more about power than it is about freedom. Sometimes this may be no more than a desire to draw attention to one's self at the expense of others: a simple case of "showing off," as the improvisor Steve Beresford sees it with disarming honesty,[58] or it may be more integral to the improvisational form such as is the case with "challenge dancing" in the world of tap dance. Constance Valis Hill gives an engaging account of this in her essay "Stepping, Stealing, Sharing, and Daring: Improvisation and the Tap Dance Challenge":

> Like improvisation in jazz, improvisation in the challenge can take form as the spontaneous creation or composition of a percussive statement in performance. More often and most generally, however, improvisation in the challenge is the act of responding spontaneously (to an *opponent*, musician, or member of the au-

dience), in the moment of performance. If the challenge is the *call*
to action, the putting forth of a rhythmic statement by the challenger, then the improvisation (or more aptly, the improvisatory
imperative) is the *response* (and not only an "Amen")—the answer to the call that is spontaneous, creative and reactive, compelling the challengee (who in turn becomes a challenger) to look,
to listen, and to respond in the moment, with any and all means
necessary. . . . [W]hat is essential in the dynamism and fierce excitement of the challenge is that it at the very least be *perceived* as
an extemporaneous, or improvised, *battle.*[59]

This is not exactly the collective love-in one has come to expect when
free-improvisors take the time to speak and write of their improvisation, but it should remind us of the aporia of freedom remarked upon
right at the beginning of this discussion. For all of the talk of dialogue,
we witness here in the "pushing and pulling" of improvisation the dialectic of negative and positive freedom, of the collective and the singular,
the "yes" and "no" of the work played out in full view of the audience.
However, regardless of the acceptance or not of the competitive dimension of improvisation, what the majority of improvisatory discourses
have in common is the assumption of a dialogical model that is played
out intersubjectively within the performance. If competitiveness does
creep into this performative interaction then it is understood exclusively
in terms of social participation and human relations rather than as being
a result of the improvisor's relation to the *work*: an aesthetic relation.
One consequence of this within the discussion of freedom and free-
improvisation is that it is inevitably framed in terms of either a negativity that strives to establish and maintain a regime of noninterference
where mutual respect for the improvisatory space of the other is a first
principle, or, conversely, a more risky positivity that recognizes a certain
desire for mastery and accepts that issues of power and the freedom to
actualize this power aesthetically are an integral part of improvisation.
The latter does not necessarily destroy the collective aspirations of group
improvisation but it certainly removes any ethical pretensions it might
have.

Negative and Positive Improvisation

Thought thus, the pursuit of negative freedom is most likely to produce
improvisations that are "hyperaware," improvisations that in their profound concern and care for the other open up a performative space that is

attentive to, responsive to, and, above all, supportive of the mark-making project of the other. At its best, such a pursuit can produce improvisations of great sensitivity and delicacy where every mark is considered, every interjection is carefully weighed and weighted, ensuring that participation in an emerging oneness effectively extinguishes the desire for empty theatricality and virtuosic self-aggrandizement. At its worst, there can be witnessed what might be described as an escalation of sensitivity where virtually every mark interferes with or intrudes into the marked space of the other. Such hypersensitivity can result in an exaggerated politeness that endlessly waits to be asked: "After you," "Oh, no, after you, please," "No, I insist, after you," "No, no, really." This would be a regime of call and response where to call would be risking an act of violence, thus leaving the improvisation awash with responses in search of a call, answers without a question. Frozen in an ecstasy or ec-stasis of mutuality, such improvisation, if it fails to attain sublimity, quickly descends into the boringness that always awaits the improvisor. Notwithstanding David Toop's predilections, waiting for twenty-five minutes to hear the sound of a jack plug being removed from an amplifier might not be everyone's idea of a fun night out! Even where participants are a little less "lowercase" the concerted considerateness for the inviolable space of the other can encourage a peaceful coexistence that, in its beautiful but suffocating harmoniousness, is every bit as boring as the frightened minimalism of the oversensitive.

Turning now to consider the strengths and weaknesses of positive freedom as an ideal pursued within free-improvisation, we will again start with the best and descend to the worst. And the best is very good: an approach to improvisation that does not stand on ceremony or wait nervously to be invited into the action but which is decisive, determined, and often disruptive of cozy, considerate communities. Such positivity might be thought in terms of calling rather than responding but this should not be confused with the posing of questions that might invite, require, or demand answers. In fact, positive freedom neither raises questions (too negative) nor does it answer questions (too heteronomous); instead, it might be described, like negative freedom, as an answer without a question, but here the similarity ends. Where negative freedom was described above as driven by answers in search of questions, positive freedom might be better grasped as an answer that gives rise to questions. The former is haunted by doubt, hesitant and puzzled as to the best way of proceeding; the latter is assured, committed, and challenging (question-raising). Maurice Blanchot identifies the same reversal in the thought of Simone Weil. He writes of her (not uncritically):

> We enter into thought . . . only by questioning. We go from ques-
> tion to question to the point where the question, pushed toward a
> limit, becomes response. . . . Such a way of proceeding is foreign to
> Simone Weil. . . . [I]t would seem that she first responds to herself,
> as though for her the answer always comes first, preceding every
> question and even every possibility of questioning: there is an an-
> swer, then another, and then again another answer. . . . Affirming is
> often for Simone Weil a way of questioning or a way of testing. . . .
> [B]y affirming and holding firmly without wavering to the move-
> ment of affirmation. . . . The kind of invisible effort by which she
> seeks to efface herself in favour of certitude is all that remains in
> her of a will as she advances from affirmation to affirmation.[60]

Such conviction can undoubtedly produce work of extraordinary authority, work that is imposing and masterful. What is more, although the
positive free-improvisor is ultimately unconcerned with respecting the
sanctity of the other's aesthetic space, such improvisation is not necessarily undialogical. On the contrary, such work can be full of dialogue as
long as it is accepted, along with Franz Rosenzweig, that we are here in
the presence of what he calls the "hearing of the eye" rather than the "true
hearing of the ear."[61] We will return to this in a moment, immediately after we have reconsidered positive free-improvisation in its worst light.

As Friedrich Schiller discovered when considering what he called
the "form-drive," the positive freedom associated with imposing order on chaos has something "barbaric" about it, an inhumanity that
rides roughshod over the sensibilities of those "savages" enslaved to the
"sense-drive."[62] Paradoxically, within collective improvisation, where
the desire for mastery is likely to be harbored by more than one, the result is more often than not chaos rather than order. And when things go
wrong in this way it becomes apparent that the opposite of negative freedom is not, as Berlin assumes, the interference of one singular freedom
with that of another but, rather, an obliviousness to the other that also
rushes headlong into boringness. After twenty-five minutes of cacopho-
nous overkill perhaps the eventlessness of "lowercase" improvisation
would be more fun after all.

Dialogics of the Ear and Eye

Returning to the subject of dialogue, it is worth reemphasizing that what
have been described above as negative and positive free-improvisations
are both dialogical, albeit differently. It would be useful to read Franz

Rosenzweig's words here before addressing this difference and then considering the possibility of a nondialogical listening that might allow us to begin rethinking the positivity of positive freedom outside of Berlin's dualism. There are many improvisors of a dialogical cast of mind that would benefit from listening to Franz Rosenzweig's following words from *The Star of Redemption*:

> Here we are concerned with a kind of hearing quite different from that required in dialogue. For in the course of a dialogue he who happens to be listening also speaks, and he does not speak merely when he is uttering words, not even mainly when he is uttering words, but just as much when through his eager attention, through the assent or dissent expressed in his glances, he conjures words to the lips of the current speaker. Here it is not this hearing of the eye which is meant, but the true hearing of the ear.[63]

On the face of it this maps well onto the above discussion, with negative free-improvisation having more than a passing resemblance to Rosenzweig's "hearing of the ear," while his "hearing of the eye" offers many (somewhat uncomfortable) insights into the nature of its positive equivalent. With this in mind it would no doubt be possible to judge the success or failure of actual improvisations in terms of their ability to originate and sustain dialogical forms that steer clear of the negative and positive poles of boringness that await timidity and arrogance alike. Ben Watson's recent book on Derek Bailey and free-improvisation, undoubtedly the most judgmental book on the subject currently available, does exactly this. Page after page (it's a long book) is devoted to detailed accounts of specific improvisations, tracing over and over again, with the obsessiveness of a true fan, the microcosmic disasters and triumphs of an endlessly shifting personnel caught up in the trials and tribulations of these little dialogues. This makes for engaging reading, but for all its promotion of and enthusiasm for its subject, this book never quite manages to bring to the fore the real ontological force of free-improvisation, which is its incomparable ability to present the beginning of art and its glorious failure to hold this beginning before our eyes. To grasp this, the most important aspect of free-improvisation, it is necessary to follow Rosenzweig outside of all dialogics into the aesthetic that, for him, is not part of but "alongside" the world, indeed a silence alongside the world. The "true hearing of the ear" is not then, as improvisors would no doubt argue, the listening to the other as artist/improvisor but, rather, the listening to the otherness of art *itself*, the silent alterity prior to all dialogue. Following Rosenzweig in this direction will bring the tragedy of this aesthetic more clearly into view:

> This is the world of art, a world of tacit accord which is no world at all, no real, vital, back-and-forth interconnection of address passing to and fro and yet, at any point, being capable of being vitalized for moments at a time. No sound punctures this silence and yet at every instant each and everyone can sense the innermost part of the other in himself. It is the equality of the human which, prior to any real unity of the human, here becomes effective as content of the work of art. Prior to any real human speech, art creates, as the speech of the unspeakable, a first, speechless, mutual comprehension, for all time indispensable beneath and beside actual speech. The silence of the tragic hero is silent in all art and is understood in all art without any words. The self does not speak and yet is heard.[64]

This is a very Kantian passage, one that should remind us of the "tacit accord" that is the *sensus communis*, a sense that must itself be sensed before the work of art can begin. For Rosenzweig, the work of art provides us with an "analogy to creation,"[65] a "language prior to revelation,"[66] a "beginning": "The epoch of creation is only the beginning—albeit the everlasting beginning—even as it is mirrored in the brief life span of the work of art."[67] The "true hearing of the ear" "hears" the silence of art at the moment of its origination prior to its re-presentation as a dialogical communicative form: a work. This silence, however, is not the dumb muteness of the unmarked space but the eloquent silence reverberating in art at the originary moment of transition from the unmarked to the marked. This is where Rosenzweig sees tragedy—the tragedy of the tragic hero—to which can be added the tragedy of the work, thus rendering art doubly tragic. Tragedy, for Rosenzweig, is the dramatization of an undialogical silence and solitude, to which we will add the silencing of this silence and the breaching of this solitude in the dialogical community of free-improvisation:

> The tragic hero has only one language which completely corresponds to him: precisely to keep silent. It is thus from the beginning. Tragedy casts itself in the artistic form of drama just in order to be able to represent speechlessness.[68]

Just as historically (and here Rosenzweig agrees with Nietzsche) the rise of dialogue heralds the decline of tragedy, so the emerging artwork only achieves communicative potency to the extent that it sacrifices what Rosenzweig calls its "tragic force."[69] The double tragedy of art, then, is that, rooted in a common sense that is universal but incommunicable—"no community originates. And yet there originates a common content"—the tragic silence of its beginning is forgotten in the working out of the artwork: the tragic loss of tragedy.

Free-improvisation is the exemplary aesthetic form because it manages to offer a glimpse of this double tragedy and it does this to the extent that it resists the *work* of art being destroyed by the artwork. To be successful improvisation must be a form of delay, an incessant interruption of the work's desire to be a work and to speak. Watson hints at such things when he describes Tony Oxley's idea of rhythm as "continual interruption,"[70] or at moments like the following: "[Robyn] Schulkowsky takes seriously the sense of singular event instilled by John Cage into modern music, so each blow seems to be delivered as if for the first time."[71]

At its best free-improvisation is not driven by a concern for the other improvisors but by a concern or care for the work itself. At its best it is by no means participatory but exclusive and excluding—collective, yes, communal, no. At its best free-improvisation is profoundly competitive, not only at the level of Rosenzweig's inauthentic dialogical "eye," which is always looking for an opportunity to speak, but also at the level of the authentic "hearing of the ear" that concerns us here. Although improvisors have different views on the legitimacy of competitiveness as a motivation for improvisation this is always considered within the parameters of an assumed dialogical intersubjective field that is thought to be either enhanced or damaged by such competitiveness, but there is another way of approaching this, as Keith Johnstone's Theatresports clearly illustrates.

Competition and Dialogue

Although fundamentally competitive, Theatresports is almost exclusively focused on the work and the working of the work rather than on the performers. The competition is between one work and another, rather than one performer and another. Performers are "judged" in relation to their skill in keeping the work working, open, and mobile rather than in response to any display of individual performative virtuosity or dialogical prowess. Indeed, many of Johnstone's techniques are designed precisely to *block* the emergence of too easily assumed dialogical relationships

within the unfolding of the work, particularly where the quest for dialogue is driven by a fear of what he calls the "alteration" necessary for
good improvisation. Recognizing that "frightened improvisors keep re-
storing the balance for fear that something might happen,"[72] Johnstone
devotes much time and space to the art of *tilting*, that is, of tilting the
balance that is ever in danger of being achieved in an improvisation, by
introducing destabilizing material into the emergent dialogue, thereby
"demolishing" or "devastating" it.[73] Tilting is a highly competitive sport,
pitting one performer against another in a struggle for power that results
in winners and losers, success and failure, but, as is clear throughout,
Johnstone is not interested in personalities, only in the work. It is the
shifting of the balance of power that is crucial, not who has it. It is the
possibility of failure or success that gives improvisation its edge rather
than who succeeds or fails:

> Players who come from show-business assume that failure has
> no value. If so, I ask them:
>
> · Which is the most famous tower?
> · Which is the most famous space shuttle?
> · Which is the most famous ocean liner?
>
> . . . Show-business pastes over inadequacies with glitz and razz-
> amatazz, but sport displays a tug-o'-war between success and
> failure. A scripted show would be wrecked if the scenography
> collapsed, and yet this could be the high point of an improvised
> show.[74]

Both dialogue and competition coexist in this model of improvisation but
are transformed by being stripped of their intersubjective garb. Johnstone's
primary concern is with the "art of making things happen," the happening of the artwork, which for him means regarding every moment of a
performance as anticipatory, as the beginning of a future yet to come. As
he says, players are "working well" when "they're giving the audience
the 'future' that it anticipates,"[75] which is not the same as giving them
what they expect. Anticipation does not simply want fulfilment; it wants
a future that is itself anticipatory, a future that retains its futurity—anticipation feeds on anticipation. To "work well," then, the improvisor must
enter into some form of dialogue with the audience, but as a listening to
the silent anticipation of that audience rather than to its rowdy interjec-
tions and reckless judgments; a silence that, as the originary sense of a
collective beginning, can be "heard" in the work too, as a silence that is

forever endangered by the dialogics of the work itself and the desire to make it a work. Improvisors are "working well," Johnstone continues, when they "care about the values expressed in the work,"[76] which, when stripped of any unwelcome moral overtones, should remind us that care for the work takes precedence over any intersubjective engagement, and that the "values expressed" in free-improvisation concern above all the value of ensuring that things continue to happen. Once understood thus, the competitiveness of Theatresports, and perhaps all free-improvisation worthy of attention, can be welcomed and encouraged to the extent that it is placed in the service of the work rather than of the competitors. This is why the virtuosity of the improvisor should not be measured in terms of technical mastery but, rather, in relation to an ability to create or mobilize strategies that keep the work happening, even if this requires sacrificing oneself and one's precious hard-won talents to the continuance of the work—the virtuosity of sacrifice. Johnstone would describe this as failing gracefully:

> Some people (often fervent capitalists and sports fans) condemn Theatresports on the grounds that it's competitive, but while "straight" theatre encourages competition . . . Theatresports can take jealous and self-obsessed beginners and teach them to play games with good nature, and to fail gracefully.[77]

To fail "gracefully" is to fail successfully. It is to recognize that such failure is necessary for the work to continue. Such failure is liberatory in two ways but also tragic on account of this very dualism. The sacrifice of performers is a necessary part of the work's happening (for Johnstone, the avoidance of boredom), but this failure liberates the artist from the task of trying to gather and hold together both the origin and the event or performance of the work within the temporality of aesthetic production: the duality of creation and preservation. And the artist *needs* to be liberated from this task in order to fully recognize its impossibility and, thus, its significance. In this sense such liberation might be best understood as an emancipation from the illusions of success that, in their foregrounding of the artist, obscure and trivialize the origin of the work of art. The liberation of the artist releases, in turn, the artwork from the gathering grasp of the singular artist, allowing it to return to its origin, which continues to happen as the singularity of production ebbs and flows. It is the liberation of the artwork from the cramped intentionality of the singular artist that ensures the continuing presence of the origin in the unfolding of the work, and it is the graceful failure of the artist that is required to keep this origin in play. To fail without grace is to lose sight of the origin, obscured or displaced by the success of the work.

Origination

This way of linking failure and origin returns us again to Benjamin and Heidegger where it is the destruction of tradition that keeps it alive. Understood as a microcosmic enactment of this destruction, free-improvisation will once again be used to exemplify this predicament and help to clarify the very particular notion of origin that is being assumed here. With a view to demonstrating the interpenetration of tragedy and mourning within aesthetic practice, it will be necessary to look more closely at Benjamin's historical categorization of origin before returning to what Caygill describes as the tragic "dialectical logic of subjectivity" to be found in Heidegger's earlier thought.

A most striking expression of Benjamin's conception of origin is to be found in *The Origin of German Tragic Drama*:

> The term origin is not intended to describe the process by which the existent came into being, but rather to describe that which emerges from the process of becoming and disappearance. Origin is an eddy in the stream of becoming, and in its current it swallows the material involved in the process of its genesis. That which is original is never revealed in the naked and manifest existence of the factual; its rhythm is apparent only to a dual insight. On the one hand it needs to be recognized as a process of restoration and re-establishment, but, on the other, and precisely because of this, as something imperfect and incomplete.[78]

As Caygill reads it in his book on Benjamin—*Walter Benjamin: The Colour of Experience*—this understanding of origin has two main methodological implications. First, that "the temporal character of origin means that the meaning of a work is never fully present [as can be] revealed by a comparison of the same work with itself over time"; second, "that critique does not possess any incontestable criteria which are immune to change in the encounter with the object of critique . . . because these criteria themselves change in the encounter with the work."[79] But isn't this problematization of reception something quite different to the existential predicament of the artist creating the work? Is the mourning of the critic before the distorting or shattered mirror of origin's history in any way comparable to the tragedy of origination witnessed in exemplary fashion in free-improvisation? In his historicization of origination Benjamin makes a distinction between origin as genesis and origin as becoming: "Origin [*Ursprung*], although an entirely historical category, has, nevertheless, nothing to do with genesis [*Entstehung*]. The term origin is not intended to describe the process by which the existent came into being."[80] But the question is, isn't it precisely the copresence of genesis and becoming in the aesthetic act, its creation *and* preservation as one tiny fragment of tradition, that separates the producer from the receiver? The problem for the artist regarding the origination of the work is not methodological but aesthetic and existential—herein lies the tragedy. This is where Heidegger's poetically inspired philosophical vision outstrips Benjamin's, entering as it does more comprehendingly into the aesthetic experience of the creative artist and the existential predicament of the originator. As critic, Benjamin receives the artwork as, to use his words, the rhythmic pulsation of an origination that has already "swallowed" up its own genesis. For him, reception demands participation in this infinite rhythm of origination, whereas for the artist, and particularly for the free-improvisor, it is precisely participation in the becoming of the work that risks obscuring the productive moment of genesis, obscuring, that is, the transition from the unmarked to the marked that gives the working of the work its necessary intensity and, Heidegger would say, its truth. Although both Benjamin and Heidegger agree that the origin is not a singular event but, rather, the infinite happening of the historicity of the artwork itself, it is only the latter that fully recognizes the predicament of the artist, suspended between beginning and ending and torn between participation and nonparticipation, dialogue and solitude, universality and singularity. This difference is rooted in the copresence of genesis and becoming in Heidegger's thought, something that recalls again his understanding of the Kantian productive imagination as both spontaneous and receptive. In this mode of thinking it is not simply that the origin is lost in the destructive preservation of tradition, and then mourned as a perpetual absence but, rather, that the "founding leap" (*ursprung*) of origination is always present as the call of the work's future. And again, it is the predicament of the artist to be suspended between the past and the future of the work. For Benjamin, the presence of the origin is the mark of its destruction as an originary past, now absent: remember the *Angelus Novus* has his back turned to the future. Heidegger too recognizes the limitations of such a "primitive" conception of origin but it is precisely the futurelessness of such beginnings that his ontology is engaged in surpassing:

> A genuine beginning, however, has nothing of the neophyte character of the primitive. The primitive, because it lacks the bestowing, grounding leap and head start, is always futureless. It is not capable of releasing anything more from itself because it contains nothing more than that in which it is caught.[81]

With wings caught up in the winds blowing out of a destroyed past, the critic can only mourn, but the artist has a different vocation and thus a different grounding in the historicity of art, indeed a grounding denied to the critic and the philosopher who are left hovering above the creative destruction of art practice at a safe distance from the existential predicament of the artist. Heidegger's thought, however, in its gathering together of the beginning, becoming, and end of the work of art, more effectively grasps the tragic logic of subjectivity as it is enacted in art practice generally and most specifically in the forms of improvisation being referenced here.

In essence, by identifying the threefold nature of the origination of the aesthetic—artist, artwork, art—Heidegger puts his finger on the forces that play upon and, indeed, are contested within freely improvised performances or productions. If it is true that the most profound promise of free-improvisation is to be witnessed in its attempt (consciously or not) to enact the origination of the artwork, and the preservation of that origination—the preservation of the event of opening that is art—then it is always the artist and/or the artwork that ultimately breaks this promise. This, the failure of art, is precisely what makes the artist and/or the artwork fascinating at the expense of art, but then without this fascination art and its promise would remain locked up and concealed in an oblivion devoid of ontological value.

The seductive and compelling lure of the work as an emerging and potentially finished structure or object begins the moment a free-improvisation is under way. Even the purity of the beginning of the work is tainted to the extent that it anticipates becoming a work and forgets or loses the sense of a collective origin from which the communicative aesthetic act derives. The desire to produce and/or witness the production of a work is something deeply rooted and shared by performers and the audience, a fact that can have a variety of consequences, as Eric F. Clarke observes, none of them particularly positive. What he is alert to is how it is the risk of failure in free-improvisation that is inspiring for the performer and rewarding for the audience rather than actual failure which, without a successful outcome in an emergent work, is largely meaningless and frustrating. He describes the scenario thus:

While all performance arts risk failure on specific occasions, for improvised performance—and in particular the extreme of free-improvisation—the potential for devastating failure in a specific performance is considerably greater. Because it dispenses with precomposed material, passed on by notation or oral tradition, and relies instead entirely on the uncertainties of construction at the moment of performance, it renounces the support and coherence that a score or memorized structure can provide. For participants in group improvisation, the challenge that this offers may be a source of inspiration and motivation, but public performance brings with it the expectation that a level of excellence and coherence will be maintained, with little tolerance for possibly well-intended but unsuccessful experiments. In other words, the requirements of public performance seem to run counter to the exploratory and experimental nature of improvisation.[82]

This raises an interesting issue regarding the audience. If the role of the audience is a crucial component in the overall performance, then what exactly is this role? Keith Johnstone's audiences directly intervene in the improvisation, demanding the removal of anyone who is boring. But what constitutes boringness? Is it the emergence or the avoidance of a work that is boring? Johnstone clearly believes the former and does everything in his power to continually "tilt" performances to keep them from falling back on well-worn principles and tried and tested methods. Clarke, on the other hand, is less convinced, suggesting that the presence of the audience introduces the demand for recognizable works, thus stifling the gleeful anarchy favored by Johnstone: "Other improvising musicians certainly offer precisely the opposite opinion—that the presence of an audience and the need to avoid breakdown leads to a certain cautiousness that diminishes innovation and experiment."[83] Whichever way one sees it there remains the question of the improvisor's relation to the work. With or without an audience (and audiences can be hard to come by in the world of free-improvisation), and in spite of the oft-expressed desire to be "in the moment," the instant an improvisation commences it begins to take on a shape, like Leonardo's reconfiguration of meaningless scribble, and it is here that the artwork and the artist become entangled.

Recognition

Why do artists make art? Why do improvisors improvise? For Hegel, as already seen, it is not the production of artworks as aesthetic objects that is the crucial issue but the recognition of the self in such works that gives art what he would call its world-historical value. This is all well and good as long as the project of art remains one that retains the dialectic of artist and artwork as the productive motor of self-recognition, but what if, as in what we are calling exemplary free-improvisation, the intention is to *disrupt* the resolution of such aesthetic labor into what could be recognized as works? In such a case the dialectic of self-recognition is in danger of stalling. If it is true that art has more to do with recognition than it does with expression then it is not surprising that improvisors are still drawn to the production of works like iron filings to a magnet: there is so much more at stake than just adding another object to the world. And even when the outcome of an improvisation is in doubt—will it break down or not?—the "excellence and coherence" (Clarke) of the performance demanded by the audience already points toward an assumed integrity that reflects back on the artist as an emergent self-consciousness. In other words, the desire for the work is really the desire for the self, which is precisely why Heidegger has to break with humanism in order to clear the work out of the way in pursuit of the Being of art.

But if the work gets in the way of the Being of art so too does the artist. However, throughout the literature on free-improvisation, and widespread among the improvising community, is a profound suspicion of any individual virtuosity or egotism that draws attention away from the collective. As Viola Spolin puts it, "Any player who 'steals' a scene is a thief."[84] As Eddie Prevost argues, "Clinging to the self in the hurly-burly of free collective improvisation is both an art and a cul-de-sac. As a mechanism of art the self must be thrown into the whirlpool of potentiality."[85] Thought within the context of the "star" system and celebrity culture, where show-biz vacuity, empty slickness, and flashy hypertechnique have long reigned supreme, such sentiments are undoubtedly refreshing, but they are also problematical. In truth, the deracinated humanism that continues to lurk in the mass obsession with the idols of the culture industry is by no means swept away by the codes of free-improvisation but, rather, rerooted in the dialogical soil of the collective, and thus rendered more immovable than ever. Such thinking does not attempt to think beyond the self but, instead, rethinks the self in terms of infinite transformation, the very becoming that, for Benjamin, obstructs our view of the origin. Staying with our two improvisors for a moment, Spolin's and Prevost's words are archetypical in the following two passages:

> True improvisation re-shapes and alters the student actor through the act of improvisation itself. Penetration into the focus, connec-

tion, and a live relation with fellow players results in a change, alteration or new understanding for one or the other or both.[86]

> The whole essence and ultimate meaning of dialogue is transformation. Conversations and interactive processes which proscribe any shift in self-knowledge, or limit its possibility, cannot therefore be generative, or productive of whatever might be produced.[87]

This celebration of alteration and transformation as the essence of improvisation in fact obscures this essence, which concerns Being and beings, not self and others or subject and object. This is chiasmal rather than ontological thinking, trapped in the interminable movement of a crisscrossing back and forth between ever-altered self and ever-altered other, sucking both into an oscillatory rhythm without genuine alterity. And one can see why: without the coherence and substantiality of the recognized (in the Hegelian sense) work, the improvising self is thrown back upon itself as the producer without a product—absolute spontaneity without origin. But the dim view taken of all self-aggrandizement within free-improvisation strips the singular improvisor of any authority such virtuosic dwelling in the now might have, resulting in a peculiar aesthetic without artist or artwork, reducing improvisation to an inexplicable anonymous process. In the face of this absurdity it is dialogue that comes to the rescue, allowing this irresolvable chiasmus to be reenacted and thus made meaningful as the infinite transformative process witnessed above. So, instead of directing the chiasmal relation of the artist and the artwork toward its essence by raising the more primordial question of the Being of art in relation to this chiasmus, such dialogical/participatory discourses simply internalize the chiasmus, thus replacing the tragedy of art with an ethics of empathic intersubjectivity. Now it is neither the artist nor the work that obscure the Being of art but the group and the entanglement in the collective that inserts the noise of incessant dialogue into the essential silence of art.

To follow Heidegger here, one would have to say that the promotion of intersubjective empathy, dialogue, and, ultimately, communion as the goal of free-improvisation falls far short of the authentic task of the artist; indeed, by confusing the very beginnings of art with its têlos nothing essential can get off the ground. To explain: Heidegger's rejection of the philosophy of empathy in *Being and Time* is based on the fact that such thinking, while claiming to provide an "ontological bridge from one's own subject, which is given proximally as alone, to the other subject, which is proximally quite closed off,"[88] confuses the unsociableness of beings with the essential solitude of art, which has nothing whatever to do with intersubjectivity or social interaction. The empathic thinking that leaves its mark on so many discourses of improvisation only busies itself with the forging of links between one self and another to the extent that it has forgotten what Heidegger describes as the "being-with" or the primordial togetherness of *Dasein*. It is only out of this collective or shared ground that the perceived problem of social fragmentation, alienation, and singularity can arise as a secondary issue to be solved by dialogue and participation in the group. Heidegger deals with the question of empathy thus:

> Not only is Being towards Others an autonomous, irreducible relationship of Being: this relationship, as Being-with, is one which, with Dasein's Being, *already is*. Of course it is indisputable that a lively mutual acquaintanceship on the basis of Being-with often depends upon how far one's essential Dasein has understood itself at the time; but this means that it depends only upon how far one's essential Being with Others has made itself transparent and has not disguised itself. And that is possible only if Dasein, as Being-in-the-world, *already is with others*. "Empathy" does not first constitute Being-with; *only on the basis of Being-with does "empathy" become possible*: it gets its motivation from the unsociability of the dominant modes of Being-with.[89]

Taking this view, the significance of collective free-improvisation can be better recognized if the dominant perspective, the whole raison d'être of which is the establishment of a collective aesthetic will, is reversed or turned back upon itself. Instead of transcending the false closure of the artwork and the myopic self-interest of the artist in an orgy of mutual transformation without end, this other perspective would seek to forego the immediate pleasures of social interaction for the sake of a commonality that can be sensed but not enacted as a collective cultural task. These words are chosen carefully. Heidegger's Kantian lineage here remains in evidence: "Being-with" and the *sensus communis* share the same understanding of an anterior and primordial commonality that, to the extent it takes on presence as a sense, originates the work of art and the artist together. The fact that the enactment of this sense of art—the improvisation—destroys this sense and fails to achieve the unconcealment of Being does not necessarily require either the surpassing of this tragic predicament in the participatory ethics outlined above, but nor does it necessarily require the negation of this enactment in a "lowercase" stasis that is in danger of mystifying nothingness rather than substantiating the Being of art. There is another way of addressing this predicament, one that will introduce, as promised, a very un-Heideggerian concept: irony.

Irony

Recalling the earlier discussion of mourning, the following words of Howard Caygill's (and Benjamin's) were cited as an articulation of the latter's melancholic lamentation in the face of the interminable destruction of tradition:

> For Trauerspiel the world was empty, a place of "never-ending repetition" with no possibility of ever becoming genuine or authentic: "For those who looked deeper saw the scene of their existence as a rubbish heap of partial, inauthentic actions." The world handed down to us by tradition is uncanny, undecipherable, always other.[90]

Reading these words again from a different perspective it could be argued that this recognition of the inauthenticity of all aesthetic acts might lead to neither mourning nor tragedy but to irony. If mourning is really taken from the vocabulary of the critic looking on rather than the artist embroiled in the work, and if the tragic is, as Caygill argues, too entrapped in the logic of subjectivity, then perhaps it is irony that allows a way into the production of artworks without the mystifications of self-involvement, submission to the logic of the work, or communion with the group.

Although there is nothing particularly comic about irony—in its essence it is closer to tragedy—it is in what might be called the comedic dimension of improvisation that a certain opening into the ontological play of Being and beings presents itself. One can identify this ironic thread running through, for example, the free-improvisation of musicians (Ben Watson calls them "the comedians") such as Steve Beresford, Lol Coxhill, Han Bennink, and even the dead-pan severity of Derek Bailey where one senses an acute awareness not just of the self but, crucially, of the forces playing upon the self as an improvisation proceeds (self, work, other). Although all virtuosos in their own different ways, such performers exhibit what could be described as a reflexive knowingness that manifests itself in an uncanny ability to be able to both inhabit an emerging work while, at the same time, observing or listening to that work as if from the outside: the inside/outside of irony. In a recent review, Derek Bailey is described, not for the first time, as having achieved a certain egolessness in his contributions to collective improvisations, as Stewart Lee writes: "[Bailey] developed an utterly individual style, at once idiosyncratic and without ego";[91] but this is somewhat misleading, not least because it fails to explain the extraordinary impact Bailey so often has on the manner in which the improvisations to which he contributes emerge. This is far from being selflessness; it is, rather, a particular deployment of the self, one that displays what the romantic ironist Friedrich Schlegel describes as the "infinite agility" of irony, a speed of movement that acts quickly to deflate the inflated, mock the portentous, and reduce the fetishism of "spontaneous creation" (as Eric Clarke aptly describes it) to knockabout anarchy. This is comic, a negative freedom-from the pretensions of the artist and the conventions and constraints of the artwork. But irony is much more than this; it is also the positive freedom-to act, to mark without further ado the unmarked space in the full knowledge that each and every mark could be other. The ironic position is not uncommitted; it is absolutely committed to the now—the moment so celebrated by free-improvisation—but committed to it in its contingency. If, as Niklas Luhmann argues, art is the "emancipation of contingency,"[92] and if free-improvisation is the exemplary art form, then it is here that we will witness this liberation most vividly.

Although it is not a word in his vocabulary, irony is everywhere to be found in Heidegger's thinking, and in particular it is the ontological movement of concealment and unconcealment that brings it into play. More than anything else it is the recognition that, at the level of aesthetic practice, the unconcealment of Being can only begin, and that while this beginning may contain its end the ontological cord that holds beginning and end together is broken by the becoming of the work. But, and this is the crucial point, as long as the occurrence of art continues to begin the beginning (so to speak), then the becoming of the artwork as a work will not destroy its origin in the Being of art—it will not destroy the "uncanny and indecipherable" truth of an authentic tradition. To the extent that it is self-conscious—"knowing"—the becoming of the work will not be destructive but ironic, and irony can destroy nothing; if it could, it would not be irony but critique. Irony does not destroy the Being of art, it brings it into view, not immediately of course, but not mediately either—it does not re-present Being in a degraded form. The irony we are speaking of is not in the form; irony is a manner of *inhabiting* forms, one that speaks out of that form in order to mark the boundary of its outside. Blanchot and Levinas speak of the "darkness" of the aesthetic outside of the illuminated space of the "day." Rosenzweig speaks of the silence of art "alongside" the world. Søren Kierkegaard, in *Fear and Trembling*, describes irony as a speaking without speaking:

> First and foremost he [Abraham] does not say anything, and in that form he says what he has to say. His response to Isaac is in the form of irony, for it is always irony when I say something and still do not say anything.[93]

Irony, then, does not say one thing and mean another; rather, it speaks in order not to speak. It does not attempt to say what is profoundly unsayable but, at the same time, it recognizes the ontological vacuity of mere silence. The silence of irony is too silent for mere silence.

What then is the function of the ironic work if it neither destroys nor presents the Being of art in all its truth? Perhaps, above all, it is irony that allows fascination to continue, the fascination necessary to draw both producers and receivers to the artwork again and again to there confront what Blanchot describes as the "image" that is neither immediate or mediate but rather the intoxicating distance that holds the Being and being of art apart. But fascination with the image is not fascination with a thing, an object, or a work, it is the fascination with a movement, with an "infinite agility" that indeed allows a passage through the work but not directly into the primordiality of Being. No, the movement of irony, while capable of shedding the skin of the work and of the artist, nevertheless obscures the Being of beings at the same time, hence the fascination. Without this movement art is lost, either in the being of artists and their artworks filling the world with ever more cultural artifacts, or in the Being of art that, as pure anteriority, has no need of artists or artworks, only Being. Irony is fascinating because it keeps all of the dimensions of the aesthetic in play—artist, artwork, art—but as that which is always absent from itself, dislocated and displaced: in play in fact. And it is free-improvisation, the most playful of art forms, that promises to enact this dislocation—the "permanent parabasis" (interruption) of irony, as Paul de Man describes it[94]—before our eyes.

Irony and the Beginning

So, free-improvisation is exemplary in the manner in which it begins. It draws our attention to the problematical nature of a beginning because it has no prescribed starting point or place. The work may or may not begin, but if it does (it will) it cannot be the thoughtless beginning that kicks off the performance of a composed work at the appointed place and time without further ado. Nor can it be the thought-full beginning that, in its overdetermination, will only risk tentative or provisional beginnings on the understanding that everything can always be taken back, erased and rethought and then begun again . . . and again, or not at all (something like the writing of this book!). When free-improvisations begin, they begin, no turning back, a dramatization of origination that acts as an important reminder that a question mark hovers above the beginning of an artwork, not so much will it or won't it begin, but how? The unmarked space prior to the beginning of the work bears the invisible inscription of a universality and commonality that can be sensed but not decoded or transcribed into the language of the artwork. The transition from the unmarked to the marked space is not a continuous act but represents, rather, a discontinuity, break, or radical disjuncture. From the first moment of an improvisation there is potential for the emergence of irony: Why this rather than that mark? The improvisation begins, but with this body, these materials, this instrument, these words, in this language, the contingency of what is there and available. The hyperawareness of the ironic improvisor is not simply a heightened self-awareness but is, rather, an awareness of the above contingency that must be affirmed if the improvisation is to begin. But of course, by no means all improvisors are of an ironic disposition, a fact borne out by the extraordinary lengths some performers go in their attempts to either commit absolutely to what is at hand in a valiant effort to essentialize the contingent and spiritualize what happens to be there and available; or, conversely, to buck the given in devising ever more impressive strategies to overcome the limitations set by contingency. The above differences are not presented here as psychological types but as possibilities within any improvisation that, in fact, can conceivably be taken up by one and the same improvisor at different moments in an ongoing performance. In a sense these are forces always at work in improvisations, strategies that may or may not be tempting depending on the different desires of the improvisor. For example, essentializing the contingent has enormous expressive potential, while bucking the contingent will appeal to those in pursuit of innovation and originality. But without the necessary ironic distance such strategies endanger the exemplary promise of free-improvisation by reducing it to the ephemerality of individual predilection and the transience of human desire. Indeed, the fact that many improvisors consciously seek a certain ephemerality in their suspicion of the recorded documentation of an improvisation requires that they develop an ability to deploy rather than surrender to the different possibilities at work within the work. Contrary to opinion, to repeat, ironists are not uncommitted; on the contrary, they commit themselves to the contingency of forms, recognizing that without commitment improvisations could never get under way. It is not a question of commitment or noncommitment but of an infinite series of commitments that are driven, not by the needs of the improvisor in search of self, but by the demands of the work in search of an aesthetic life beyond the instant of its origination.

At its best free-improvisation is utterly compelling and, let us be clear, not on account of any microcosmic aesthetic utopia that is too often peddled in its name. And, notwithstanding the above reflections, the most compelling improvisations of all are by no means those governed by the knowingness of irony. In actuality it is the radically contested nature of free-improvisation and the spectacle of this contest at the point of delivery that demands attention and, indeed, allows our participation or intervention. The struggle enacted before our eyes (and ears) does, however, have only psychosocial significance at the level of the performers and their respective positions within the intersubjective space, and so is merely incidental to our central concern, which, in reality, is the more essential struggle of aesthetic forces and the ontological significance of this struggle as a moment in the existential tragedy of Being and beings. It might be remembered that the following passage was cited much earlier as an illustration of Howard Caygill's misgivings regarding the early Heidegger's "tragic" vision of subjectivity. Be that as it may, as a description of free-improvisation it could hardly be bettered:

> By introducing the dialectical logic of subjectivity . . . [Heidegger] transforms the paradox of tradition into the agonal and tragic struggle of the subject. The resolute subject struggles with tradition in the guise of fate and destiny, and in the struggle finds freedom. . . . The struggle clears the space for a moment of decision, one in which the past and future may be gathered and granted significance in the present.[95]

Perhaps what resonates most here is the recognition that the freedom of free-improvisation is not something that is enacted or expressed therein as the given substance of the performance but is, rather, something the improvisation allows us to *find*. Free-improvisation then is not the embodiment of freedom but a *search* for it in the here and now of the work's becoming. In a sense it is the negative freedom that is necessary to free the improvisor and the improvisation from the forces that would devastate it: past works, the artist, the work, the other, the collective. This, the clearing of an aesthetic space that brings the improvisor to the "moment of decision," requires, however, more than brute negativity, which is why the concept of irony has been introduced to allow a more nuanced account of the manner in which the forces at work within the work can be identified, occupied, and held at bay. In this way an ironic positivity is introduced into the destructiveness of negative freedom, which allows the work to emerge and open out into (and this is the irony) the space cleared by the work but tragically inaccessible to it as a work. To find freedom is not to be free, not least because the space cleared by the artwork at the decisive moment illuminates the very freedom that originates the artist and the artwork and that, in its becoming, is lost. Yes, it is true that the becoming of the artwork obscures its origin, but the loss is not absolute—how could it be? Absolute loss could result in neither mourning nor tragedy but only absolute forgetfulness, a blank and aesthetically insignificant oblivion. Instead, the origin is lost and found, darkened and illuminated by the artwork: concealed and unconcealed.

Thought ideally, free-improvisation begins in freedom and ends with freedom before it, but it is itself unfree. This observation is not critical, it is affirmative. There are degrees of unfreedom from the most ignorant to the most knowing, and to know one is unfree (the tragic knowledge of the ironist) is, perhaps, itself a kind of freedom.

3 Mimesis and Cruelty

Improvisation saves the day for pasta dish. **Tara Duggan**

Pasta is the anti-jazz: Improvisation destroys it. If you want something as good as you could get in Italy, you have to follow a recipe. Religiously. **Diane Seed**

: : :

If you were planning on going out for an Italian meal whose advice would you take, Tara Duggan's or Diane Speed's? Certainly, as Keith Johnstone himself admits, in the culinary world (as in the world of theater) improvisation is by no means a guarantee of quality or an excuse for its absence:

> Why should an audience be expected to lower its standards if they know that a show is unscripted? Would a disgusting meal taste better if the waiter said, "Ah, but the chef is improvising!"[1]

Needless to say, for Johnstone a disgusting improvised pasta dish would be more likely to cast doubt on the chef than on improvisation. And, notwithstanding Diane Seed's hard line (the Adorno of pasta cooks), the enormous popularity of Erica de Mane's *Pasta Improvvisata: How to Improvise in Classic Italian Style* would suggest that the risk of disastrous Italian cuisine has not put the majority off of improvisation *per se*; on the contrary, it is something of a buzzword, as the Ideas in Food Web site, with its promotion of the "art of improvisation," would seem to confirm.[2] Be that as it may, this chapter will adopt Diane Seed's "anti-jazz" pasta position as its starting point in recognition of the fact that not all of those who come into contact with improvisation are as convinced of its merits as are our would-be kitchen extemporizers and those who encourage them.

Leaving (reluctantly) the world of pasta, we can allow the American architect Richard Meier to set the tone here:

> Improvisation, I wish never to hear that word again. When you build a building, you determine the parameters, you work out the values, you get them right, and then, when things change, you pull the building down, and you start again.[3]

Although such unbending opposition is rare there is a hardcore of self-proclaimed anti-improvisors who, if for no other reason than their eminence, demand attention. Adorno, Boulez, Berio, John Cage, Gavin Bryars, Artaud, and even Derrida (a complicated case) have important and not always kind things to say on the subject that cannot be avoided if a serious case for improvisation is to be made.

Immanent Critique

Staying with the antijazz theme we might begin with Theodor Adorno's long-running and much-discussed negative engagement with popular music in general, jazz in particular, and, at the most specific, his repeated attempts to debunk the claims and practice of jazz improvisation. Although it is certainly true that he speaks out of a formalist tradition that is hardly renowned for its enthusiasm for improvisation as a structural principle, and while, as has been widely recognized, he speaks at a level of abstraction that is often unilluminating as far as specific works are concerned, this should not be allowed to obscure the fact that Adorno's project is an immanent one. The all-too-common accusations regarding his so-called elitism when confronted with popular culture fail to acknowledge this, a fact reiterated on many occasions by Adorno himself. Indeed, the very notion of immanent critique championed by Adorno, and evident in his engagement with jazz improvisation, is itself posed as a direct challenge to transcendental critique, which, in its arrogant attempt to find an Archimedean point above and beyond culture, ends up "despising the mind and its works."[4] Thus, as an immanent critic

Adorno does not, for example, use composition to judge and condemn improvisation but, through the mediation of negative dialectics, allows improvisation to judge *itself*, and thus fail to meet its *own* standard. He describes immanent critique as follows:

> Immanent criticism of intellectual and artistic phenomena seeks to grasp, through the analysis of their form and meaning, the contradiction between their objective idea and that pretension. It names what the consistency or inconsistency of the work itself expresses of the structure of the existent. . . . Where it finds inadequacies it does not ascribe them hastily to the individual and his psychology, which are merely the façade of the failure, but instead seeks to derive them from the irreconcilability of the object's moments. It pursues the logic of its aporias, the insolubility of the task itself. . . . A successful work, according to immanent criticism, is not one which resolves objectives in a spurious harmony, but one which expresses the idea of harmony negatively by embodying the contradictions, pure and uncompromised, in its inner structure.[5]

Instead of castigating Adorno, then, for his uncomprehending aloofness and rarefied abstraction, it might be more fruitful to listen more carefully to what he actually says. This, in turn, might remind us not only of the complexity of his engagement with popular culture but, perhaps more surprisingly, suggest a model of improvisation that is in fact considerably more powerful than those offered by improvisors themselves in their efforts to mount a defense against him or those like him. In particular, what should be highlighted at the outset is the trouble Adorno goes to in ensuring that what he describes as the "complicity" of the critic in what is under critique is acknowledged and worked into the movement of critical thought. As he says: "Even the implacable rigor with which criticism speaks the truth of an untrue consciousness remains imprisoned within the orbit of that which it struggles."[6] Taken seriously, this admittance draws Adorno into the orbit of improvisation where its guiding principles are not rejected but, on the contrary, embraced, and then tested. Only then does the dialectical logic described above come into its own and the real task of critique begin.

Pseudo-Individualization

Above all else, it is the principles of individuation and freedom that Adorno discovers to be the founding ideas that inform what he describes as the "ballyhoo" surrounding jazz improvisation, but which of course have a hold over him too. The achievement of individuality requires a principle of free choice that runs right through the Western tradition of postromantic art and its legitimating discourses. Such discourses put increasing weight on individual acts of creation, subjectivity, intentionality, and originality, thus forging a language (or "terminology" as Adorno describes it) rich in possibilities for the self-promotion of improvisation. In truth it is primarily this language that is the problem for Adorno rather than improvisation itself or the principle of free individuality, which, if only as a hopeless hope, he shares. In a sense improvisors are betrayed by this language, which, in short-circuiting the immanent dialectical work necessary to establish and recognize the aporia of subjectivity, leaves them with little more than a stock of clichés, offering no real insight into the complexity or potential of their own practice. To be clear, Adorno, along with the jazz improvisor, wants individuality, wants freedom, wants improvisation to be the genuine embodiment of these principles, but the failure of art to realize its *promesse de bonheur*, and the stark recognition of this failure, is where the genuine critical engagement with individual freedom can begin. To sidestep the issue is, for Adorno, to remain within the "pseudo-individualization" that he sees as the hallmark of all popular music, with jazz improvisation, given its own ideology of authenticity, being its most insidious vehicle.

Pseudo-individualization is, for Adorno, the "necessary correlate" of the increasing standardization of mass cultural production within developed capitalism. Just as Althusser identifies the "interpellation" of the subject as the existential lure of ideological apparatuses,[7] so Adorno charts the emergence of improvisation alongside the increasing dominance of the jazz standard and its formularization of musical space and time. So often accused of being remote from, even ignorant of his target, Adorno, in the following passage, puts his finger exactly on the spot where the ideology of jazz improvisation is at its most vulnerable and, in spite of the common retort that such a critique is hopelessly out of date, remains deeply problematical in the overhyped postmodern jazz revival spearheaded by performers such as Wynton Marsalis and the legions of neo-Coltraneans. They might want to read the following:

> Even though jazz musicians still improvise in practice, their improvisations have become so "normalized" as to enable a whole terminology to be developed to express the standard devices of individualization. . . . This pseudo-individualization is prescribed by the standardization of the framework. The latter is

so rigid that the freedom it allows for any sort of improvisation is severely limited. Improvisations . . . are confined within the walls of the harmonic and metric scheme. In a great many cases, such as the "break" of pre-swing jazz, the musical function of the improvised detail is determined completely by the scheme: the break can be nothing other than a disguised cadenza. Hence, very few possibilities for *actual improvisation* remain.[8]

In essence this is not a rejection of improvisation any more than it is a rejection of individuality. Indeed, the issue for Adorno is precisely that the language or jargon of free individuality alone cannot be actualized when it is spun around a standardized framework that gives it the lie. No, the above amounts to a *defense* of "actual improvisation," which is to say, reading the actual with Adorno through Hegel, an improvisation that is substantial to the extent that it genuinely works through the dialectic of individuality and framework—of subject and object—thus opening both up to the aporias that, if faced, would resist the immediate gratification of the pseudo. Read in this light, what Adorno is suggesting here is that, contrary to John Cage who insists that "you can't improvise structure," but only "form, material and method,"[9] "actual improvisation" would of necessity have to work down into and through the melodic and rhythmic structure itself rather than merely playing, no matter how adventurously, on the surface. Jazz improvisation, as Adorno understands it, falls far short of this, a shortcoming that is made worse by exaggerated claims to the contrary, which work in league with the forces of order that legitimate improvisatory disorder, safe in the knowledge that the standardized structure remains secure. But again, it is more the claims of improvisation that incite the apparent violence of Adorno's critique than it is the improvisatory project itself, which, to repeat, is something he ultimately embraces.

Rhythm

Just to make this point, throughout his writings on improvisation he is particularly keen to cast doubt on the much-heralded emancipation of pulse and the all-too-apparent suppleness of rhythm typical of jazz throughout its history. Once again, he is quick to point out that such experimentation, for all of its immediate virtuosity, has no structural impact whatsoever. The following is a typical passage taken from "Farewell to Jazz":

The apparent variety of rhythmic constructs can be reduced to a minimum of stereotypical and standardized formulae. But

then—and this explains the stereotypical quality—the rhythmic achievements of jazz are mere ornaments above a metrically
conventional, banal architecture, with no consequences for the
structure, and removable at will. . . . The "false bars," which essentially constituted the supposed rhythmic charm of jazz, have
their essence precisely in the fact that rhythmically free, improvisational constructions complement each other in such a way
that, taken together, they fit back into the unshaken schema after all.[10]

Taken to its "logical conclusion" such rhythmic experimentation would,
Adorno rightly claims, jeopardize the easy "consumability" of jazz, transforming it into an "art music" without the secure standardized structure
of the popular. He uses Stravinsky's "jazz experiments" as an example.
But these remarks should be read carefully if the familiar accusation of
elitism is not to reemerge. Yes, it is true that the case of Stravinsky does
allow Adorno some leverage in his attempt to prise open the rigid structures of pseudo-individuality, but this does not exempt Stravinsky himself from receiving the very same treatment when the critical gaze falls
upon his own "experiments." This is Adorno's response in *Philosophy
of Music*, in which, once again, it is the failure to go beyond surface disruption that remains the issue:

Rhythmic structure is, to be sure, blatantly prominent, but this
is achieved at the expense of all other aspects of rhythmic organization. Not only is any subjectively expressive flexibility of the
beat absent . . . but furthermore all rhythmic relations associated
with the construction and the internal compositional organization—the "rhythm of the whole"—are absent. Rhythm is under-
scored, but split off from the musical content. This results not in
more, but rather in less rhythm than in compositions in which
there is no fetish made of rhythm; in other words, there are only
fluctuations of something always constant and totally static.[11]

This is not by any means an isolated example. Although Adorno often
pits one artist against another, this is more a strategy to keep the dialectical movement of his thought in motion than it is a substantial component
of his critical method, which is immanent and thus unconcerned with
calling upon external or transcendent authorities. This is why the common reading of *Philosophy of Music* as pro Schoenberg/contra Stravinsky
fails to recognize that the real substance of the book is to be found at the

level of immanent critique and not in the point scoring of musicological factions. This, incidentally, is why one also finds an incisive critique of Schoenberg's use of rhythmic structure,[12] leading one to conclude that it is not personalities that Adorno is concerned with, and not even specific works, but the complete radicalization of the rhythmic sense, one which points beyond all given musics toward, among other things, "actual improvisation."

Memory

There is one final example from Adorno that picks up again on rhythm but also introduces the related theme of memory, which will allow this discussion to be developed further. Here Adorno is speaking of Wagner:

> The key to Wagner's form would lie in the fact that the conductor has to know the work by heart: the analysis of form serves as an aid to memory. . . . The giant packages of his operas are divided up by the notion of striking, of beating time. The whole of the music seems to have been worked out first in terms of the beat, and then filled in; over great stretches . . . the time seems to be an abstract framework.[13]

Once again, Adorno is perturbed by the deceptive disjuncture between surface malleability and structural rigidity, which creates the illusion of individual freedom where none exists, thereby reminding us that pseudo-individualization is by no means unique to jazz improvisation. But introducing the question of memory into the analysis of musical structure raises some interesting issues regarding, in different ways, both free-improvisation and idiomatic improvisation (which would include jazz). As we have already considered free-improvisation, some of the implications of Adorno's thoughts on memory will first be retrospectively mapped back onto some aspects of that discussion.

What is interesting at this juncture is the way in which the issue of memory divides Adorno from other critics of improvisation such as, for instance, the composers Luciano Berio and Pierre Boulez. In Adorno's case, any form of mnemonics reminds the performer and the audience of their place within a structure of aesthetic time that exceeds and determines the performative moment:

> Among the functions of the leitmotiv can be found, alongside the aesthetic one, a commodity function, rather like that of an

advertisement: anticipating the universal practice of mass culture later on, the music is designed to be remembered, it is intended for the forgetful.[14]

The apparent freedom of the improvisor—the risk taking and spectacle
of spontaneity—is rarely the inspired abandonment that it appears to be
or is promoted as. Improvisation requires a powerful memory: memory
of the parameters of an instrument, of the body, of available technology,
the parameters of a work's structure and one's place within it at any one
time, the parameters of an idiom, a genre and its history, its possibilities. For Adorno, all of these memories, both voluntary and involuntary,
become fused and encoded in formulae, clichés, predigested chunks of
aesthetic matter where everything new is really old. Clearly, if improvisation is to have any value for Adorno—"real improvisation"—it would
have to become more Nietzschean, more forgetful, indeed, a "music of
forgetting" as Nietzsche describes it, what he calls "monological art."[15]
The logic of Adorno's argument is that such a music of forgetting would
be the only way of avoiding the clichés that pass for improvisation, a
logic pursued, as already suggested, by many free-improvisors. Pierre
Boulez, however, takes a different view, regarding free improvisors as
being handicapped by, as he puts it, an "inadequate memory." Far from
being a strategy to avoid clichés, it is, for him, precisely the instanta-
neousness of free-improvisation that is itself *responsible* for the production of such clichés, as he explains in a conversation with Célestin
Deliège, speaking of contemporary free-improvisation:

> There is no set course of any description; there is merely elabo-
> ration for and of the moment, because the memory is put out of
> action by material that is usually too rich or complex . . . and the
> memory cannot recall in detail the material that has gone before.
> So the memory only comes into play for extremely banal criteria
> and clichés such as, for instance, repeated notes or notes sepa-
> rated by long silences.[16]

There is clearly some truth in Boulez's complaint that so-called free-
improvisations are in fact often determined by a fairly rigid set of tacit
assumptions that result in a degree of predictability that would appear to
go against the spirit of such performance. But this is precisely the predicament of the free-improvisor as described in the last chapter—the struggle against the work becoming a *work*—and one that often produces the
most successful improvisations. Indeed, notwithstanding the cogency of

Boulez's remarks, perhaps it is free-improvisors more than any other art-ists (including famous composers) who are *most* aware of the dangers of clichés, which, of course, does not stop them from falling back on them. Derek Bailey suggests as much when he acknowledges that "habits—technical habits and musical habits (clichés)—are quite consciously uti-lized by performers,"[17] an observation made without any suggestion that this contradicts or compromises the freedom of free-improvisation.

But to bring this discussion back to the question of memory and im-provisation, it is interesting to note that, while both Boulez and Berio have difficulties with the idea and practice of free-improvisation, they are more sympathetic to what they both call improvisatory *gestures* rooted in a fixed structure of memory that saves the instant of performance from a descent into the contingency of a private psychodrama or, as Boulez puts it, "a collective psychological test which only shows up the most basic side of the individual."[18] Berio's sympathies lie with jazz im-provisation, which he depicts as the "rapid extraction of musical mod-ules and instrumental gestures from the great reservoir of memory."[19] Of course, it is precisely the gestural nature of jazz improvisation that troubles Adorno, the worry being that the very nature of the gestural is fundamentally conservative, allowing a show of surface spontaneity to conceal and impede the transformation of an inherited fixed structure. Speaking of which, Boulez, in his positive reference to Indian and Bali-nese improvisation, is perfectly direct in his identification of the *fixity* of the musical and cultural tradition that allows genuinely valuable impro-visation to take place:

> Improvisation has found its most explicit expression in vari-ous civilisations where it was associated with precise basic rules learnt over countless generations, that leave the way open for a spontaneous invention that is basically connected with gesture. Once gesture has been codified, you can have last-minute impro-visation, because it is now based on something. This happens in Indian civilisations where the qualifications and regulations for improvisations are extremely strict; the same is true of Bali, where models are absolutely fixed. Improvisation is then simply a kind of variation on a basic model.[20]

This seems straightforward enough, assuming one accepts the rather alarming rigidity that runs through this particular (serial composer's) model of improvisation. But when Boulez speaks approvingly of "codi-fied" gestures being "based on something" it raises the question as to whether he and Berio are really speaking of the same thing, of the same kind of memory. Is a "great reservoir of memory" necessarily the same thing as "precise basic rules learnt over countless generations"? Perhaps it is, but it would be nice to think that the function of memory within improvisational practice is able to exceed the strictly delimited temporality of codification that is typically assumed by such theorizations of gesture. True, neither Berio nor Boulez seem to have a problem with gestural improvisation, either as an idea or a practice but, nevertheless, it is difficult to see what kind of coexistence is possible for the gestural and the improvisational. If, for the latter, valuable improvisation is only possible when it is "based on something," does this "something" have to be thought exclusively in terms of learnt basic rules?

The case made for free-improvisation in the last chapter was built upon a "memorial aesthetics" without mourning that made an attempt to think the Heideggerian and Benjaminian origin of art alongside the idea of universality to be found in Kant's *sensus communis*. The task of remembering the beginning in the becoming of the work was the "something" that attempted to save free-improvisation from itself, from its individualism and its collectivism, from the artist and the artwork. In the present discussion, where the critique of improvisation is the issue, it is significant that once again the very same issue of memory needs to be addressed in order to save improvisation, not from itself this time, but from its enemies. The aim here is not to launch a countercritique that would shield improvisation from its opponents but, rather, to consider how such opposition might be incorporated into a more powerful model of improvisation.

To begin by refining further our understanding of Adorno's perspective on memory, it was suggested earlier that, following Nietzsche, perhaps a "music of forgetting" would be the closest approximation to a radically free improvisation, one that avoided the endless regurgitation of a stockpile of clichés and standardized formulas. The essential thing to grasp is that to forget one must have something else to remember. One might say that active forgetting is really remembering, that it is the forgetting necessary for real memory to be remembered. Notwithstanding Adorno's infamous allergy to the "jargon of authenticity," there is more than a hint of Heidegger in this dialectic of forgetting and remembering that suggests a proximity between the former's aesthetic theory and the latter's ontology of originary art that is not always acknowledged. It is clear that, for Adorno, what needs to be forgotten is a particular way of remembering, one caught up in what he calls a "dreamless" world "in which all memories of things not wholly integrated have been purged":[21]

the world of jazz. Having said that, however, every so often, as with his reference to "actual improvisation" and "real improvisation," Adorno seems to allow a momentary return of repressed memories through the medium of jazz *itself* when he speaks of the "element of excess, of insubordination" and the "recollection" of jazz's "anarchic origins."[22] At such moments, moments of "real improvisation" perhaps, the memory of the known, the "rehashing of basic formulas where the schema shines through at every moment,"[23] gives way to a sudden awareness of an aesthetic dimension of the work that the familiar mnemonics of performance obscure. But how does this happen? What is the difference between improvisation and "real improvisation"? The problem Adorno has with jazz improvisation is its pseudo-individualism, something he shares with many free-improvisors who, for that very reason, prefer to work in groups. At the same time, however, he is also throughout his work profoundly resistant to any identification with the collective. So, in keeping with his negative dialectics that steadfastly refuses to settle upon either the subjective or objective poles of art practice—artist/artwork—Adorno's fleeting (and infuriatingly undeveloped) reference to "real improvisation" speaks not of the individual or the collective but of "oppositional groups" improvising out of "sheer pleasure." This is a strange statement for Adorno who almost never speaks of art in terms of pleasure. He is indeed alluding to a strange moment, when the forgotten pleasure in the intertwining of subjectivity and objectivity, of the individual and the collective, is remembered within the dialectical movement of oppositional improvising groups breaking open the surface of the artwork to expose its repressed origin in what Heidegger would call Being and Adorno calls the *spirit* of art. By thus thinking improvisation in terms of oppositional groups he is able to suggest a mode of aesthetic expression that avoids the triviality of the subjective—"if expression were merely a duplicate of subjective feelings, it would not amount to anything"[24]—while, at the same time, dialectically dynamizing objectivity by making its expressive potency dependent not on the intrinsic qualities of form but on the mimetic acts of artists. Such acts, if thought in terms of oppositional groups, manage to hold collectivity and objectivity apart, something that is vital if art is to retain its expressive value in the face of collective standardization. But first this has to be remembered, as Adorno writes:

> Art is imitation only to the extent to which it is objective expression far removed from psychology. There may have been a time long ago when this expressive quality of the objective world generally was perceived by the human sensory apparatus. It no

longer is. Expression nowadays lives on only in art. Through expression art can keep at a distance the moment of being-for-other which is always threatening to engulf it. Art is thus able to speak in itself. This is its realization through mimesis. Art's expression is the antithesis of "expressing something."[25]

Mimeticism

As is clear, Adorno's aesthetic theory promotes a mimeticism that, it should be emphasized at the outset, has nothing whatever to do with imitating or copying that which is already given. Perhaps the best way to grasp this would be to start where Adorno himself most likely first encountered a different way of thinking mimesis, in the work of Walter Benjamin. In his 1933 essay "On the Mimetic Faculty" Benjamin makes a distinction between what he calls the "commonplace, sensuous area of similarity" within which the familiar notion of mimesis operates, and his concept of "non-sensuous similarity,"[26] which *produces* rather than re-presents or reproduces affinities between the subjective and the objective. Where Benjamin speaks of the mimeticism of language, Adorno broadens this into a feature of all aesthetic practice, sharing with his friend the view that, with the "decay of the mimetic faculty," art increasingly becomes "an archive of non-sensuous similarities, of non-sensuous correspondences."[27] This is how Benjamin's essay begins:

> Nature creates similarities. One need only think of mimicry. The highest capacity for producing similarities, however, is man's. His gift of seeing resemblances is nothing other than a rudiment of the powerful compulsion in former times to become and behave like something else. Perhaps there is none of his higher functions in which his mimetic faculty does not play a decisive role.[28]

As is clear here, the production of similarities is not presented by Benjamin as the reduction of difference to the same but as the very *production of difference*, if that is how we understand the "powerful compulsion" to become "like something else." It is the becoming rather than the resemblance that is important here, a distinction that ensures that mimesis remains a productive rather than a reductive movement. Adorno speaks of a mimetic "non-conceptual affinity"[29] with the other that, as Martin Jay observes, "involves a more sympathetic, compassionate, and noncoercive relationship . . . between non-identical particulars, which do not then become reified into two poles of subject/object dualism."[30] In the

same vein Adorno speaks of "aesthetic behaviour" as "assimilating itself
to the other rather than trying to subdue it." It is the movement of this
assimilation, its becoming as a process of mimesis that keeps the artwork
and the artist agile:

> Aesthetic behaviour . . . is a process set in motion by mimesis, a
> process also in which mimesis survives through adaptation. This
> process shapes both the relation of the individual to art and the
> historical macrocosm. It congeals in works of art in so far as they
> represent immanent movement, tension and the possibility of re-
> lease of tension.[31]

It is this, the idea that mimesis sets aesthetic behavior in *motion*, that
begins to point ahead to a different model of improvisation that will increasingly concern us. It is a model that situates improvisation within
rather than outside of reproduction and representation while, of course,
problematizing both terms.

If mimesis is thought productively rather than reproductively then
representation too needs to be addressed differently. This is already signaled by Benjamin who in his essay on epic theater discusses representation within the context of "the interruption," the disruptive dramatic
movement *par excellence*. In so doing he is keen to separate representation from reproduction in the following manner:

> The task of epic theatre . . . is less the development of the ac-
> tion than the representation of situations. "Representation" here
> does not mean "reproduction." . . . Rather, the truly important
> thing is to discover the situations for the first time. (One might
> equally say "defamiliarize" them.) This discovery (or defamil-
> iarization) of situations is fostered through the interruption of
> the action.[32]

Thanks to the concept of interruption, the discovery described here is
not passive, the situation is not the re-presentation of that which is already given but the sudden flaring up and recognition of the new within
the old, the unfamiliar within the familiar. As with his understanding
of the infinite differentiation (or differencing) of mimesis, so here again
Benjamin draws out the uncanniness of representation, the way in which
it removes rather than reproduces presence, thus allowing the movement
of presencing to interrupt the fixation with (and the fixity of) what is
present. Just as mimesis can be thought not as the making of one thing

similar to another but, rather, as the movement that makes something other than itself, so representation too, once cut free from a postulated originary presence, is precisely the manner in which "un-sensed similarities" interrupt the "sensed similarities" of any given situation. Interestingly, Derrida, like Benjamin, also draws sustenance from the ambiguities of the German word for representation (*Darstellung*). In a discussion of Artaud's "theater of cruelty" he demonstrates how representation introduces absence rather than presence into aesthetic space:

> The stage, certainly, *will no longer represent*, since it will not operate as an addition, as the sensory illustration of a text already written, thought, or lived outside the stage, which the stage would then only repeat but whose fabric it would not constitute. The stage will no longer operate as the repetition of a *present*, it will no longer *re*-present a present that would exist elsewhere and prior to it.[33]

For Derrida the end of representation is, at the same time, the beginning, the place or the opening of a space (*"espacement"*) where the real uncanniness of what Derrida calls "original representation" interrupts the self presence of the all-too-familiar situation. Similarly, it is this, the alterity of the aesthetic, its enigmatic quality, that gives rise to what Adorno describes as the "shudder" of art. To "shudder" is to remember, not the history of represented codes, but the prehistory of that which art is only the "after-image." As for Adorno, it is (surprisingly for an "elitist") the circus that makes him "shudder":

> Art as *mnemosyne* is this kind of retaining operation. The instant of appearance in works of art is the paradoxical union or balance between a vanishing and a preserving tendency, for works of art are static and dynamic at the same time. Artistic genres below the standards approved by culture, genres such as the tableau in circus and variety shows, probably even the mechanical water fountain of the seventeenth century, candidly blurt out what serious art tries to hide in its bosom as some kind of secret *a priori*. They too are enlightened because they seek to translate the memory of shudder, incommensurable as it was in prehistorical times, into such terms as can be understood by man.[34]

What is immediately evident is Adorno's recognition that the artwork represents a moment of appearance and disappearance. Clearly, part of

Adorno's attraction to the circus and variety shows is that the vanishing quality of such performances—their ephemerality—makes manifest the dialectic of concealment/unconcealment that is obscured by the claims of the artwork within the context of a culture industry driven by the desire for the consumption of works. This is the other side of the Adornian coin: on the one hand he seeks to liberate art from the pseudo-subjectivity of the improvisor, while here, on the other, it is the pseudo-objectivity of the artwork, one that endures only by keeping its vanishing moment "secret," that Adorno seeks to dialectically problematize. On a number of occasions in *Aesthetic Theory* he even goes beyond the ephemerality of the circus into the pure transience of pyrotechnics:

> Ernst Schoen once praised the unique nobility of fireworks, the only art that does not want to endure but is content to sparkle for an instant and then fade away. Perhaps this is a model for critically interpreting the temporal arts, i.e. drama and music, in terms of the reification that is constitutive of them and yet degrades them.[35]

It is, perhaps, not too much of a leap from this instantaneous aesthetic back into the model of free-improvisation presented in the last chapter. What both have in common is a deep-seated suspicion of both the inspired subject and the reified object. Of course, Adorno wants to break with the inspiration of the individual improvisor precisely because it is the product of the very reification that it appears to deny, but so too does he want to resist the powerful and ever-present temptation to identify with an ideology of collectivity that would seek to dress reification up in the humanist clothes of dialogics—the dubious preciousness of the "I-Thou." Where, in the last chapter, the movement of the improvisor was described in terms of the beginning of art and the task of keeping that beginning in view as beginning, here it is the language of mimesis that has been foregrounded and, in particular, the manner in which the representational movement of the mimetic faculty defamiliarizes the familiar by interrupting situations that are in danger of becoming or indeed have become reified.

Cruelty

But, what kind of improvisation takes place in the circus or variety shows, in Brechtian theater, or, for that matter, in the "theater of cruelty"? In some ways it is easier to determine what such improvisation

is not. It is not the so-called freedom associated with individual interpretation, nor is it related to the expressivity associated with subjective
feeling. Similarly, it is not to be associated with the call and response of
collective interaction thought within an organic, empathic totality. To
reintroduce Artaud here, in spite of his avowed opposition to improvisation it would seem that his problem concerns the nature of "inspired"
acting rather than improvisation *per se*:

> My shows have nothing to do with Copeau's improvisations. . . .
> [T]hey are not committed to the whims of an actor's rough and
> ready inspiration, especially modern actors who once they step
> outside the text plunge blindly on. I would not care to entrust the
> fate of my shows and theatre to that kind of chance. No.[36]

Like Adorno, he inherits a model of improvisation that is determined
by the relationship between the improvisor and an authoritative text, one
that assumes an empathic interpretative dialogue with that text. Although
Adorno sometimes alludes to a model of "real improvisation" outside
of this particular nexus, the fact that his immanent project never directly
proposes an alternative to the jazz standard means that this task is left in-
complete. The case of Artaud is rather different given that the whole "theater of cruelty" project is more about the affirmation of the new rather
than the negation of the old. And it is this sweeping away of the old theater of the text that exposes the actors "who once they step outside of the
text plunge blindly on." The problem is that by sweeping away the text
Artaud must also sweep away improvisation and improvisors, as indeed
he does—but, as with Adorno, perhaps not entirely. There is one section
in a letter to Jean Paulhan that, again with a frustrating degree of irresolu-
tion, hints at another model of improvisation, one that radically reconfig-
ures the relationship between text, performance, and performer:

> Theatre will no longer be based on dialogue and the little dia-
> logue remaining will not be written out, pre-arranged or deter-
> mined *a priori*, but will be made up on stage, created on stage,
> correlating with the other language, with the required postures,
> symbols, moves and objects. But all this objective groping among
> one's material, where Words appear a necessity, resulting from
> a series of condensations, shocks, stage friction, all kinds of de-
> velopments—(in this way theatre will become a genuine living
> operation, it will retain that kind of passionate pulsation with-
> out which art is pointless)—all this groping, all these experiments

and jolts will nevertheless culminate in an *inscribed* composition, every last detail decided on and recorded by means of notation.[37]

Although insistent on the necessity of notation and inscription it is significant that, for Artaud, this is the *culmination* rather than the origination of performance. For all of its strictness or "cruelty" the codification of gestural space is not imposed from a linguistic source prior to the theater but, and these are the crucial words, *"made up on the stage."* In some respects these views have some affinities with the Wagnerian notion of fixed improvisation (and Artaud is extraordinarily Wagnerian in so many respects) where the final work, the text, image, composition, or whatever, represent a final fixing of an improvisational process. As Wagner puts it in *The Destiny of Opera*, the "most perfect form of art" would be a "mimetic-musical improvisation of consummate poetic value fixed by the finest artistic judgement."[38] There is a reversal here, with inscription coming *after* rather than before improvisation, effectively shifting the state of fixity to the end rather than to the beginning of the work. A major influence on Artaud's thought is the Balinese theater but, as Berio and Boulez agree, the improvisation that takes place within this context uses the fluidity of gesture to disguise the fixity of its source. The "theater of cruelty" works in exactly the opposite way. Its eventual form emerges out of what Artaud calls the "groping" among the objective material, a series of "experiments" or (we would say) improvisations that are eventually notated and fixed, thus disguising the unfixity of their source. In short, one is fixed then improvised, the other is improvised then fixed: this is why the "theater of cruelty" is cruel. If the performers are involved in the improvisations that provide the material to be fixed, then the experience of producing the very structure that will be eventually imposed upon them mercilessly certainly has an element of cruelty quite distinct from the joyous gestures of Balinese, Indian, or flamenco improvisors. The latter are always already within an aesthetic situation that is fixed, whereas within the "theater of cruelty" the performers are responsible for the production of the situation only then to witness its rigorous codification. One might say they see fixity coming into being or witness the beginning of fixity. This reversal has a direct bearing on the distinction signaled earlier between Berio's "vast reservoir of memory" and Boulez's "countless generations of fixed rules" in that it allows us to gain a more profound sense of the unfixity of the fixed. In short, it allows us to remember the manner in which our memories become memorable as a cultural tradition and codified heritage. In a sense we are speaking here of a memory of memory or memory of remembrance that, in trying to think outside of a history of aesthetic forms, raises again the issue of the origin or Being of art and, with it, the possibility of "actual improvisation," a mode of performance or practice that might give expression to this more essential engagement.

For all of his talk about the necessity of absolute obedience to the newly formulated laws of the "theater of cruelty," Artaud insists that any performance worthy of attention must have the "passionate pulsation" of life, which raises the question, how is this passion to be expressed outside of the all-too-familiar strategies of individual inspiration? Answering this question brings Artaud and Adorno together. What both want is an art that is expressive but that avoids, indeed critiques, the trivial capriciousness of the inspired individual. This leads them both into the promotion of a mimeticism that is at once expressive and objective. Adorno brings expression, objectivity, and mimesis together in the following way:

> Aesthetic expression is objectification of the non-objective. Put more precisely, through its objectification expression becomes a second non-objective substance, one that speaks out of the artifact rather than out of the subject. Even so, the objectification of expression, which coincides with art, cannot do without a subject that produces expression and thereby, to use a bourgeois phrase, gainfully employs his mimetic impulses. Art is expressive when a subjectively mediated, objective quality raises its voice to speak.[39]

What is being remembered here is not a history of forms ever ready to be plundered for expressive content but the originary movement from the nonobjective to the objective that constitutes art and, indeed, provides it with its expressive substance. The importance of mimesis within the context of this originary movement is that the expressive moment is integral to the mimetic act of finding objective equivalents for nonobjective substance. What gives the mimetic impulse expressive power is not its success or failure in fixing subjective intention in an objective artifactual otherness but, rather, in its ability to re-present the dissonance between the unfixed and the fixed, between the "pulsation" of life and the code. The expressive dimension of mimesis then has nothing to do with *what* it copies but concerns instead its dual nature as that which produces similarities while also satisfying the "powerful compulsion" to become "something else." It is not feelings but the codification of feelings in objective gestures that is expressive, not because these gestures speak or show this expressive substance but precisely because they don't. Similarity assumes otherness, and it is this otherness that intrudes into every mimetic act and that makes it pulsate, but it is the pulsation of dissonance that has the "life" required by both Adorno and Artaud, not the dead harmoniousness of an impossible mimetic sameness. Indeed, as Artaud himself admits, where he says "cruelty" he could just as easily say "life":

> The idea being that because life, metaphysically speaking, accepts range, depth, weight and matter, it accepts evil in direct consequence and everything inherent in evil, namely space, range and matter. All of which culminates in consciousness and anguish, and consciousness in anguish. Life cannot fail to exercise the blind severity all these contingencies bring or else it would not be life. But cruelty is this severity and this life which exceeds all bounds and is practiced in torture, trampling everything down, that pure inexorable feeling.
>
> Therefore I said "cruelty" just as I might have said "life" or "necessity," because I wanted especially to denote that the theatre to me means continual action and emergence, above all there is nothing static about it, I associate it with a true act, therefore alive, therefore magic.[40]

Within the context of the "theater of cruelty" the imposition of the masks and gestures arrived at through the contingencies of improvisation is not, then, in any way comparable to the rigors of, for instance, Balinese theater where the "evil" of this "blind severity" is not part of the show. The intensity of engagement Artaud demands is one that requires the performers to continually bare the scars of their own submission to an emerging logic that is "cruel" precisely because it is eternally emerging with an inhuman severity that is not grounded in a genuine strictness that could be definitive or foundational. Certainly, Artaud seeks formulas but he does so from one moment to the next. Yes, he speaks of codifying precise gestures while admitting, in the same breath, their pointlessness: that's why he's "cruel."

> The main point: to see the relationships, learn the formulae, to find the right formula each and every moment.
>
> To put useless, pointless gestures back in useful environments, relinking them with primal laws, making them conform with everything.[41]

Accepting that improvisation takes place prior to the fixing of the work, the question remains, is there a place for improvisation at the moment of performance itself or is this sacrificed to the "cruel" spectacle that ensues?

The difficulty is that we are used to thinking of improvisation as the un-fixing of the fixed at the moment of performance or practice whereas here we must consider the possibility of a form of improvisation that reverses that movement. If the expressivity of art concerns the dissonance of the mimetic act understood as the othering of the self in search of objective similarities or correspondences, then what kind of improvisation could carry this over into the performance itself? Certainly not the pseudo-individualism and blind inspiration rejected by Adorno and Artaud, modes of improvisation that are far too at home in their aesthetic surroundings to bring the cruel contingency of the given into view. A more promising direction to go in would be via Benjamin's reading of Bertolt Brecht's epic theater where he lays stress on the manner in which it is incumbent upon the actor to refuse empathy and engage instead in a mode of performance "based on distancing."[42] The fact is, creating distance or, better, expos-ing the distance between actor and character, performer and code within the mimetic act, is not something that can be inscribed. No matter how "cruel" Artaud becomes in his pointless legislation, the *sense* of cruelty can only be created by the performer, just as the defamiliarization of the situation can only be fully achieved in Brechtian theater by the distancing of the actor, something that cannot be written into the drama. This is why Brecht himself thought productions of his plays often failed. As he says, for example, of the Deutsches Theater production of *Mother Courage*, "the central aim of the epic theatre was not achieved. Much was shown, but the element of showing was absent."[43] It is this concern with the act of showing that emerges as a key element in the model of improvisation that is trying to be grasped here. The difference between showing and not showing is not something that can be inscribed into the play by the play-wright; it is, rather, an aspect of performance that can only be achieved if the performer finds ways to both occupy the theatrical space while also drawing attention to that space as marked through and through. This is where the relationship between irony and improvisation once again pre-sents itself as a crucial issue.

Irony

Brecht acknowledges the importance of irony in his theory of the theater, a fact noted by Benjamin, who rightly sees it as a major platform for his didactic aims,[44] but neither gives any attention to how this might affect the improvisatory dimension of performance. The reason for this, per-haps, is that the ironic position, with its exaggerated self-consciousness and cool reflexivity, would appear to stand for everything that is contrary to the spontaneous immediacy of improvisation. This is true but that is exactly what is needed here, a model of improvisation that can operate within the context of Artaud's reversal of the fixed/unfixed duality. Obviously, by its very nature irony can work in both directions, fixing or unfixing as the case may be. In the last chapter, although the ironist was positioned between the artist and the artwork with a view to bringing the Being of art into view, there was nonetheless a certain emphasis placed on the ironic *unfixing* of the work and the interruption of the working of the work congealing into a *work*. On this occasion the ironist will be cast in a different role, as the fixer of the unfixed, not in order to create a work but to *show* how a work becomes a work, to show the movement from the unfixed to fixed. The irony being that the fixed is never as fixed as it seems, and the tragedy being that the destruction of the unfixed by the fixed is the inescapable price paid for human expression in art. But how does such irony enter into improvisatory practice?

Returning to Adorno's pseudo-individualized jazz improvisor, instead of understanding the exposure of the formulaic nature of this genre as a critical strategy it is perfectly possible to imagine a mode of improvisation that *itself* draws attention to the standardization at its root by deliberately focusing on clichéd patterns of performance that *show* how expression is fixed precisely by enacting it. This might be thought of as a kind of performative auto-critique, but in truth irony is more of a deconstructive than a critical strategy, sharing with the former an affirmative nature that knowingly occupies the given rather than being intent upon negation. Deconstruction does not destroy structures; rather, it shows how structures become structures and, simultaneously, shows the contingency of that becoming. Contingent or not, the structures are always there, which is where Derrida's problem with improvisation lies. As he responds to a question in *Points*:

> I do not know why I go off in this direction, while improvising, rather than others, so many other possible directions. What is important here is the improvisation—contrived like all so-called free association—well, anyway, what is called improvisation. It is never absolute, it never has the purity of what one thinks one can require of a forced improvisation: the surprise of the person interrogated, the absolutely spontaneous, instantaneous, almost simultaneous response. A network of apparatuses and relays—and first of all language, the element of this finite interview I am speaking about—has to interrupt the impromptu, put it beside itself, set it aside from itself. A battery of anticipatory and delaying

devices, of slowing-down procedures are already in place the moment one opens one's mouth . . . in order to protect against improvised exposition.[45]

This is a very typical Derridean response to the question of improvisation, one that expresses a desire for the spontaneous and the impromptu but which, at the same time, must affirm the network of structures that would seem to prevent or "protect" one from improvising and improvisation, respectively. But perhaps it is Derrida's rather limited model of improvisation that creates the difficulty here, relying, as it does, too heavily on strangely orthodox notions of pure instantaneity and creative novelty that could never stand up to deconstruction's scrutiny. The suggestion here, however, is that it is possible to conceive of a model of improvisation that is itself knowingly situated within the very networks that would seem to preclude it. Not only does this make improvisation possible, in many respects it offers a way of understanding how Derrida *himself* improvises, a discussion that we will return to in the last chapter. For the moment it is enough to indicate that the presence of standardized or clichéd patterns of performance and the consciousness of them does not prevent improvisation; on the contrary, it merely changes the form that it takes. Nor does this ironic model of improvisation necessarily imply satire, pastiche, or empty virtuosity, tempting though they may be for the performer. All of the above are avoidable if the dialectic of contingency and fixity is kept on show. This might be thought of as the other side of "cruelty." Yes, it is cruel to fix aesthetic acts in contingent codes and formulas that then take on the disciplinary force intended by an Artaud, and yes, the degree of cruelty would no doubt be lessened to the extent that contingency is removed, but it is precisely the contingency of art that gives it its intensity. A *necessary* art would have as much passion as an arranged marriage, as much aesthetic force as a pie chart. The contingency of art is a constant reminder that, in spite of appearances, everything could just as easily have been different even though the artwork shows us that things nevertheless turn out much the same. Drawing attention to this sameness can be humorous but it can also be a poignant reminder that without the fixing of infinite possibility into contingent repeatable patterns of actual practice the expressive voice falls silent and the aesthetic becomes a nonsense. It is the insubstantiality of art that explains its intensity, the lack of determination at its core that makes the collective acceptance of and submission to the rhetoric of forms, the tropes, figures, codes, and formulae, the clichés, all the more urgent.

The moment of improvisation is the moment in which everything could be different and yet things turn out much the same. Improvisation could, perhaps *should*, be a beginning but in reality it is usually just a continuation. But rather than using this as a critical lever against improvisation, as does Adorno, it is perhaps more constructive to consider just *how* the improvisor is able to occupy particular fixed structures, to draw attention to their fixity and the contingency of their origin, while at the same time molding these into an artwork of real expressive and communicative intensity. Although we might accept that most improvisation is governed by a set of underlying formulae that, once recognized, must temper our unbridled celebration of innovation, novelty, and freedom at the level of practice, this should not be allowed to obscure the fact that an artist's or performer's relationship to the structures that constitute their aesthetic horizon is by no means as static or as predictable as some critics seem to assume. Even if we accept, with Boulez, that most improvisation is predictable, this should not obscure the fact that such predictability can itself be the product of an *active* engagement with given codes of aesthetic practice and not merely with their passive acceptance. When Boulez remarks that "we were listening to a group improvising, and I amused myself by describing what was going to come next; it is very obvious,"[46] does this have to be accepted as a criticism? Quite apart from the fact that almost all composed music is itself pretty predictable (Handel, Mozart . . .) what exactly is wrong with predictability? Keith Johnstone actually *demands* obviousness as a way of liberating improvisation from the false hegemony of unpredictability:

> Many students block their imaginations because they're afraid of being unoriginal. . . . The improviser has to realize that the more obvious he is, the more original he appears. I constantly point out how much the audience likes someone who is direct, and how they always laugh with pleasure at a really "obvious" idea. Ordinary people asked to improvise will search for some "original" idea because they want to be *thought* clever. They'll say and do all sorts of inappropriate things.[47]

If predictability and originality are not contraries, perhaps a more fruitful avenue of enquiry would be to look into *how* and *why* improvisors engage in predictable strategies of performance or practice rather than bemoaning the fact or wasting time explaining why they shouldn't—they're going to anyway.

The ironic model of improvisation that keeps ebbing and flowing as we proceed is undoubtedly open to misinterpretation. Irony has a bad name: conceited, aloof, unengaged and calculating, shifty and two-faced, inauthentic. Not a great start perhaps, but then why can't ironic improvisors be like everybody else? Certainly those responsible for the discourses around improvisation have done their best to imprison it in a quasi-ethical totality of care and enabling, rooted in utopian visions of commitment and authenticity, but this should not blind us to the fact that intense improvisatory gestures can certainly be ironic. The much-heralded hyperawareness of the improvisor should not be limited to an intersubjective, empathic awareness of the dialogical other, but should, rather, extend to the more fundamental issue of the beginning and continuation of the work. Above all else, the hyperawareness of the ironist can be described as an acute consciousness of the working of the work, the being of the work, and the position or positioning of the self within this work. In the last chapter we concentrated on the beginning of the work and the task of maintaining this sense of a beginning during the work's continuation, the tragedy of the work being the inevitable destruction of the beginning by the continuation. In this chapter we are more concerned with the continuation of the work and the manner in which this continuation opens the improvised work up to the charge of being formulaic and predictable: the fixed masquerading as the unfixed. Where an ironic model of improvisation is helpful is not only in its ability to preempt the critic's accusation of fixity by drawing attention to this itself, but also in the way in which it can offer some insight into the fixing process, the way in which works continue beyond the instant of their origin. To claim that intense improvisatory gestures can be ironic is to recognize that it is not just a question of remembering "at the last moment" the possibilities made available by the "countless generations" of codes and rules but, rather, of making aesthetic judgments that, to recall Kant, bring into conjunction the individual act and its universal communicative force, subjective feeling, and common sense.

Kant is no ironist (although his work is by no means without irony) but his account of judgment as the transition between singularity and universality is certainly capable of grounding an ironic consciousness, not least because the aesthetic judge (like the ironist) stands above or outside of both the felt immediacy of production *and* the sensed commonality of reception. Thus, to the extent that an improvisatory gesture is judged and not just remembered at the "last minute," it can be better thought of as a reflective moment that is intended to achieve a communicative viability that has real intensity. And as we have seen before with Kant, it is the taking up of the standpoint of the universal other that introduces intensity into the artwork. Not the dialogical other at play within the work, but the sensed other *prior* to the work's beginning. In essence, irony is no more than the hyperawareness that one would expect to emerge if the Kantian account of aesthetic judgment is taken seriously and pushed in the direction of production rather than reception. If it is accepted that individual feeling and collective sensibility must be thought together, but without collapsing one into the other, then the proximity of judgment and irony becomes clear. The judgment necessary to make a work can never be reduced to the immediacy of simple "yes" and "no" decisions; on the contrary, the "yes" of the beginning and the aesthetic decisions that allow a work to continue beyond this originary "yes" while also keeping it in view are heavily mediated by a reflective process that must carefully weigh the dual needs of individual expression and collective communication. This is the source of intensity.

Recognizing, even during Kant's lifetime, that the figure of the ironist emerges out of this expressive/communicative predicament, Friedrich Schlegel's conception of romantic irony as an engagement with the "impossibility and yet necessity of complete communication"[48] can already be seen as a radicalization of Kant's judgment of taste. Standing between the expressionist and the communicator, the ironist brings real intensity to the predicament of the artist by introducing a hyperawareness of the predicament they (expressionist/ironist/communicator) are all in, and then proposing strategies that allow this predicament to be negotiated productively. If we remain with our conception of improvisation as the enactment of the aesthetic predicament, then the ironic improvisor will here allow us to see exactly why improvisation is predictable and what the purpose of this predictability is.

We have already seen how improvisors themselves can be well ahead of the critics when it comes to an awareness of the clichés and formulae that underpin their practice, a knowingness that can be both humorous and poignant. What concerns us here is a different aspect of this same hyperawareness. Although it might be true that much improvisation is more fixed or predictable than many improvisors would like to admit, this does not change the fact that such work can have immense impact nonetheless. Why is that? Kant's account of aesthetic judgment can offer at least part of an answer if his postulated *sensus communis* is accepted as a way of explaining the gravitation of aesthetic production/reception around universally recognized gestural patterns. But such a view can only take us so far in the pursuit of a more nuanced understanding of the real agility necessary to produce works that are both deeply felt and communicable.

One shortcoming of Kant's aesthetics is that the ahistorical and acultural nature of his conception of a *sensus communis* is not properly discussed within the historical and cultural context of actual aesthetic judgments and the production and reception of specific works. What this means is that, although Kant acknowledges the failure of aesthetic judgments to meet the demands of absolute consensus grounded in a *sensus communis*, he does not express any interest in the different *ways* in which aesthetic judgments fall short of universal validity and the impact such failure has on the subsequent judgments. Thinking Kant and Heidegger together, if the *sensus communis* is the (ahistorical) origin of art then the tragedy of this origin's preservation/destruction in actual singular aesthetic judgments and subsequent artworks is a historical one that passes through the codes, formulae, and clichés that have concerned us throughout this chapter. Similarly, the mimetic faculty that we have identified as the vehicle for the expressive content of art must also be thought historically if the nature of improvisation is to be properly understood. It is to Benjamin's credit that he raises this as a central question:

> It must be borne in mind that neither mimetic powers nor mimetic objects remain the same in the course of thousands of years. Rather we must suppose that the gift for producing similarities . . . , and therefore also the gift of recognizing them, have changed in the course of history. The direction of this change seems determined by the increasing fragility of the mimetic faculty. . . . The question is whether we are concerned with the decay of this faculty or with its transformation.[49]

This indeed is the question and, as will be shown, the decay and transformation of mimesis are inextricably linked.

Mimesis and Transformation

In Adorno's account of mimesis it is the re-presenting of the transition from subjective feeling to objective form that gives art its expressive potency. His critique of improvisation is that the consciousness of this transition is lost the moment that subject and object appear to have been separated in dubious notions of individual freedom when in reality they are drawn ever more tightly together through the onset of a subterranean standardization. This may be true, but what Adorno fails to explain adequately is the process behind the onset of the dreaded standardization. *Why* is it that some forms (and not others) become standardized, and is pseudo-individualism the only consequence once they do? Perhaps an oversensitivity to the dangers of reification on Adorno's part blinds him to the fact that it is not just a question of desolidifying the formulaic and interrupting the overfamiliar, but also of explaining, if not why particular forms are attractive in the first place, then at least acknowledging that they are. It is not that the mimetic faculty just happens to be activated by an abstract desire to make one thing similar to another, nor is mimesis simply the unreflected seeking of an objective otherness. No, it is a particular mode of re-presentation, of repetition, that carries within it a consciousness and memory of the promise and the betrayal of aesthetic forms. The mimetic act does not copy the world, it copies other mimetic acts, it re-presents specific patterns of transition from one thing to another not in order to retrieve past styles but to retrace the originary movement of art. Mimeticism imitates the working not the work, the saying rather than the said. Of course, one can only arrive at the working *through* the work, the saying *through* the said, which is why the desolidifying force of Adorno's negative dialectics is so important, but having set everything in flux the question remains: Why one pattern of movement rather than another? On what grounds does the artist, performer, improvisor decide (whether after much deliberation or instantaneously) to imitate one or another pattern of mimetic acts? And, to return to Benjamin's question, how are these aesthetic choices (or judgments) transformed over time?

Exercising aesthetic judgment at the point of production requires the artist to make choices, not just between one mark or another but one pattern of marking rather than another, a pattern with a history, an accretion of mimetic acts that resonate in a very particular way. Adorno's critique of improvisation assumes that the performer's aesthetic choices always take place *within* one standardized pattern of mimetic acts. In other words, as Berio and Boulez agree, such performances are based upon a series of movements within a codified history of gestures rather than *between* different histories or *across* mimetic traditions: between, that is, one mark and another rather than one marked space and another. This, of course, can be true of any art that stakes its reputation on overly simplistic notions of autonomy, but there is every reason to believe that a great many artists, performers, and improvisors are only too well aware of their place within particular codified structures, the boundaries between one structure and another, and the possibility of movement between these structures and the expressive histories they carry with them. Although the aesthetic choices necessary to create an artwork are always determined by one structure or another, this does not mean that the artist is necessarily the plaything of the given or simply "in play" as Hans-Georg Gadamer might put it.[50] In reality, most artists are far more knowing than they are given credit for, in spite of the apparently ingenuous discourses of authenticity that clog up the art world. In fact, it is power rather than authenticity that attracts most artists to one mimetic pattern rather than another. The artist is rarely interested in art for its own sake; the artist is interested in what the work can *do*, its communicative efficacy, its expressive intensity, its facilitation of mimetic movement. This interest demands an acute awareness of the ways in which the history of mimetic acts does indeed, to return to Benjamin, indicate a process of decay and transformation, or, to express this more clearly, a process of decay that demands of the artist the necessary transformation to re-new, revivify, and reempower the mimetic faculty through the discovery of new or forgotten gestural strategies. Aesthetic forms grow old and tired, their textual richness and the promise therein become threadbare, schematic, and formulaic. The mimetic movement such forms allow is increasingly reduced to well-worn gestural paths demarcated and authorized by ever-more sclerotic codes of practice. But artists don't need critical theorists to tell them this, given that the process of decay and transformation, and the consciousness of it, are so often the very lifeblood of their art practice. Perhaps, if one considers the fundamental contingency of the artwork and the recognition of this contingency by the artist, it should not come as too much of a surprise to discover that artists are themselves extraordinarily aware of the forms and formulae they and their works occupy. It is precisely *because* everything could be different that the artist comes to a fuller recognition of why things are as they are, or why they might need to be transformed. Even without looking at the development of this reflexivity into full-blown irony, if art can be considered to be the emancipation of contingency then the aesthetic dimension can be thought of in essentially rhetorical terms, as an ever-shifting network of tropes and figures that are temporarily persuasive rather than eternally true, powerful rather than authentic. Such a view fits much better with the idea that what counts in art is not so much what is authentic, original, or unpredictable but, rather, what is persuasive at a particular moment in history. In this regard the artist is no longer thought of as the unwitting dupe of ideological aesthetic apparatuses but as the active judge of possible mimetic strategies. Although anything is possible not everything is aesthetically persuasive or powerful at any one time, and this goes for the unpredictable as well as the predictable. The deeply antirhetorical and nonironic nature of modernism has left its mark on the critical discourses that surround art and improvisation in particular. The valorization of originality, novelty, innovation, and un-predictability obscures the fact that within an artwork or a performance the new is not always powerful and the formulaic is not always sterile. For all of the apparent radicalism of such avant-gardism, in reality such an ideology of permanent revolution is much closer than it knows to the commercial world that it so often despises. When Boulez castigates im-provisors for lacking innovation, like it or not he is really speaking the language of business, as the following section from the Amplify Your Ef-fectiveness Web site neatly illustrates:

> CJ, a second-level manager, wants her company to be innovative. She sees many first and second level managers receiving awards for their improvisation—being fast on their feet. But her com-pany seldom recognizes innovation—inventing and using new methods. CJ believes that until her peers and upper management put more emphasis on innovation and less on improvisation, the company's results will be much less than what they could be.[51]

In terms of a company's results there may be something in this, but as an aesthetic ideology it is deeply problematic, not least because the intended results of an artwork are far from clear. And even if such things as mar-ket share, profitability, and investment potential are by no means alien to the contemporary artist (far from it!), this does not change the fact that there is no necessity for the artwork to be innovative or original in order for it to be viable aesthetically or commercially. If this is accepted then the (very Boulezian) distinction made by the Amplify Your Effi-ciency people between backward-looking improvisation and forward-looking innovation in the following contribution raises more questions than it answers:

> Improvisation is about ad-hoc invention of ways to do the stuff we already claim we do. It's reactive and backward looking: "To do X, which we've promised/claimed, we suddenly realized we need a solution to Y, so let's do this random thing." Improvi-sation seeks to solve the immediate delivery, without creating something re-usable.[52]

Again, this might be all very well within a managerial context but once such thinking infiltrates the art world, which it did long ago, then the very question of the origin becomes obscured and with it our under-standing of originality too. Perhaps it is partly the exaggerated claims made by some improvisors regarding the originality of their work that has encouraged critics of improvisation to identify this, its apparent strength, as its Achilles heel. But then, at its best, it is precisely improvisation that raises the stakes of the debate by suggesting another way of thinking originality altogether.

Put in a nutshell, the dominant view of originality and the aesthetic ideology that promotes it casts the artist in the role of originator and demands that the artwork interrupts the continuity of history with the mark of the new. In other words, originality is situated within the domain of the artist and the artwork. From the outset we have been trying to hold onto a different way of thinking the origin and the nature of origination, one situated in art rather than in the artist or the artwork. It is not the question of being original that is essential but the manner in which the origin of art can be kept in view. Thus, originality is not tied to the new, to the most recent or the not-yet, but to the *beginning* of art and the tracing of that beginning in the expressive history of mimetic gestures, clichés, and formulae. The new and the old, the unpredictable and the predictable, innovation and re-novation are all part of a concept of originality thought historically as the preservation of the origin within the endless destruction of tradition. CJ, the second-level manager, is critical of improvisors for being "fast on their feet," a trait considered "reactive and backward looking" by Steve Smith (the second contributor above), but this fails to do justice to the agility of the improvisor and in particular to what Schlegel describes as the ironic consciousness of "eternal agility,"[53] which we can again introduce into the discussion here: the ironic improvisor being the most fleet-footed of all. Admittedly, improvisational agility should not be judged only in relation to what might be called the play of the immediate situation, where momentary brilliance can indeed disguise the fact that nothing very substantial has really been achieved, nothing "re-usable," as Smith describes it. Instead, the full significance of the improvisor's "looking back" and hyperreactivity to a given situation should be more properly considered as a very knowing and, indeed, much more substantial engagement with a history of mimetic gestures that requires the ironist's sensitivity to cultural decay and the improvisor's skill in transformation.

Originality and Predictability

Critics of improvisation demand, then, the reusable, the invention of methodologies and repeatable codes, not realizing that it is precisely innovation that constantly creates the need for further innovation, innovation that insatiably consumes itself. But, appearances notwithstanding, the ideology of innovation turns out to be not quite as disintegrative as it looks, precisely because it never interrupts *itself* as the dominant logic of becoming any more than it does the new as its immovable têlos. The reassuring linearity of innovation attempts to evade contingency by pressing action into the service of endless novelty, but all this does in the end is rob the unpredictable of any vestige of unpredictability it might have: when everything is unpredictable, unpredictability becomes the most predictable thing imaginable. Thought within the commercial context of brainstorming "imagineers" such predictable unpredictability is, no doubt, just what is required to keep market position, but when confronted with the emancipated contingency of art such a polarization of improvisation and innovation is as sterile as it is shortsighted. So much the worse then that critics of improvisation from within the arts, such as Boulez, have signed up to the same ideology, forgetting that the contingency of art is not something to be evaded but, rather, it is something to be embraced and celebrated as the means by which the more essential originality—the mimesis of art's originary movement—can be sustained. What Boulez fails to understand or acknowledge is that the so-called predictability of improvisation is where the discussion should *begin*, not end. To repeat the question he fails to address: Why does the predictable have such impact? Perhaps it is because, to invert the ideology of innovation, there is something unpredictable about predictability, an uncanniness that interrupts the situation not with the radical otherness of the new but, rather, with what might be called the alterity of the given. When Benjamin, following Brecht, speaks of the defamiliarization of the familiar *produced* by the mimetic faculty as it transforms one thing into another in ever-changing ways over time, he is working with a notion of infinite interruption that is closer to Hegel than to the "spuriousness" of eternal innovation described above. The "quotable gesture" that disrupts the smooth ideological surface of the theatrical (or aesthetic) space is not drawn from a beyond that pulls the situation outside of itself into the new but is, on the contrary, the eruption of the othering (or transformative) power of the mimetic faculty as it allows the situation to *return to itself* as difference. It is not then, as Berio and Boulez assume, that the gestures of the improvisor merely play upon the smooth and continuous surface provided by a history of fixed codes. Although this may be true of much that passes for improvisation (so much the pity), this does not alter the fact that things only really get interesting when this surface is broken open not by gestures originating outside of this or that history of forms, but by the force of difference within it.

Irony and Interruption

We have already suggested that, within the context of Artaud's theater, an improvisational dimension might be identified, or at least imagined, around the manner in which attention could be drawn to the "cruelty" of necessarily submitting to the fixing of gestures into arbitrary ("pointless") codes—the enactment of fixity. To develop this idea further, it is important to remember that it is the contingency of art that allows it to interrupt itself. If the "cruelty" of art can only be sensed by somehow making the process of fixing apparent, but also if a pure freedom prior to all fixity is inconceivable, then it is only through the interruption of one arbitrary code by another that the familiar returns to itself as unfamiliar, thus bringing itself into view. When Paul de Man talks of the "permanent parabasis"[54] of Schlegel's irony, its logic of interruption, it should be remembered that the ironic position is never a critical one outside of the object of irony, but a movement within it (immanent), an infinite "becoming" as Schlegel describes it, but one that mirrors rather than transcends the given. Describing romantic poetry in his famous "Athenäum Fragment, No. 116," Schlegel's words apply equally to the irony that is at the heart of this concept of poetry:

> It can—more than any other form—hover at the midpoint between the portrayed and the portrayer, free of all real and ideal self-interest, on the wings of poetic reflection, and can raise that reflection again and again to a higher power, can multiply it in an endless succession of mirrors. It is capable of the most variegated refinement, not only from within outwards, but also from without inwards.[55]

Schlegel speaks of a hovering between the "portrayed and the portrayer," and in a sense much of this book so far has probably been trying to do just that in its attempt to offer an account of improvisation that avoids both the pseudo-individualism of the artist on the one side and the dubious totality of the work on the other. Heidegger's triangulation of artist, artwork, and art is one way of attempting this, while another is Adorno's mimeticism with its intention of breaking with the crude binarism of subject and object, artist and artwork. Part of the reason for pursuing this ironic midpoint is not so much to resolve the disputes that have arisen between improvisors and their critics but to try to arrive at a more nuanced and, indeed, more powerful model of improvisation, one that relates more effectively to the complexities of actual practice. So, for instance, the following discussion between the composer Gavin Bryars and Derek Bailey might be resolved by finding a midpoint between their positions but, ultimately, achieving such a synthesis is less interesting than using their polarization to reveal and begin to address the deeply aporetic nature of improvisation itself. This is part of their discussion:

> GAVIN BRYARS: One of the main reasons I am against improvisation now is that in any improvising position the person creating the music is identified with the music. The two things are seen to be synonymous. The creator is there making the music and is identified with the music and the music with the person . . . and because of that the music, in improvisation, doesn't stand alone. It's corporeal. My position . . . is to stand apart from one's creation. Distancing yourself from what you are doing. Now that becomes impossible in improvisation. . . .

> DEREK BAILEY: A lot of improvisors find improvisation worthwhile, I think, because of the possibilities. Things that can happen but perhaps rarely do. One of those things is that you are "taken out of yourself." Something happens that so disorientates you that, for a time, which might only last for a second or two, your reactions and responses are not what they would normally be. You can do something you didn't realise you were capable of. Or you don't appear to be fully responsible for what you are doing.[56]

Clearly these two are talking at cross purposes, so a resolution of their differences would be difficult to achieve. The distance Bryars is talking about is *between* the artist and the work, favor being given to the work because, as a conception, he believes it does not have to be embodied. Bailey, on the other hand, is talking about what might be described as a distance *within* the self, one that is sensed (no matter how briefly) within the work/performance as what Bailey calls a "disorientation," and what we have been calling an interruption. Notwithstanding this confusion, it is clear that both Bryars and Bailey are keen to resist what Adorno would call identity thinking: improvisor with improvisation, improvisor with him/herself, improvisation with itself, the reduction of difference or differences to the same.

But, to ask the question from the position of the "hovering" ironist, why should the validity of improvisation be at stake when it is perfectly possible to conceive of a model of performance that is in fact *driven* by the very process of distancing? And not the distance associated with the compositional and disembodied conceptuality of Bryars or the "inspired" self-transcendence intended by Bailey but the opening up of a distance within and between the artist and the artwork, one that draws out the link Schlegel makes above between ironic "hovering," reflection, and the infinite productivity of mimesis ("endless succession of mirrors"). Irony is not transcendent but immanent; its flight takes place *between* singularity and universality, across the gap between subjective feeling and objective sense (*sensus communis*). Infinite reflection here avoids the charge of "spuriousness" by being thought literally as the mirroring of the given by itself over time, although in the case of irony the mirror is an instrument of *misrecognition* rather than the "recognition" demanded by Hegel. The ironist and the ironic artwork forever return into themselves but always as other or as the movement of a mimetic othering that, in reflecting infinite difference, produces the work in all of its uncanny origin-ality.

To think improvisation along these lines is to conceive of something that manages to break the synonymy of improvisor and work that so disconcerts Bryars while also avoiding the apparent autonomy of the work and the subsequent diminution of performative responsibility that seems to attract Bailey. Indeed, the model of improvisation being suggested here is particularly keen to emphasize the responsibility of the improvisor for every aspect of the work, not just the moment of performance but also the tradition of which it is a part and the originary mimetic impulse that this tradition struggles to preserve. What this entails also is a responsibility for the alterity that interrupts the familiar situation—the very point where Bailey begins to deny it—such that the distance between improvisor and improvisation is not mystified but recognized for what it is as an integral part of the continuation of the work beyond the instant of its beginning. This is, of course, true of all art, but the role of improvisation, perhaps above all else, is to *show* us how the distance between artist and artwork, which both Bryars and Bailey seem to want, is not something merely given, but something enacted by the artist or performer. To be sure, improvisors experience, indeed seek out, moments where they appear to perform "out of their skin" but such apparently transcendent instances, while they might indeed exceed the boundaries of what a particular performer might think they are capable of, inevitably rehearse in one form or another aspects of a tradition that the improvisor is situated within and responsible for. In one sense, perhaps, Bryars is seeking to evade responsibility by setting his composition (his "conception") free into a world of performance that he does not have to work to sustain, whereas Bailey is embroiled in a mode of practice that, in endlessly enacting and reenacting the beginning, continuation, and end of art, is infinitely more engaged in the task of ensuring that the otherness of the aesthetic is allowed to return into itself as the productive unfamiliarity identified by Benjamin. And while it might be true that the interruption of the familiar with the unfamiliar is something that seems to exceed the responsibility of the individual performer, this does not change the fact that such moments of interruption are by no means random, despite the widespread confusion of improvisation with chance. On the contrary, it is the improvisor who decides (or should decide) how to negotiate and manage the tropes and figures, codes and formulae within the contingency of any particular performance. Anything could happen but only certain things will, everything could be different but this time it will be like this: such is the nature of improvisation and, even when the unwonted occurs, the improvisor is still responsible for ensuring that this serves the continuation of the work rather than the mystification of the artist. Playing "outside oneself" is really allowing the alterity of art the space to play, and it is part of the improvisor's task to produce this playful space, not by standing next to the work and pointing at it, as Bryars suggests, but by entering the space of the work and working ceaselessly to "unravel" it, with an ironic agility able to keep the *permanent parabasis* aesthetically productive and disruptive.

Chance

Bryars says he sees the improvisor and the improvisation forever tied together in an unhealthy embodied unity in which the work is forged physically before our eyes. He is also disturbed by the sight of the improvisor rehearsing a stockpile of personal clichés all day only to then perform them in the evening as the authentic embodiment of the self "within the moment"—another version of pseudo-individualism. And quite apart from its inauthenticity, the identification of performer and work leads Bryars to conclude that one exhausts the other. As he says of his own career as an improvisor:

> I began to find improvisation a dead end. I could only get out of improvisation what I brought to it. . . . I found more and more with improvisation . . . that I got no more out of it than I brought to it. I was limited by my own personality and by that of the people I played with. . . . I found the situation usually produced less than the sum of its parts. It was not possible to transcend the situation I was playing in.[57]

This critique is not without substance but, unlike with Adorno, it lacks the immanence necessary to properly engage with the strengths and weaknesses of its target. Bryars has a "position" outside of improvisation, one that is intended to authorize and legitimate his critique and which introduces into the evaluation of his own past as an improvisor a set of criteria that, he believes, improvisation cannot meet. Chief among these are transcendence (of the situation), as seen above, and distancing (as seen below):

> My position, through the study of Zen and [John] Cage, is to stand apart from one's creation. Distancing yourself from what you are doing. Now that becomes impossible in improvisation. If I write a piece I don't even have to be there when it is played. They are conceptions. I'm more interested in conceptions than reality.[58]

It is certainly true that the improvisor is inside rather than outside the situation, but is that necessarily a failing? As we have argued throughout, the essential difference between the critic and the artist is that, as Benjamin, Howard Caygill, and Jay Bernstein all confirm, the critic looks on from outside, remembering and mourning the lost origin from within a "destructive" history that they are powerless to transform. The tragic dimension of art, microcosmically enacted by improvisation, concerns, as Caygill identifies, the existential situation where the subject enters into a singular struggle with the dialectic of preservation and destruction within what Adorno would call the "expressive" history of mimesis. For improvisation, it is not a question of transcending the situation, as Bryars would wish, but of interrupting it. The distance of the ironist is one that is enacted within the work as a process or *espacement* that forever slips from one code to another, between one encroaching totality and another. The concept of distancing that Bryars takes from Cage delights in shirking the responsibility normally shouldered by the author of a work. To look on gleefully as chance intervenes and takes on its own responsibility for the work's ultimate fate certainly removes all improvisation from the situation as it removes all irony (in spite of Cage's knowing grin), but, regardless of the merits of such an approach, it is difficult to grasp the claimed superiority of the work produced when measured against the possibilities of improvisation. Although it is easy to see the difference between improvisation and fixed modes of composition in any genre there is some confusion around the question of chance and the aleatoric as regards their perceived overlap with improvisatory methods. To be clear about this, chance can play its part in virtually *any* creative practice, no more or less so in improvisation. It is not the intervention of chance that is important but what the artist does with it, how it is worked. Relating the role of chance to the contingency of the artwork and the aesthetic situation at any one time, if art *is* to be thought of as the "emancipation of contingency" what would be the most radical way of acting upon this? The implication of Bryars's position (as with that of Cage) is that removing oneself from the working of the work allows the contingency of that work to be truly emancipated from a localized embodiment that limits its realization to the given situation and the prescribed "devices" of the individual performer: but is this true? Surely, in spite of all claims to the contrary, it is precisely chance or aleatoric art that *fails* to emancipate contingency, fails, that is, to emancipate it from *itself*. Contingency is emancipated not by stepping aside and leaving it to the determination of fate but, rather, by setting it free into a situation that is fundamentally *set against* the contingent, as is improvisation. If (as he does) Berio finds Cage's work boring this is because it does not emancipate contingency but leaves it imprisoned within the fixity of its own pointless and all-too-predictable unpredictability. Adorno says much the same when he too recognizes the iron law of chance beneath the surface playfulness of aleatoric art and the dubious liberatory message of its legitimating discourses.[59] Of course, improvisors themselves are often guilty of confusing their own art with the aleatoric, a fact that can obfuscate the actual role of chance within improvisation, which should always be thought of as a beginning rather than an end. Perhaps more improvisors should listen to Martin Davidson, the managing director of Emanem, a record label that specialized in improvised music, when he writes in his "New Musical Dictionary":

> *Chance Music*: Often lumped together with improvisation even though the two methods are diametrically opposed. One has humans completely in charge, whilst the other makes humans totally subservient to random outside events. John Cage, the leading chance music advocate, was very much against improvisation, saying that improvisors resort to habits. This is often true, but not necessarily a problem if the habits are good.[60]

The point is well taken as a reminder that stepping outside of the work in the name of conceptual and/or transcendent "distance" may not be as radical or as emancipating as it seems.

Second-Order Observation

It doesn't necessarily follow, then, that distancing oneself from the performance of the work offers a vantage point that is superior to the improvisor's in its reflexivity and conceptual breadth. When, for instance, the choreographer Victoria Marks, in her essay "Against Improvisation," describes how she places "great value on being an author who stands in the wings while other people do the dancing—an impossibility for the improvisor,"[61] the question might be asked: What reflective insight does this give that is not available to the performer? While the dancer cannot physically be in two places at once and thus may not see the whole performance there is no reason to believe that an improvisor cannot enter into what Niklas Luhmann describes as a "second order observation" where self-observation is always already filtered through the observation of the other, thus embedding in the work what Luhmann calls the "observational directives" to be followed by the observer of that work:

> The unique meaning of the forms embedded in the work of art . . . becomes intelligible only when one takes into account that they are produced for the sake of observation. They fixate a certain manner of observation. The artist accomplishes this by clarifying—via his own observations of the emerging work—how he and others will observe the work. He does not need to anticipate every possibility, and he can try to push the limit of what can still be observed, deciphered or perceived as form. But it is always assumed that the point is to observe observations. . . . The same holds for the observer. He can participate in art only when he engages himself as an observer in the forms that have been created for his observation, that is, when he reconstructs the observational directives embedded in the work.[62]

In fact, the model of ironic improvisation mooted throughout assumes precisely this level of reflexive observation. Perhaps Marks, in common with many others, underestimates the self-reflexivity of improvisation. Certainly her conviction that improvisation "offers immediate gratification" as distinct from the "long-term relationship" of choreography would suggest as much. Indeed, one might even argue that improvisation is the art of deferred gratification par excellence, which is precisely why the unreflective celebration of "being in the moment" is so misleading, ignoring as it does the fact that the moment, understood as interruption or "tilting," endlessly and necessarily defers the work becoming a *work*, and it is the *work* that gratifies. As a compromise it might be admitted that it is, perhaps, the act of deferring itself that gratifies the improvisor, but then this endless deferral is only possible to the extent that the improvisor is both inside and outside the work, observing and observed, singular and universal, doubled up with irony.

It is not, then, that the choreographer (or the director, or the composer) can, as Marks seems to assume, simply look on as an improvisation takes place, using it merely as a resource or as material to be "transformed into carefully worked and reworked choreography, down to the smallest detail."[63] Such a view pays insufficient attention to the "observational directives" that are already very much at work in the improvisation as it unfolds before the eyes of the onlooker. It is not simply a matter of fixing the unfixed but of drawing out the fixity of improvisation itself, the "network of apparatuses and relays," the "battery of anticipatory and delaying devices" that Derrida believes protects us from improvisation but which, in reality, are integral to it. Yes, the fixing of improvisation may be "cruel" but this should not blind us to the fact that such cruelty is attracted to and fascinated by the cruelty that is already embedded in improvisation itself, that takes place "on stage" prior to being fixed. Perhaps this helps explain why improvisors are attracted to the thought and theater of Artaud in spite of his contempt for the vagaries of improvised interpretation. If the "theater of cruelty" represents the most rigorous fixing of dramatic action into "pointless" codes, then what gives it the life and "pulsation" that Artaud demands is the fact that what is being fixed is the mimetic process of fixation itself, the expressive transition from the unmarked to the marked space that improvisation allows to begin again and again. To "show" this does not require the interpretive or expressive virtuosity that is all too easily mistaken for improvisation but, rather, what we much earlier called a feeling for feeling, and to which we might add a sense of sense.

The Element of Showing

How is this shown? Or how is the "element of showing" shown in improvisation? What we are looking for is not the familiar improvisatory gestures that would have us believe that the generations and generations of fixed codes are there and available merely as launching pads into a realm of performative freedom and dialogue untrammeled by the inhuman cruelty of discipline and impossible rigor. What we are looking for does not have this transcendence nor does it possess the emancipatory characteristics of a negative freedom in which the improvisor heroically pushes beyond the limits and constraints of the work while, at the same time, retaining the ethical substance necessary to accommodate the other in an empathic universe of mutual respect and enabling. This has all been seen before, but the "element of showing" is something different, something sensed not so much in but *around* the way a movement is performed, a sound delivered, a word spoken, a mark marked, a space or gap between the showing and the shown: *espacement*. Thus, the difference between an improvised and a nonimprovised gesture is infinitesimal, not a difference of degree but, one might say, of existential quality, something more to do with the way in which a performer inhabits a performance, a form of "dwelling" quite different from being "at home" in the work.

Susan Leigh Foster speaks eloquently of improvisation in terms of the known and the unknown and sees the improvisor's engagement with the known as crucial. It is a pity, then, that she cannot resist being tempted back into the language of transcendence the moment the unknown is addressed:

> The *unknown* is precisely that [the *known*] and more. It is that which was previously unimaginable, that which we could not have thought of doing next. Improvisation presses us to extend into, expand beyond, extricate ourselves from that which was known. It encourages us or even forces us to be "taken by surprise." Yet we could never accomplish this encounter with the unknown without engaging in the known.[64]

Perhaps this chapter has, above all, been trying to gain some purchase on the way in which, as Foster rightly says, the known has to be engaged with—not, however, in order to "extricate ourselves" from it or "expand beyond" it but, rather, as a way of repositioning the discussion of improvisation within the situation that it permanently interrupts. Foster understands this better than most but appears not to have quite found the language or an appropriate mode of address to really do justice to this (the most essential?) aspect of the improvisor's art. Just as showing the shown has been part of what we have been pursuing here, so knowing the known (as opposed to knowledge) has similarly been an issue throughout, which explains why the knowingness of irony has been an important part of our own mode of address. Generally speaking, discourses on improvisation are sadly lacking in irony both at the level of form and of content, which is a pity when one considers the undoubted insight of the following statement, one that is crying out for a more ironic sensibility to really put it to work. It is Susan Leigh Foster again:

> The performance of any action, regardless of how predetermined
> it is in the minds of those who perform it and those who witness
> it, contains an element of improvisation. The moment of waver-
> ing while contemplating how, exactly, to execute an action al-
> ready deeply known, belies the presence of improvised action.[65]

It is precisely this, the contemplative wavering within predetermination
that characterizes irony and that, thought together with improvisation,
allows us finally to say that the way in which the improvisor can show
us the mimetic transition from one thing to another, from the unfixed to
the fixed, is in that moment of reflection, of hesitation, reservation, and
decision prior to each gesture. Not the anteriority of a history stretching
back over generations, but the concentration of all that memory in the
"yes" and "no" of the now about to begin. This is not a question of going beyond the known but of *entering into* it again and again.

4

Improvisation, Origination, and Re-novation

It is an attempt to give oneself, as it were a posteriori, a past in which one would like to originate in opposition to that in which one did originate.

Friedrich Nietzsche

Can we *only* think back? No, we can also think ahead—and that is thinking proper. In such thinking we are capable in a certain way of knowing with certainty what once was. Strange—are we to experience something that lies behind us by thinking forward? Yes, we are. Then what is it that already was; what will come again when it recurs? The answer to that question is: whatever will be in the next moment. **Martin Heidegger**

: : :

The doubts raised throughout the last chapter regarding the true significance of improvisation—its standardization, predictability, and its lack of innovation—do not change the fact, whatever value they may have, that the reception of improvised art practice seems to have no problem whatsoever with pseudo-individualism or the eternal recurrence of the same. Indeed, it is probably fair to say that the majority of those attracted to improvisation, whether as producers or receivers, are precisely *not* in search of the unheard of, the unseen, or the unimaginable—the dialogical discourses of improvisation speak too loudly against that. As with any other art form, it is the recognition and reappropriation of the given that the vast majority find attractive. It is the ability of the improvisor to inhabit the given, to make a home and play within it, thus parading an apparent freedom beyond the reach of nonimprovisors, that validates much that passes as improvised art. Perhaps this is especially true within the context of the cultural logic of postmodernism where the very modernist dialectic of backward-looking improvisation and forward-looking innovation presented by the Amplify Your Effectivity group in the last chapter seems oddly out of touch with a reality that appears to have no problem in thinking innovation and backward-looking improvisation together and affirming both. Admittedly this has resulted in a great deal of work that could barely be described as innovative or improvised, but this does not seem to have disheartened those who only desire what is always already there, ready to be reproduced over and over again.

This sounds bad, and in many ways it is. Just think of the smug confidence of the virtuoso with a technique that glitters on the surface of aesthetic forms that are assumed, resumed, and consumed as prefabricated chunks of performative cultural capital, forever ready-to-hand to be repeatedly mastered by the master. Or think of the dubious automatism that is too easily and too often promoted as a quasi-spiritual force surging through the veins of the improvisor without regard for the manner in which the automatic is, in truth, the product of training, rote learning, and an absolute embeddedness in the given to the point of forgetfulness. Think too of the communicative community that arises both within and around the world of improvisation, a community full of its own communality and its own communicability, brimming with a dialogical openness to the other that is only conceivable on the unspoken assumption that this otherness is forever reduced to the same.

Yes, that does sound bad and, indeed, it is intended as a direct provocation for those content with a model of improvisation that appears to have no inkling of the extraordinarily complex interweaving of the old and the new or the possible significance of the ways in which the given is given again and again. But nevertheless it cannot be denied that one real strength of the retro logic of postmodernism is that it resituates innovation within what has been rather than what is to come, thus liberating the discussion of improvisation from its longstanding obsession with the new.

The There *and the* Given

This reorientation must, however, first establish exactly how the given is *itself* given. Having already spoken of improvisors working with what is there and ready-to-hand, the question needs to be asked at the outset whether what is *there* is the same as what is *given*, in other words, are the *there* and the *given* identical? Certainly, if Heidegger and Levinas are to be believed, there is an important difference here which encourages them both to make a distinction between *there is* (Levinas's *il y a*) and *it gives* (Heidegger's *es gibt*). This is how they express it in turn:

> In *Being and Time* [p. 212] we purposely and cautiously say, *il y a l'etre*: "there is/it gives" ["es gibt"] Being. *Il y a* translates "it gives" imprecisely. For the "it" that here "gives" is Being itself. The "gives" names the essence of Being that is giving, granting its truth. The self-giving into the open, along with the open region itself is Being itself.[1]

> PHILIPPE NEMO: A moment ago you evoked the *"es gibt,"* the German "there is," and the analysis Heidegger made of it as generosity, since in this *"es gibt"* there is the verb *geben* which signifies to give. For you, on the other hand, there is no generosity in the "there is"?
>
> EMMANUEL LEVINAS: I insist in fact on the impersonality of the "there is"; "there is" as "it rains," or "it's night." And there is neither joy nor abundance. . . . Neither nothingness nor being. . . . One cannot say of this "there is" which persists that it is an event of being.[2]

The importance of the above distinction for Levinas, as part of his life-long resistance to what he sees as the primacy of Being in Heidegger's thought, cannot be overestimated but the aim here is not to restage yet again the dispute between an ontology of Being and an alterity ethics that motivates Levinas's oeuvre, and which in turn fuels the philosophical industry that has sprung up around it over recent years. Instead, our intention here is to suggest that, thought together, Heidegger's *es gibt* and Levinas's *il y a* offer some very real insights into different but complementary aspects of what might be called the ontology of and alterity of improvisation respectively.

If, to get things under way, we accept Amplify Your Effectivity's argument that improvisation is backward looking then perhaps it would be wise at this juncture to dispense with the unnecessarily oppositional notion of innovation and replace it with a more appropriate term such as re-novation, the act of re-newing, of making the old new. The necessity of shifting the emphasis in this way is to allow a clear distinction to be made between those (pseudo) modes of improvisation, briefly sketched above, and, to borrow Heidegger's vocabulary, more authentic strategies to be addressed below. That is to say, to make a distinction between forms of improvisation that might be described as canny, as opposed to the uncanniness that will be the main focus here.

To clarify this distinction: canniness might be understood as an intuitive grasp of the cultural marketplace and the necessary strategies to position improvisation within that context of consumption as a spectacle of freedom and expression, but also as the word suggests (especially in the German *Heimlich*) it assumes a profound and fundamental at-homeness both within the given forms of improvisation and the cultural milieu in which they are promoted and consumed. Uncanniness (the *Unheimlich*), on the other hand, speaks of an incessant unsettling of the given with all of its overbearing familiarity, resulting in a fascination with the manner in which the given is given in ever-new ways. This, while not preventing the formation of cultural communities around what we have called re-novative improvisational practices, certainly problematizes them, not least because dialogue and empathy (the lifeblood of communality) are each unsettled too. Perhaps it would be useful to think of a commonality *without* community where what we share is not something that can be easily spoken of in the social realm but which, nonetheless, inhabits it as a silent bond or, as Heidegger puts it, a stillness within the "idle talk" of the "they." Indeed, in his famous discussion of the call of conscience in *Being and Time* it is precisely silence and stillness that characterize the uncanny:

> Only in keeping silent does the conscience call; that is to say, the call comes from the soundlessness of uncanniness, and the Dasein which it summons is called back into the stillness of itself, and called back as something that is to become still. Only in reticence, therefore, is this silent discourse understood appropriately in wanting to have a conscience. It takes the words away from the common-sense idle talk of the "they."[3]

Here Heidegger gives one glimpse among many of the ways in which he is working to open up a rift between the *there* and the *given*. Particularly noteworthy here is the linking of the *there* to the "they," a move that it is important to understand correctly. Although often difficult given what he has to say on the subject, it is necessary nonetheless to take Heidegger at his word when he claims that the "they" and all of its accompaniments— "idle talk," "everydayness," "averageness," "leveling down," "publicness," "inauthenticity"—are not terms of derogation but fundamental aspects of any phenomenology of the *there*. Before, that is to say, we can begin to raise the ontological question of the "origin of the work of art" we must first of all acknowledge that we only come to art in the first place thanks to the "they." As Heidegger says, "we take pleasure and enjoy ourselves as *they* take pleasure; we read, see, and judge about literature and art as *they* see and judge."[4] Thus we are *all* part of the "they," Heidegger included. There is no Archimedean point outside of the "they" that would allow the necessary leverage to critique the *there* any more than there is a metaphysical exit that would free us from the homeliness of the home. It is not a question of being free but of allowing Being the freedom to be, something to be thought within the *there* and not beyond it. But before turning to this it is important not to forget the place of improvisation in the above.

The premise of this chapter is that, notwithstanding the critique of improvisation's formularism and pseudo-individualism, it is precisely this situatedness within the *there* that would seem to give both improvisors and their audiences such enormous pleasure—the pleasure of the "they" no doubt. The blatant fact that so much improvisation merely regurgitates a past that is never really past because it is ever-present as the there and available, that's one thing, but that we should actually take pleasure in the eternal recurrence of the same is another, certainly depressing in many respects and yet maybe not altogether so. The pleasures of repetition, indeed the desire for repetition, would suggest an ever-returning absence or void in everything the "they" is capable of producing and receiving, a lack that is felt but not faced or addressed. Certainly, the pseudo-individualism that works across the surface of this infinite sameness as an illusory force of differentiation that fools almost everyone fortunate enough not to have read Adorno should be treated with some suspicion, but that does not mean that it should be dismissed entirely. Just as the pseudo and the formulaic allow Adorno to allude to a "real improvisation" that nevertheless remains beyond the grasp of his negative dialectics, so too the manner in which the pleasures of the "they" conspire to conceal the abundance of what the *given* could give (the gift of *es gibt*) can also be recognized as what Heidegger has described as the necessary error or errancy of our engagement with the world that is *there*. In "On the Essence of Truth" Heidegger sets this up in the following way:

> The insistent turning toward what is readily available and the ek-
> sistent turning away from the mystery belong together. They are
> one and the same. Yet turning toward and away from is based
> on a *turning to and fro proper to Dasein*. Man's flight from the

mystery toward what is readily available, onward from one current thing to the next, passing the mystery by—this is *erring*.

Man errs. Man does not merely stray into errancy, because
as ek-sistent he in-sists and so already is caught in errancy. . . .
Errancy is the free space for that turning in which ek-sistence
adroitly forgets and mistakes itself anew. The concealing of the
concealed being as a whole holds sway in that disclosure of specific beings, which, as forgottenness of concealment, becomes errancy. . . . By leading him astray, errancy dominates man through
and through. But, as leading astray, errancy at the same time contributes to a possibility that man is capable of drawing up from
ek-sistence—the possibility that, by experiencing errancy itself
and by not mistaking the mystery of Da-sein, he will *not* let himself be led astray.[5]

Crucial here is the recognition that pseudo-individualism, although it leads
the improvisor and the audience "astray" into an ersatz freedom that
is determined through and through, nevertheless in this *movement* of
errancy—from one standardized formula to another—it actually *preserves* the freedom necessary for the transition from the *there* to the *given*
to remain a possibility. Put another way, the *there* is not simply there, it
is given thanks to the to-ing and fro-ing of human ek-sistence/insistence,
which, however, forgets this movement and thus conceals the very freedom that entraps it in the canniness of the everyday. In a sense, then, it is
not a question of freeing the erring self from error so much as recognizing the free space that errancy presupposes and "turning" the movement
within that space toward different possibilities, toward the "mystery"
that error itself preserves and negatively indicates through concealment.

Listening

How does this turning take place? What is it that could remind the forgetful self of the mystery that "idle talk" so effectively conceals? And, regarding improvisation, what is it that transforms looking backward into an
authentic ontological and aesthetic event that is far more essential than
mere innovation? One certainty is that the turning, although in response
to a call from beyond the self ("from beyond me"),[6] nonetheless takes
place within the *there*. This is where the famous discussion of conscience
in *Being and Time* begins to resonate with some of the improvisational
ideas being pursued here. In particular, it is the manner in which the call
of conscience—the "it calls"[7] prior to the "it gives"—leads Heidegger

to promote hearing, listening, and hearkening as "the primary and authentic way[s] in which Dasein is open for its ownmost potentiality-for-being."[8] It is this primordial listening, one that does not need to be restricted to the ear, that represents the movement necessary to turn toward the "mystery" of what is there, that is a prerequisite for the kind of improvisation we want to talk about.

As with so much else, what might be called the ontological significance of listening has suffered within the realms of improvisation—where it has regal status—by being cuffed to a rampant dialogism that cannot hear beyond the everyday mechanics and machinations of social interaction played out within the aesthetic domain. Where Heidegger's line of thought opens things up is in its refusal to limit listening to the dynamics of mere intersubjectivity, an intersubjectivity that only too often has near terroristic status within groups forged by improvisatory practices. An example: the pioneering and highly influential British improvising drummer John Stevens, founder of the Spontaneous Music Ensemble in the mid-1960s and now accorded something approaching godlike status in the annals of improvisation, often described himself as "the Ear." His model of listening, in common with many improvisors, was conceived dialogically as question/answer, call/response, yes/no and so on, a listening to be sure but closer again to Franz Rosenzweig's "listening of the eye" where the interlocutors are always *looking* for an opening in which to respond and for a way of speaking even when silent. Rosenzweig puts it like this:

> For in the course of a dialogue he who happens to be listening also speaks, and he does not speak merely when he is actually uttering words, not even mainly when he is uttering words, but just as much when through his eager attention, through the assent or dissent expressed in his glances, he conjures words to the lips of the current speaker.[9]

This, the "listening of the eye," fills space with sound even when there is silence, while the proper "listening of the ear" hearkens to the silence of art. It is a double listening, hearing both the sound of what is *there* and the silent presence of what, with Heidegger, we are calling the *given*. Indeed, like Rosenzweig, Heidegger is keen to distinguish his notion of a "call" that is "hearkened" from any dialogics of communication: his too is an aesthetics of silence.

> The call dispenses with any kind of utterance. It does not put itself into words at all. . . . *Conscience discourses solely and constantly*

> *in the mode of keeping silent.* . . . What is "called" is not to be tied
> up with an expectation of anything like a communication.[10]

In other words, the call/response model to be found in Heidegger's hermeneutics of conscience should not be confused with its counterpart in
the world of improvisation or in the discourses that surround it. Where
the latter represents a commitment to the other as interlocutor and col-
laborator within a communicative community of producers and receivers alike, the former is different in that it is not a question of responding
to the call of an other but of listening to the call and response of Being
itself. This is a difficult idea to explain but a beginning might be made
with the following words of Heidegger's:

> But is it at all necessary to keep raising explicitly the question of
> *who* does the calling? Is this not answered for Dasein just as un-
> equivocally as the question of to whom the call makes its appeal?
> *In conscience Dasein call itself.* . . . Ontologically, however, it is
> not enough to answer that Dasein is *at the same time* both the
> caller and the one to whom the appeal is made. When Dasein is
> appealed to, *is* it not "there" in a different way from that in which
> it does the calling? Shall we say that its ownmost potentiality-
> for-Being-its-Self functions as the caller?[11]

By thus replacing the "who calls?" with the "it calls" Heidegger effectively shifts the emphasis away from the human, all-too-human desire for
empathy that is of no serious interest to him. Instead we find a mode of
listening that witnesses what might be called the self-differencing of the
there as it is "called" by its own "potential for Being." But *how* does the
"it" of the "it calls" call? Certainly not by talking back to the "idle talk"
of the "they"; there is no question of there being an interior dialogue
within being itself, a communicative self-communion. On the contrary,
the "call" avoids the "publicness" of dialogue by remaining silent. But,
thinking with Nietzsche (as Heidegger does here), there is silence and
there is silence, and it is that silence that is *too silent for silence*, a "long
bright silence"[12] that is not dialectically opposed to sound but *inhabits* it,
beneath the voice—*sotto voce*—that is the silence that concerns us.

Of course, it should be remembered we are only concerned with
Heidegger's account of the "call of conscience" to the extent that it
might cast some light on a particular mode of improvising that is noteworthy for its embeddedness in the *there*, a backward-looking practice

that may or may not have aesthetic value depending on the degree to which the *there* and also the *given* are drawn upon at the moment of production. Turning toward the "mystery" of being, while opening up our discussion of improvisation to the possibility of its own being, is itself in danger of becoming overly mysterious if some concrete examples are not given to provide a way into the ontological substance of this thought.

Ask someone to improvise . . . what happens? More to the point, ask someone who has no experience of improvisation to improvise and see what happens . . . if anything. Indeed, telling someone to improvise almost guarantees that nothing will happen, such is the intimidation of such a demand: Why is this? It would appear that the difficulty so often associated with improvisation has something to do with the way in which it seems to freeze the would-be improvisor in a terrifying space somewhere between the old and the new—the marked and the unmarked—yet unable to enter either. Classically trained musicians dread the removal of the score behind which they hide and which protects them from the appalling improvisatory void that opens up between them and the audience. The actor without a script, the dancer without choreography (even the professor without notes) have all faced the same horror, where there seems to be no way forward or back and where everything just stops for what seems like an eternity. At this moment, a moment of dread as Kierkegaard so perfectly describes it, the subject is confronted with a vertiginous freedom that is as thrilling as it is appalling:

> Thus dread is the dizziness of freedom which occurs when the spirit would posit the synthesis, and freedom then gazes down into its own possibility, grasping at finiteness to sustain itself. In this dizziness freedom succumbs.[13]

Everything is *there* in its place, ready-to-hand, but nothing is *given* except nothingness itself, which only makes a bad situation worse. At such moments the improvisor can either tumble headlong into the void in the vain hope that some kind of beginning can be marked (this, as we have seen, is the anxious leap out of which free-improvisation attempts to forge a style) or, more likely, the decision will be made to retreat back into the there-ness of the *there* and its secure but ungiving facticity. It would be easy to see this retreat as a loss of nerve in the face of the new, and certainly Adorno would describe it as the aesthetic cowardice necessary for the dreaded culture of standardization to take hold, but such a turn could be looked at differently.

Comedy

Take, for instance, the inexperienced stand-up comic faced with first night nerves and a baying audience. The most likely scenario will be a rather desperate clinging to a set of tried and tested gags that, within such an anxious void, will be as predictable as they are unfunny. But such a collapse in the face of the dread-full possibilities of improvisation does not signal the end of improvisation but precisely its beginning. Although it is true that falling back on the formulaic will almost certainly remove the comedy for the novice, this does not by any means kill off the improvisational possibilities therein, as even the most cursory glance at the performance of an effective stand-up will confirm. What is *there* for the funny and the unfunny comedian alike is more or less identical: same mother-in-laws, same genitalia, same racial and gender stereotypes, same political hypocrisy and religious bigotry—nothing new there. And if it is the ability to improvise that marks the difference between one and another, the good and the bad, this has almost nothing to do with the invention of new material on the hoof but, rather, with the manner in which the *there* is *given* differently. The re-novative production of the new out of the old, difference out of the same, the absurd out of the obvious, is what makes us laugh and as often as not it is improvisation that facilitates this, the comedic differentiation of the *there* and the *given*. But is it the improvisor who is responsible for giving this difference or is it something that "calls" from within the *there* itself, something that the improvisor hears? To consider the latter view and make a turn toward the "mystery" (or the funny side) of the *there* would be to acknowledge that the task of the improvisor is not necessarily one that is impelled to transcend or surpass what is ready-to-hand so much as it represents a desire to return to the familiar and the formulaic, a fact that might give the angst-ridden novice in retreat from the improvisatory abyss some grounds for hope.

Certainly, the fainthearted and the inexperienced might be driven back into the *there*, back into the arms of the "they," while the experienced improvisor is more likely to volunteer this return, but that does not change the fact that the "call" that gives itself within the *there* is available for all once they (those within the "they") have learned how to listen.

But what is funny? What do the "they" (that means us) laugh at? Obviously there is no simple answer to such questions as even the most cursory glance at the multitude of humorless books and essays on the subject will confirm (and the "humorous" ones are even worse), but it is likely that any answer worth considering will acknowledge the fact that, notwithstanding the obvious appeal of out-and-out zaniness, it is the unfamiliarity of the familiar that not only alienates us from the certainties of everydayness but which also illuminates, through laughter, the slippage between the *there* and the *given*. This is what stand-up comics (and existential philosophers) would call the absurd, but it is important to understand that absurdity is not produced by the comedian during flights of comic fantasy but is, rather, something recognized or heard calling within the *there* itself. Thus, the cherished autonomy of the improvisor needs to be thought differently, no longer as a negative freedom-from the stockpile of tried and tested gags but as the positive freedom-to move among and within the comedic formulas or clichés that are there in an endeavor to remain alive to the manner in which what *is* there gives itself to itself as well as to those who have learned, thanks in part to the improvisor, to hear this, the self-calling of being. This sounds very grand, but it doesn't have to if we consider for a moment the notion of comic timing.

All are agreed that timing is an essential part of comedy but unfortunately it is usually conceived only superficially as the delivery of a punch line without sufficient attention being paid to the comedic structure that the punch line completes or resolves. Such inattention overlooks the prior insight that at particular moments within an improvised performance certain avenues will open up while others will go dead. Some comic clichés will speak while others will remain, for the moment, clichéd. The aesthetic judgment necessary to sense or feel the *there* giving itself differently, the recognition of what Heidegger calls the "abundance" of the *it gives* concealed by the "everydayness" of the *there*, it is this judgment above all else that, cast at the right time, is crucial for an improvisation to (in the case of comedy) be funny. In other words, good timing says much more about the *beginning* rather than the *end* of an improvised comic sketch. It is about grasping what is given in the *there* as *it gives* and also having the necessary (ironic) agility to escape the *there* once the giving ceases and, along with it, the humor. In this respect, Charles Baudelaire's famous essay "Of the Essence of Laughter" both hits and misses the mark at the same time, correctly identifying the "permanent dualism" of the comic but situating this dualism within the self as a dialectic of "greatness" and "wretchedness" or of "superiority" and "innocence." Below are two examples of his thinking:

> Since laughter is essentially human it is essentially contradictory, that is to say it is at one and the same time a sign of infinite greatness and of infinite wretchedness, infinite wretchedness in relation

to the absolute being, of whom man has an inkling, infinite greatness in relation to the beasts. It is from the constant clash of these
two infinities that laughter flows.[14]

Artists create the comic; having studied and brought together
the elements of the comic, they know that such and such a crea-
ture is comic, and that he is comic only on condition that he is
unaware of his own nature ["innocence"]; just as, by an inverse
law, the artist is an artist only on condition that he is dual and
that he is ignorant of none of the phenomena of his dual nature
["superiority"].[15]

Without wishing to deny the plausibility of this account of the comic it
has to be said that Baudelaire presents us with a rather jaundiced view of
what counts as funny, one that in its overdependence on a particularly
unpleasant model of knowingness (he himself describes it as "satanic"[16])
reduces comedy to the play of the *subject* rather than the dualism of a
self-differencing *being* that can only be heard from inside the *there* at
the moment it is given. It is not just a question of grasping the essence
of what is or is not funny but of identifying the nature of improvisation
within the very different models of comedy outlined above.

Straight away it should be clear that the Baudelairean perspective immediately takes us back to where we started, that is to say to a model of
improvisation that is all too familiar with what is there and which has no
trouble in transforming the superiority of ironic knowingness into a performative virtuosity that is as impressive as it is reactionary and unsavory
to boot. But if, as Baudelaire rightly observes, there can be identified a
"permanent dualism" in comedy, and if this can be transported from the
realm of the all-knowing self into the mystery of a self-differencing being then the task of the improvisor takes on a very different import. Far
from being an "evil" figure, the improvising stand-up might be thought
of as one who takes on the responsibility of ensuring that the dualism of
being—of the *il y a* and the *es gibt*—is not concealed by being collapsed
into itself but is, rather, revealed in the laughter of the "they."

Admittedly, this is a rather odd take on Heidegger's (deeply unfunny)
ontology, but if one considers that, for him, the problem of being is
rooted in the forgetting of Being, and that this is rooted in the failure
to recognize the potentiality of the *there* to reveal the abundance of the
given, then any improvisatory strategy that can hear, and allow us to
hear or remember *how* to hear this difference, is going to have some ontological value.

If, for example, one thinks of the comic end of the improvisations directed by the British director Mike Leigh, in plays/films such as *Abigail's Party*, *Nuts in May*, or *Life Is Sweet* or, more recently, of the hugely successful work of the British comic writing and acting duo Ricky Gervais and Stephen Merchant in *The Office* and *Extras*, it is apparent that the strong reliance on improvisatory techniques results in a profound embeddedness in what could be described as a hyper-there-ness that is *so* familiar that it becomes almost monstrous in its cringe-making everydayness. Keith Johnstone is adamant that the mark of a good improvisation is often its *obviousness* precisely because, as the work of Leigh and Gervais confirm, it is the obvious that is so unsettling, so uncanny—even horrific. Here we are concerned with the overpowering and suffocating *presence* of the "they," indeed a hyperpresence that brings the there-ness of the *there* into view as if for the first time, thus giving it anew.

Where the stand-up comic falls back on the pregiven but ever-shifting (improvised) structure of the gag, so within the improvisational context provided by Mike Leigh, for instance, the performers fall back on obvious stereotypes that are funny not because they feed our sense of superiority in the face of wretchedness, as Baudelaire would have us believe, and not (as a rather stony-faced Adorno and Max Horkheimer argue during their critique of laughter in the *Dialectic of Enlightenment)* because they satisfy our dubious desire to "deride" the other.[17] No, both of these accounts completely miss the fact that in many cases we laugh at a point of sudden recognition and/or revelation, at a moment when the predictable, the humdrum, the run of the mill, and the same-old-same-old stop (if only momentarily) boring, irritating, or infuriating us and show their funny side. This side is not added by the comedian, it is not bolted on to the *there* as a quirky or bizarre ornamentation designed to invite derision, but it *speaks to* the comic performer and through the performance to us, as long as we have learned how to hear this silent difference within the same, have developed, that is to say, a sense of humor.

In the writing of Gervais and Merchant—*The Office* and *Extras*—the hyperpresence of the *there* as filtered through the crushing ordinariness of everyday stereotypes and clichés is not presented as an antidote to (or critique of) the threadbare tradition of stand-up comedy or televisual sitcoms. On the contrary, the real sophistication of these two shows is that they both construct a highly complex comedic structure that achieves much of its effect through the juxtaposition and the interpenetration of the comic and the real. This sets up a series of comic dualisms that each in their own way highlight the difference between the *there* and the *given*. We have already mentioned the hyper-there-ness of the *there* that in *The Office* is encoded in the quasi-documentary fly-on-the-wall style with all of the realist associations this carries with it. As with all realisms the real is not simply presented as the *there*, it is, rather, re-presented as that which only becomes real (or realistic) by having another side of reality made manifest, for example, its simplicity, nobility, harshness, heroism, or, in this case, its funny side. Just as Heidegger suggests that moods such as boredom, where nothing seems to be happening, offer a kind of phenomenological insight into the Being of being, so it is the long, unedited (realist) takes, particularly in *The Office*, that have the effect, through a multitude of apparently insignificant details (a raised eyebrow, the flick of a piece of paper, the munching on a Scotch egg) of simultaneously drawing us into the dense web of the everyday while also alerting us to the potential for estrangement that the signs of the real, in all of their arbitrariness, contain.

The funny side of this, however, is only fully revealed with the advent of David Brent (Ricky Gervais) whose response to the boringness of the everyday (and all of his team in the office are indeed extraordinarily boring) is to be, or at least seem to himself to be, a funny man. What makes David Brent funny is that he is so excruciatingly unfunny, and where Gervais and Merchant's timing is so impeccable is in ensuring that Brent's hapless attempts at humor are so utterly ill-timed. Of course, having the comedy operating in two registers like this does risk descending into the cruel derision and superiority already encountered but this is avoided thanks in large part to a certain poignancy that attaches itself to the David Brent character, one that allows us to witness, with some discomfort, his entrapment in a set of tired comic clichés that unfailingly miss the mark. But, to repeat, this has less to do with the clichés and more to do with the sense of comic timing that he so painfully lacks. In a sense, he is the world's worst improvisor, which is sad, but then he is also funny once placed within the larger improvisatory structure of *The Office*, which is timed to perfection.

The same disjunctive dualism can be seen operating in *Extras* where it is the bewigged sitcom character starring in the comedy within a comedy, *When the Whistle Blows*, who enacts the dialectic of the clichéd ("are you 'avin' a laff?") and the real: Andy Milman's (Ricky Gervais) deadpan relations with his agent (Stephen Merchant) and friend Maggy (Ashley Jensen). Here the poignancy of the entrapment within the clichéd is further intensified by being recognized and suffered by the Milman character *himself* who resents the formulaic nature of his own comic success. But this stepping back from the formulaic, while bringing it more clearly into view, does not escape it; on the contrary, *Extras* itself is every bit as clichéd as the embedded *When the Whistle Blows*. Playing the famous guest stars against type, the sexual innuendo, the bad taste, the ineptness, and the egocentricity are all part of a comic tradition that is expertly drawn upon by Gervais and Merchant, thus turning us toward the funny side of the real, which is indeed both mysterious (why do we laugh?) and yet all-too-familiar (because we always have).

Earlier we described free-improvisation as the enactment of the beginning of art, to which we later added a discussion of its continuation in the (sometimes "cruel") irony of "infinite agility." Here we want to highlight the role of repetition within this continuance and the way in which the abundance of the *given* can be seen to flare up within the thereness of the *there* to the extent that the cliché (the epitome of repetition) can be recognized, as it is in comedy, as a privileged site for the unconcealment of being. Heidegger, of course, isn't laughing, but this doesn't change the fact that, at its best, comic improvisation can be seen to enact the disjunctions outlined above in such a way that the self-calling of being can be heard resonating not within the anonymous rumbling of the Levinasian *il y a* but in the far from anonymous "idle talk" of the "they." Whether we laugh at or with the comedian we are really laughing at ourselves as both other and the same, at a moment of re-cognition and re-novation that allows the becoming of knowledge to be known again as the sudden revelation of the new in the old.

Il y a

Prior to its fixity in the dualistic structures described above, the improvisatory stream of comic consciousness is characterized by an uncanny sense for the ridiculous as it inhabits the everyday. But the ridiculous— the uncanny in its humorous guise—is fleetingness itself and needs the mobility and agility of improvisation to register its trace. As with all improvisors, the stand-up comic needs to develop a hyperawareness of what gives at every moment and be able to snatch what is given in all of its abundance from out of the clutches of the *there* (and snatching is rarely rude within improvisation) before it reverts to the "everyday." Contra Baudelaire and Adorno, the ridiculous has nothing whatsoever to do with ridicule; it is, rather, an alterity that shines through the same, thus revealing the difference within repetition. This is also where it becomes clear why Heidegger's recognition of what might be called the ontological entanglement of the *there* and the *given* is a more productive way into the question of improvisation than is Levinas's separation of the *there* and the *given*, which leaves us with an "impersonal being" that gives rise to "horror and panic,"[18] and that, for him, requires us to seek "escape" from the *il y a* into the responsibilities of the ethical—hardly the best way into improvisation. Levinas articulates it thus:

> To escape the "there is" one must not be posed but deposed; to make an act of deposition, in the sense one speaks of deposed kings. This deposition of sovereignty by the *ego* is the social relationship with the Other, the dis-inter-ested relation. I write it in three words to underline the escape from being it signifies. I distrust the compromised word "love," but the responsibility for the Other, being-for-the-other, seemed to me, as early as that time, to stop the anonymous and senseless rumbling of being. It is the form of such a relation that the deliverance from the "there is" appeared to me.[19]

It is certainly true that Levinas has deeply felt political reasons for stripping the *there* of the generosity of its Heideggerian givenness, as the following remark in *Difficult Freedom* makes evident: "None of the generosity which the German term '*es gibt*' is said to contain revealed itself between 1933 and 1945."[20] Nevertheless, this (somewhat uncharacteristic) confusion of the sociopolitical and the ontological leaves him with a notion of otherness that, while resonant ethically, is too absolute to be very meaningful existentially, let alone aesthetically. By placing the *il y a* between, or outside of, the presence of being and the absence of nothingness respectively, Levinas is resisting the reduction of the other to the same, a violence that he detects in the so-called generosity of the *es gibt*. But the problem with this strategy is that it completely removes the there-ness of the "there is," only retrieving it once the *il y a* has been "ethicized" (as Rudi Visker describes it)[21] in the "infinite" relation of the "face-to-face" that grounds Levinas's alterity ethics. But this retrieval is itself problematic in that it assumes a phenomenology of time that, in its desire to provide a temporal underpinning for the intersubjective dissymmetry that is necessary to retain the alterity of the "face-to-face" relation, introduces a radical notion of futurity that can only be thought as an absolute breaching of the temporal totality of the same. The problem with this is that it wipes out the old with the new, a new that, as Levinas describes it, "would explode, immaculate and untouchable as alterity or absolute newness."[22]

To transpose such thinking back into the domain of free-improvisation would, no doubt, be an excitement given the totally uncompromising notion of novelty operative there. Yet for all of its rhetorical force the strictly nonsensical Levinasian notion of the *il y a* reconfigured as the "impossible exigency"[23] of an infinite, absolute, and impossible futurity really doesn't make much sense as either the origin or the ambition of improvisatory practice: nothing is *that* new. Better, then, to remain with Heidegger who, instead of leading us away from the irresponsible enjoyment of the everyday toward the absolute alterity of an absent God "faced" in the alterity of the Other, returns us instead to the things themselves in all of their there-ness.

Unlike Heidegger, and perhaps also for political reasons, Levinas rarely speaks of Nietzsche, a fact that signifies a deep-seated aversion to the all-important notion of recurrence that is conceived by the latter as the very vehicle of the new. As seen above, the miraculous untouchability of the new is only thinkable for Levinas as the absolute breaching of all temporal continuity in a now without ties. Indeed, even Henri Bergson's attempt to radicalize our experience of duration in terms of "creative evolution," where novelty is promoted above all else, fails to measure up to Levinas's "impossible exigency," contaminated as it is by the oldness of thought itself and in particular by the necessity of thinking the future in terms smuggled in from the past. In other words, even the "flow" of Bergsonian duration is for Levinas really a form of recurrence or repetition that reduces the other (the futurity of the future) to the same and its eternal return.

Unsurprisingly, it is not difficult to detect such thinking in the world of improvisation. It is, after all, extraordinarily seductive and resonates well within those discourses of freedom that in a quasi-Nietzschean way promote the "active forgetting" of history as a preliminary to creative novelty. But the apparent breaching of temporal or historical continuity in the thought of Nietzsche should not be confused with the pristine ahistoricism of Levinas's unthinkable futurity. Above all it should be remembered that for Nietzsche the "unhistorical sense" that he famously describes in "The Uses and Advantages of History for Life" is understood by him not as an end but, on the contrary, as a *beginning*. The "unhistorical" state, far from being a denial of the continuity of history is, rather, the necessary preparation for a historical consciousness that is powerful enough to face, not the alterity of a fractured time, but both the real challenge of historical accomplishment and the appalling spectacle of its eternal recurrence as the same. This for him, and contra Levinas, is the true site of difference and alterity: the difference within the same/the same difference.

Eternal Recurrence and the Will-to-Power

Within the domain of Nietzsche's thought the new and the old are not separable but entwined in a far more complex (and aesthetically fruitful) relationship, one that allows, as Heidegger demonstrates in his *Nietzsche, Vol. 2*,[24] eternal recurrence and the will-to-power to be thought together. This entanglement will now allow us to recall again the manner in which Heidegger himself insists upon the necessity of thinking preservation and destruction together, which, in turn, can also be thought alongside his working together of the Kantian productive and reproductive imagination in *Kant and the Problem of Metaphysics*. (Just as a reminder: "For the power of the imagination is also and precisely a faculty of intuition, i.e., of receptivity. And it is receptive, moreover, not just apart from its spontaneity. Rather, it is the original unity of receptivity and spontaneity.")[25] In Nietzsche's case the same weaving together of the old and the new can be clearly detected in the "Uses and Disadvantages of History," a piece that is too often mistaken as a celebration of the "unhistorical" and the new alone. In truth, its real challenge is the reevaluation of what it means to *create the past*, in a sense to destroy one history while creating another:

> The best we can do is to confront our inherited nature with our knowledge of it, and through a new, stern discipline combat our inborn heritage and implant in ourselves a new habit, a new instinct, a second nature, so that our first nature withers away. It is an attempt to give oneself, as it were *a posteriori*, a past in which one would like to originate in opposition to that in which one did originate.[26]

Amor fati is embraced by Nietzsche, but at the same time transformed into a creative modality by being rebranded as an act of will: to be able to say of what has passed, "thus I willed it." As Heidegger rightly concludes, Nietzsche's ambition is to straddle both the philosophy of being and the philosophy of becoming—Parmenides and Heraclitus respectively—in such a way that the there-ness of the *there* (*il y a*) and the giving of the *there* (*es gibt*) are held apart in the experience of the eternal recurrence of the same. As we can see above, as early as the "History" essay of 1874, it is the giving of oneself a past that, as the "it was" eternally returning as the "there is," allows Nietzsche to think "the same" in a radically different way to the violence of the Levinasian "totality." Otherness does not have to be thought as an alterity constantly under threat from the same but, as Nietzsche shows, might also be understood as a component of, indeed the *crucial* component *of* the same: indeed, that which *makes* the same the same. Before trying to explain this, the following passage from

Heidegger's *Nietzsche* will provide much of the conceptual material necessary to make sense of Nietzsche's position:

> Can we *only* think back? No, we can also think ahead—and that is thinking proper. In such thinking we are capable in a certain way of knowing with certainty what once was. Strange—are we to experience something that lies behind us by thinking forward? Yes, we are. Then what is it that already was; what will come again when it recurs? The answer to that question is: whatever will be in the next moment. If you allow your existence to drift in timorousness and ignorance, with all the consequences, then they will come again, and they will be that which already was. And if on the contrary you shape something supreme out of the next moment, as out of every moment, and if you note well and retain the consequences, then this moment will come again and will have been what already was: "Eternity suits it." But the matter will be decided solely in your *moments*. It will be decided on the basis of what you yourself hold concerning beings, and what sort of stance you adopt in their midst. It will be decided on the basis of what you will of yourself, what you are *able* to will of yourself.[27]

"Being in the moment," the catchphrase of so many improvisors, speaks of an occupation of the now that, in its hyperawareness of the presence of the present, aspires to an obliteration of the past in the name of a future always about to happen. Nothing could be further from Nietzsche's (and Heidegger's) conception of the decisive moment where the will wills backward and forward simultaneously, "by means of the will to will oneself once more and yet again. The will to will back all the things that ever have been. To will forward to everything that ever has to be." Here it is the creative act of self-giving alone that is worthy of recurrence. It is the giving that returns eternally, not the taking of the *there* that, for all of its perennial ready-to-hand-ness, is more often than not misrecognized as difference, thus obscuring the real location of difference in the recurrence of the same. The will to "will back all things that have ever been" is not, contrary to appearances, some half-crazed philosophical megalomania intent upon the legislation of all otherness for all time: far from it. To understand each moment as the giving of oneself not only a past but an origin—an eternal self-origination or beginning—represents, if anything, the greatest *risk* to the attainment of power and the dreaded reduction of difference to the same. To state what should be obvious: the "will-to-power" is not synonymous with the possession of power. On the contrary, this, one of the most misunderstood Nietzschean concepts, would be better thought as a radicalization of the much less controversial Kantian account of the power-to-will, with the emphasis falling on the will rather than on power. Deleuze makes a similar point when he observes the following in *Difference and Repetition*: "Those whom Nietzsche calls masters are certainly powerful men, but not men of power, since power is in the gift of the values of the day. A slave does not cease being a slave by taking power."[28] Thought thus, it is really the *lack* of power in the face of necessity, fate, or the *there* that is behind the demand for what is also recognizable as a radicalization of Kant's categorical imperative: act as if one's private maxim were to become a universal law. Here it is the "as if" that betrays the absence of power, and it is the fictional nature of all that is associated with the "as if," as Hans Vaihinger has demonstrated in his *The Philosophy of "As If,"* which should remind us that the willing of the eternal return is better understood as a challenge and a provocation that, as with all fictions, allows action and movement in the face of deadlock and stagnation. What is more, in common with Kant's categorical imperative, Nietzsche's "will-to-power" is purely formal. He does not tell us *what* to will but only that whatever one wills it should be willed *as if* it would return eternally as a self-given origin. A consequence of this formalism for Kant is that the absence at the heart of his moral philosophy encourages him to introduce the sublime into his critical system as a way of articulating the mystery unaccounted for in either his epistemology or his aesthetics. "Beyond good and evil," Nietzsche's formalism, stripped of the futurity of the Kantian moral ought, offers something closer to what might be described as an alterity aesthetics of being where self-imposed ethical maxims are replaced by aesthetic judgments and creative acts. This thought of eternal self-origination introduces a radical otherness into the experience of temporality that both breaches time's continuity (Levinas's exigency) while also keeping both the new (difference) *and* the old (the same) in play. And here again is the complexity: the newness of the new, its difference from the old, its break with the continuity of time, is valued by Nietzsche not because of its novelty but as the decisive place or moment where the old *begins* again. Certainly, the new is always different in some way or another if for no other reason than the next moment is always other and as yet unwilled. But as Heidegger expresses it above, it is the "stance" toward this, the mystery of being that the will-to-power wills to return eternally as the same: the same stance, the same resolution to produce each moment as a new origin of a past to come. Deleuze, again, expresses this well:

> The eternal return does not bring back "the same," but returning constitutes the only Same of that which becomes. Returning is the becoming-identical of becoming itself. Returning is thus the only identity, but identity as a secondary power; the identity of difference, the identical which belongs to the different, or turns around the different. Such an identity, produced by difference, is determined as "repetition." Repetition in the eternal return, therefore, consists in conceiving the same on the basis of the different.[29]

It is in this respect that only the difference of each originary moment is capable of returning as the same. Paradoxically, then, it is difference that produces the same, the same difference, if you will. Perhaps Heidegger's words will add something to this:

> The sense is that one must shape Becoming in being in such a way that *as becoming* it is preserved, has subsistence, in a word, *is*. Such stamping, that is, the recoining of Becoming as being, is the supreme will to power. In such recoining the will to power comes to prevail most purely in its essence.[30]

This takes us right back to both the ontological interpenetration of preservation and destruction as well as Benjamin's understanding of the persistence of the origin of the work within the work itself as a perpetual presence and possibility. On this occasion the question arises: How is the eternal return of the same experienced and acted upon by the self-giving, auto-originating artist/improvisor?

Difference and Diversity

In trying to answer this it might be useful to introduce a distinction Deleuze makes between difference and diversity, one that fits very well with the underlying principles of this discussion. He writes, in *Difference and Repetition* again, that "difference is not diversity. Diversity is given, but difference is that by which the given is given, that by which the given is given as diverse."[31] Where Deleuze says "diversity is given" we would say diversity is *there*, and that difference is that by which the *there* is *given* as diverse. The experience of return is not an experience of sameness but of diversity. That Nietzsche often speaks of recurrence in terms of the exact repetition of previous states does not change the fact that the *experience* of such repetition will nevertheless be one of diversity precisely because the experience of diversity is itself an integral part of that which returns. This manner of thinking may offer some insight into how and why the backward-looking, formulaic mode of improvisation affords such pleasure to so many producers and receivers alike. In spite of the "same sameness" (Kierkegaard)[32] of such improvising, the *experience* is nevertheless one of difference, and certainly out of such diversity can be forged a culture of choice that is as inviting as it is ideological. For it should not be forgotten that, more often than not, the concept of "choice" serves the forces of reaction rather than liberation, diversity obscuring the fact that beneath the appearance of difference everything remains the same. But just as the diversity of the *there* disguises its sameness, so the sameness of the *given* disguises its difference. Contrary to appearance, what is appalling about the eternal recurrence of the same is not its unbearable sameness but, rather, the ever-repeated demand to *make a difference* in the face of that sameness. And it is the fact that this sameness is disguised as difference that makes the task of the improvisor that much more difficult, thanks in large part to the fact that it is such diversity that magnetically draws improvisation away from the difference it wills. Nietzsche often says that the strongest will of all is the will *not* to will,[33] thus describing the resolution necessary not to succumb to the attractions of mere diversity and its illusions of infinite novelty and the pseudo-individuality that so easily accompany it. Not to will, however, is not the negation but the redeployment of the will, placing it in the service of a desire and resolution to re-originate the past in the future: not to will is to will *differently*. This clearly overlaps with our account of free-improvisation as the enactment of the beginning or the origin of the work of art as a model of performance. This is the case here too except that instead of sacrificing the work of art for the sake of the working of that work, understood as an ongoing opening of origins, and instead of a resistance to the dubious totality of the "completed" *work* that forever forecloses this creative process of origination, here it is a particular "stance" within the totality of what is *there* that introduces an improvisatory moment into the repetition of the same.

By all accounts, as a musician Nietzsche was an accomplished improvisor; indeed, Rudiger Safranski reports in his biography that "in 1877 Nietzsche devised a hierarchy of things according to the pleasure they afforded. Musical improvisation was placed at the pinnacle, followed by Wagnerian music."[34] But as both the extant examples of his own musical compositions and his oft-repeated expressions of aesthetic taste confirm, he was by no means the avant-gardist he is sometimes claimed to be. Indeed, even his writing—the real pinnacle of his improvisation—although presented as an "untimely" "philosophy for the future" is engaged above all with the re-origination of the ancient thought of being and becoming. As already established, the demand that we act *as if* the next moment will return for all eternity as the "thus I willed it" tells us nothing regarding *what* should be done, only *how* we should do it: how the will should will. Old or new, innovative or not, the important thing is the "stance" toward the moment to come—it is this that makes possible the re-novative improvisation we are pursuing here. One thing that is certain, however, is that even in his earliest writings, such as, for instance, *The Future of Our Educational Institutions,* Nietzsche always places discipline and obedience to exemplars above those so-called freedoms (academic or whatever) that encourage a laissez-faire attitude to the engagement with the all-too-enticing diversity of the *there.* Such a mimetic pedagogy makes heavy use of the somewhat dubious notions of mastery and the master, which, as Derrida among others acknowledges, are certainly open to misunderstanding and misappropriation.[35] But in essence Nietzsche's conception of mastery is best understood as a radical reiteration of the Kantian account of genius in which, once again, it is the *giving* of the *there* to itself that is the central issue. Just as for Kant, where the notion of genius has nothing to do with innovation but describes, rather, the legislative principle of nature giving the law to itself through art,[36] so the issue for Nietzsche too is to grasp and imitate the manner in which the master is able to will his or her own determination. Noteworthy here is Kant's observation that two "primary properties" of genius are *originality* and *exemplarity*,[37] a concatenation that is intended to signify the ability to originate exemplary rules for others to follow. But again, this is a productive mimeticism that, far from advocating the passive obedience to a rule or set of rules, is, rather, promoting the imitation of the aesthetic *act* of originating rules. Just to make this distinction clear, Kant replaces the concept of imitation with that of "following," as can be seen in the passage below from the *Critique of Judgement*:

> Seeing, then, that the natural endowment of art (as fine art) must furnish the rule, what kind of rule must this be? It cannot be one set down in a formula and serving as a precept—for then the judgement on the beautiful would be determinable according to concepts. Rather must the rule be gathered from the performance, i.e. from the product, which others may use to put their own talent to the test, so as to let it serve as a model, not for *imitation*, but for *following*. The possibility of this is hard to explain. The artist's ideas arouse like ideas on the part of the pupil, presuming nature to have visited him with a like proportion of

mental powers. For this reason the models of fine art are the only means of handing down this art to posterity.[38]

Here, where it is not a question of "do what I say" but "do what I do," the trajectory of thinking that leads from Kant to Nietzsche (and on to Heidegger and Deleuze) should be evident, beginning with the transformation of the Kantian concepts originality and exemplarity into the Nietzschean "will-to-power" and "eternal recurrence" respectively. An effort will now be made to pull the above strands together and conclude with the consideration of a model of re-novative improvisation that, thanks to this manner of thinking, will allow us to identify and describe an improvisatory mode that is too often obscured by its "pseudo" improvisatory twin.

We began with the claim that improvisation and innovation are opposed on account of the former's tendency to be backward rather than forward looking. Within the context of our own postmodern retroculture, however, it was suggested in reply that innovation and the recurrence of the past were by no means seen as opposites by those improvisors and their substantial audiences drawn to the many forms of improvised recycling. However, in an effort to both hold onto the notion that improvisation can indeed be backward looking while also wanting to transform this insight into something more than the legitimation of dead-tired formulaic and standardized styles, a distinction was made between the *there* and the *given* as a way of opening up a space for "real improvisation." In order to do this it was necessary to take Heidegger's ontology of a self-calling being (reverberating between the *il y a* and the *es gibt*) and incorporate it into the existential predicament of the Nietzschean self-giving self, willing the future as the origination of a past to come. Having thus shifted the register from the ontological to the existential as a way to begin a dramatization of the *there*, the promised remarks on re-novative improvisation will now be offered as a retracing of our steps toward the ontological issues underpinning and validating such a mode of aesthetic production and performance.

Nietzsche's Moment

One thing to say immediately is that we must start by breaking with the moment of improvisation, that is to say, the "being in the moment" so celebrated by improvisors across the board. The work of this chapter so far has been dedicated to establishing the fact that improvisation does not have to be thought as a total immersion in the now, understood as a break with or breaching of the continuity of a totalized temporality.

The importance of Nietzsche and Heidegger in the rethinking of improvisation is that they dynamize time by locating the decisive moment both
before and *after* the self-presence of the present that has proved to be so
attractive to so many hyperaware improvisors.

How would Nietzsche have improvised? Probably impossible to say,
but for all of his promotion of an "active forgetting" that, as he says himself, reduces existence to something approaching the dumb unhistoricality
of the contented cow chewing on the cud (not much improvising there),[39]
forgetfulness can only be achieved if something else is remembered. And
it is this, the radical reconfiguration of memory, that represents a transformation of what it means to improvise. Above all else, what needs to
be forgotten is the rich diversity of the *there* obscuring as it does the eternal recurrence of the same, which, once recalled or (better) once allowed
to "call" again, introduces into the improvisatory act an exemplariness
that, if "followed," allows the desired difference to be introduced into the
repetition of the same. True, Nietzsche has nothing but contempt for followers, as can be witnessed in Zarathustra's consistently harsh treatment
of the motley "yea-saying" crew that trudge up and down the mountains
behind him, but then these are far from being the kind of disciples he has
in mind when he famously announces that the teacher is best repaid by
not being followed. To follow, to *really* follow, is not to follow. So why
then is musical improvisation considered by Nietzsche to be the "pinnacle of pleasure"? Partly perhaps because of the experience of a certain
freedom, one that attracts most improvisors to improvisation, a freedom
in Nietzsche's case from both followers and following. But, having said
that, Nietzsche is deeply suspicious of such a negative form of freedom-
from as well as, perhaps surprisingly, the solitude that accompanies it,
hence Zarathustra's ultimate desire to always return to the "rabble." The
negative freedom-from, driven by a belief in the freedom of the will, figures large in the world of improvisation and, as we have seen, as a logic
of production it draws the improvisor away from the idiom, the style,
even the work when taken to the limit. In many ways Nietzsche moves in
exactly the opposite direction, promoting not the freedom *of* the will but
the freedom *to* will. Nietzsche's concept of the "strong will" represents
an attempt to resist the vacuity of the free will and its laissez-faire attitude
to the diversity of each moment. The discipline and obedience he promotes in its place recognizes that with freedom comes responsibility, responsibility for that which is willed, for its persistence in the future, for its
return as a past that is willed and can thus be willed again. As an improvisatory strategy we are, then, no longer referencing the irresponsibility of
the ecstatic moment, stripped of its idiomatic cultural accoutrements and

their continuity in time (a pure Dionysianism unrelated to art because stripped of the Apollonian). Instead, we witness with Nietzsche the outlines of a model of "idiomatic improvisation" (Bailey) that communicates something of the mystery of being by showing how the *there* is *given*, by showing how the unfixed is fixed—this time without irony.

Where the ironist is hyperaware of both the necessity of fixing the unfixed in given aesthetic structures and the contingency of these structures, Nietzsche's "stance" toward contingency and the fictions that temporarily (for the ironist) create the appearance of necessity is somewhat different. The ironist, aware of the tragic contingency and partiality of each and every idiom, style, and gesture, nevertheless inhabits and mobilizes what is *there* for the duration of its aesthetic productiveness. But this, ultimately, is always an act of taking rather than giving. In a way, ironists, trapped in the diversity of the *there*, might be considered indistinguishable from the "they" if it were not for their knowingness, which the former presumably lack. Although we have already tried to make a strong case for irony, one that recognizes its tragic predicament, nevertheless Nietzsche's tragic knowledge differs in that for him it is not a matter of being thrown into the *there* but, rather, of being responsible for the *giving* of what is *there* in all its contingency and fictionality. And even if the "as if" of this giving or willing is an acknowledgment of the partiality of what is *there* to be *given* this does not alter the fact that the giving itself must be absolute and exemplary. Derek Bailey acknowledges something very similar to this when discussing both Indian music and flamenco:

> No idiomatic improvisor is concerned with improvisation as some sort of separate isolated activity. What they are absolutely concerned about is the idiom: for them improvisation serves the idiom and is the expression of that idiom. But it still remains that one of the main effects of improvisation is on the performer, providing him with a creative involvement and maintaining his commitment. So, in these two functions, improvisation supplies a way of guaranteeing the authenticity of the idiom.[40]

As a model of idiomatic improvisation this shifts the emphasis away from the substance of the idiom itself, placing it instead on the responsibility for the continuation of the idiom through acts of re-origination and re-novation. However, such a concern for the becoming of the work undoubtedly leaves its mark not only on the improvisor, as Bailey observes, but also on the being of the work too. The bringing together of the old and the new in improvisatory gestures that are intent on repeating/re-originating in the "next moment" the known, with an intensity of commitment and spontaneity that would belie this knowledge, communicates something more than the self-satisfied virtuosity that too often blights the work of those too deeply situated within their idiom. Perhaps it would be more accurate to speak of something *other* rather than something more, an alterity that, by introducing a certain absence into the work (its future as a past) dis-locates both it and its creator, placing them both outside of rather than in the moment, another reminder of Derrida's words: "there, where there is improvisation, I am not able to see myself, I am blind to myself."[41] Such improvisation takes place within our world, familiar to all, but what allows it to be *given* as the same, that is, as the same ever-returning resolution on the part of the performers to re-originate the *there* by *giving* it to itself anew—it is that which makes the difference. It is a difference that can be sensed, seen, heard, and felt as the alterity that returns in the eternal recurrence, the difference within the same. Perhaps it is this that "calls" the performer into the work again and again, not in order to merely rehearse the *there* but to re-novate it by giving it this time "as if" for the first time and for all time.

As T. S. Eliot has expressed it, "to be original with the minimum of alteration is sometimes more distinguished than to be original with the maximum of alteration," a view that might alert us to what could be described as the microscopic dimension of some improvisatory strategies. Certainly the gestural nature of much improvisation has a tendency to bring into view a particular aesthetic movement that is often identified with the improvisatory moment itself. In many cases this may well be the case, as most self-proclaimed improvisors would no doubt testify, but not always, a fact that leaves some modes of improvisation unrecognized and unaddressed. By shifting the emphasis away from the moment to the *willing* of and the *return* of the moment an attempt has been made throughout this chapter to prepare the way for an understanding of improvisation that, instead of reading it off from the surface of its performative gestures, becomes sensitized to a productive dis-location of the work that situates improvisation not *in* the work but, rather, in the "stance" toward it and its ever-returning resonance. This dis-location is, of course, itself still part of the work to the extent that the manner in which the improvisor enters into the work opens up the microscopic gap between the *there* and the *given*, which is also the space of an improvisatory practice that takes on the responsibility to repeat the same in such a way that each and every repetition makes a difference.

Conclusion: Improvising, Thinking, Writing

I believe in improvisation, and I fight for improvisation, but with the belief that it is impossible. **Jacques Derrida**

: : :

As even a cursory glance at the word will make evident, to conc-lude is to bring the ludic dimension of the text into a state of collusion with itself so that the differences within it, the contradictions, errors, and absurdities are made to make a certain sense. But this is by no means the same thing as the sense of an ending, one that would do justice to the sense of (or for) a beginning that has occupied us throughout. Just as the beginning of a work and the continuation or repetition of that beginning has from the outset been situated within a free play that precedes it, so its end must similarly allow this play to succeed it, in such a way that even the end can be understood as a beginning.

The Philosophy of Improvisation

Speaking reflexively, it would be true to say (and probably all too obvious) that the current text's mode of production and method of construction has itself been improvisatory throughout. As Deleuze insists, philosophy is not *about* anything, and we would agree with him that "treating philosophy as the power to 'think about' seems to be giving it a great deal, but in fact it takes everything away from it."[1] If, to continue with Deleuze, the real task of philosophy is the creative act of inventing concepts[2] then a philosophy of improvisation should be less concerned with talking about improvisation and more engaged in the bringing into being—the becoming—of a concept of improvisation. When asked by an interviewer whether he thought he had created any philosophical concepts, Deleuze replied: "How about the ritornello? We formulated a concept of the ritornello in philosophy."[3] But how often in his work does Deleuze talk about the ritornello? Hardly ever, precisely because the work itself is the enactment of the infinite becoming of the ritornello. Another example: Deleuze speaks of Heidegger's invention of the concept of Being as veiling and unveiling,[4] but clearly those expecting the latter to offer a discussion of Being will be disappointed not least because, as Deleuze provocatively insists, philosophy has nothing to do with discussion: "The phrase 'let's discuss it' is an act of terror."[5] No, the movement of Heidegger's thought is itself intended to be the veiling and unveiling of Being. To be sure, a philosophy of improvisation dedicated solely to "thinking about" improvisation would indeed take much from philosophy, but just as important, it would take much away from improvisation too, a fact that, no doubt, motivates Derek Bailey's dismissal at the beginning of his book on the subject:

> There is no general or widely held theory of improvisation and I would have thought it was self-evident that improvisation has no existence outside of its practice. Among improvising musicians there is endless speculation about its nature but only an academic would have the temerity to mount a theory of improvisation.[6]

Such sentiments are all too familiar across the whole range of improvisatory practices from the free-est to the most standardized, where an ingrained anti-intellectualism and antiacademicism reigns supreme. But it would be wrong nevertheless to confuse a theory of improvisation with a philosophy of improvisation.

Bailey is right—there is no widely held theory of improvisation. Given that most theories aspire to universality, this must be considered something of a failure, one that is reflected in much of the discussion among improvisors who, like it or not, leave their cherished realm of practice and become theorists the moment they open their mouths to speak. Theory, no matter how flawed, initiates discussion among theorists and practitioners and inevitably spins an intellectual web around the practice, which many, though not all, of those same practitioners quickly come to resent. Those attracted to the theoretical turn, the initiators and perpetrators of discussions, are, however, profoundly handicapped by the absence, not of a theory of improvisation as suggested by Bailey, but by a *concept* of improvisation. Without a concept the theorization of improvisation is little more than a distraction and rightly treated with suspicion by practicing improvisors. But, that said, the practice of improvisation is itself unable to invent a concept of improvisation—why should it, such a concept would not guarantee good improvisations. No, this task is for philosophers, not practitioners, and what is more, it is a task that requires invention and creativity, not discussion—philosophers and practitioners do not need to speak to each other.

This should not be misunderstood: no one is suggesting that philosophy "knows better" than practice, just as there is no arrogance implied or intended in the suggestion that philosophers can create a concept of improvisation without the help of practicing improvisors. Indeed, is it possible to think of improvisation outside of its practice? Perhaps not, but then this begs the question as to what constitutes improvisatory practice. It is certainly possible to reflect upon the nature of improvisation without engaging with the work of specific practitioners who, to be honest, often obscure what might be called the ontological significance of what they do, thus blocking the creation of concepts. In fact, some of the crucial differences between theory and philosophy are located here: the former is parasitical, the latter is not; the former is collective, communicative, and reproductive, the latter is solitary, incommunicative, and productive. So if, to return to Deleuze, philosophy is the invention of concepts then perhaps it is this "creative act" as he describes it that can and should be understood as a practice. In other words (and unlike theories-of) a philosophy of improvisation does not separate itself from improvisatory practice but (re)locates this practice within the productive movement of philosophical thought itself, thus liberating it from the dubious openness of discussion and theoretical disputation. But what kind of practice is this, and in what ways is it improvisatory?

Methodology and Method

As an initial step it might be useful to make a distinction between the two seemingly overlapping but different concepts of methodology and method. Any *theory* of improvisation worth considering would, presumably, have to be capable of grounding a methodology that, in turn, should itself be able to form the basis of a teaching, a fact borne out by the instructional nature of so many books on improvisation. Although often complicit in this themselves to the extent that they are tempted by the theoretical turn, most improvisors are rightly suspicious of methodologies that draw improvisatory practice into what Blanchot describes as the "tranquil discursive continuity" of the university.[7] But unlike in the academic world where the absence of a methodology is synonymous with an absence of credibility, improvisation can get along quite happily without this type of rigor. But, to be clear, the lack of a methodology does not mean "anything goes." Far from it, and this book has throughout been at pains to return again and again to the multiplicitous figurative orders that play on each and every improvisation and the degrees to which the improvisor can be aware of this overdetermination. The consciousness of such orders—gestures, clichés, formulas, repetitions—demands a different kind of rigor, one that is methodical rather than methodological, with irony (again) being the most methodical method of all.

On the subject of method it is very significant that Blanchot introduces René Descartes on the first page of the main text of *The Infinite Conversation* as one of the "dissidents"[8] situated outside of the university system. It is his understanding of the Cartesian method that, it will be suggested, points toward a mode of what might be called philosophical improvisation:

> As for Descartes, if the *Discourse on Method* is important, be it only in its freedom of form, it is because this form is no longer that of a simple exposition (as in scholastic philosophy), but rather describes the very movement of a research that joins thought and existence in a fundamental experience: this being the search for a mode of progressing, that is, a method; this method being the bearing, the mode of holding oneself and of advancing of one who questions.[9]

Where Blanchot's engagement with Descartes differs from the academic mainstream is in his sensitivity to the interpenetration of thought and existence that gives rise to the particular *movement* of research—a "mode of progressing"—that, in its existential singularity, cannot ground a methodology. An unorthodox reading maybe, but one that finds corroboration in Descartes' own text as the following passage makes evident:

> I shall be delighted to show in the Discourse [*Discourse on Method*] what paths I have followed, and to represent *my life* as it were

> in a picture; in order that everybody may be able to judge of my methods for himself.
>
> My design, then, is not to teach here the method everybody ought to follow in order to direct his own reason rightly, but only to show how I tried to direct my own. . . . I offer this work only as a history, or, if you like, a fable, in which there may perhaps be found, besides some examples that may be imitated, many others that it will be well not to follow.[10]

This, the situating of research within the particularity of a life, recalls Kant's insistence that all aesthetic judgments, being singular, cannot be taught as a methodology but only exemplified as a "manner," thus providing self-legislated rules for others to imitate in their own self-legislation.[11] And, indeed, the manner in which Blanchot himself proceeds exemplifies this particular grasp of method, promoting as it does an engagement that is not committed to any one recognizable theoretical (and, by default, methodological) position: phenomenology, structuralism, hermeneutics, deconstruction . . . and so on, but is rather improvised around an experientially rooted set of themes that are intensified over time through a combination of affirmation, concentration, and repetition. This, in turn, leads to a mode of what he describes as "research" that is radically unmethodological while, at the same time, being almost obsessively methodical, not only from work to work but from moment to moment. Witnessed in his writing is the articulation and configuration of a fragmentary and pluralistic thought that restlessly moves through or along theoretical perspectives *in search* of an order to be provisionally affirmed rather than a truth to be confirmed.

Teaching

In order to offer up a concept of improvisation then, it is not enough for philosophy to survey Hegel-fashion the phenomenological or existential movement of improvisatory practice from the still point of absolute thought: such a strategy would be irrelevant to practicing improvisors. But having said that, such relevance is not really the issue here. In truth, a philosophy of improvisation is not intended for improvisors, it is intended for philosophers, with a goal of conceptually enriching *philosophy*, not improvisatory practice. However, this does not change the fact that any philosophy of improvisation must create or be engaged in the creation of a concept that bears the inscription of its *own* creation, the aim being not to describe or explain improvisatory practice but to reveal how it comes into being as the eternal origination addressed repeatedly in the present book. To be sure, the improvisatory movement of this origination may not be as evident as the gestural figurations typical of most improvisatory forms but, as Deleuze writing of Nietzsche's "nomadic" thought reminds us, the most intensive movement can happen on the spot, barely noticed and unacknowledged: "The nomad is not necessarily one who moves: some voyages take place in situ, are trips in intensity . . . the journey is a motionless one, . . . it occurs on the spot, imperceptible, unexpected and subterranean."[12] In many ways Deleuze's nomadism is our improvisation just as his nomad is our improvisor. Similarly, his concept of "ritornello," which, it will be recalled, he offers as one of his main contributions to the creative practice of philosophy, itself bears the mark of its improvisatory becoming that will also be drawn upon below. The same could be said of Heidegger's "Being," Blanchot's "research," and Derrida's "différance," all of which in their different ways are originated by and are the origin of a movement of thought and being that might be described as improvisatory. In fact, as so often in this book, it is the particular ontological hermeneutics of Heidegger that once again lays the ground for all of the thinkers under consideration. As such, it is not just the concept of Being as veiling and unveiling that is crucial but, rather, the *manner* in which he addresses the ontological question, and in particular the movement of this address understood as a rhetorical and a pedagogical task. Put another way, Heidegger's philosophical *practice*, the performative dimension of his ontological project, presents us not just with a text but with a method of progressing that constitutes a teaching. Intent on exemplification rather than the initiation of discussion, such a manner of teaching joins thought and existence as Blanchot describes it in such a way that Being is unveiled/veiled without there being the "knowledge transfer" demanded by the corporate methodologies of contemporary educationalists. Writing very much under the influence of Heidegger, Maurice Merleau-Ponty's account of the teaching/learning experience offers a good way into the rhetorical/pedagogical performance under review. He writes in *The Phenomenology of Perception* of the orator (and Heidegger is certainly a master of oratory):

> The orator does not think before speaking, nor even while speaking; *his speech is his thought.* . . . The orator's "thought" is empty while he is speaking and, when a text is read to us, provided it is read with expression, we have no thought marginal to the text itself, for the words fully occupy our mind and exactly

fulfill our expectations, and we feel the necessity of the speech. *Although we are unable to predict its course, we are possessed by it.* The end of the speech or text will be the lifting of a spell.[13]

Bewitchment by the orator can without doubt constitute a teaching in certain circumstances, albeit one devoid of a body of knowledge that can be passed from teacher to student. As Merleau-Ponty affirms, "nothing really passes between them," and yet "the fact is we have the power to understand over and above what we may have spontaneously thought."[14] But, and this is the point, it is a power that is produced by the *movement* of the teacher's thinking into an unpredictable exteriority that is radically absent from given forms of knowledge. By all accounts this describes very well Heidegger's manner of teaching, creating in his case a pedagogy where ontological hermeneutics and rhetoric, working in tandem, become the vehicle for the unveiling/veiling of Being. Anticipating Merleau-Ponty's observation that nothing passes between teacher and student yet there is transformation, Rudiger Safranski grasps the same absence at the core of Heidegger's singular but famed teaching when he recalls Karl Jaspers's comments on his friend:

> It is astonishing how Heidegger manages to captivate us. . . . Admittedly, his students then will have felt much the same as we do today—that one is drawn into his thought until one arrives at the moment of rubbing one's eyes in astonishment and asking oneself: that was quite something, but what use is the . . . experience to me? Karl Jaspers strikingly formulated this experience with Heidegger's philosophizing in his notes. . . This is what Jaspers said about Heidegger: "Among contemporaries the most exciting thinker, masterful, compelling, mysterious—but then leaving you empty-handed."[15]

Writing and Thinking as Performance

While recognizing that those unsympathetic to Heidegger's manner of philosophizing might indeed concur that he leaves us empty-handed, this takes on a different significance when considered within the context of improvisation. No one is suggesting of course that Heidegger was a keen improvisor but that does not change the fact that the relationship between the movement of his thought and the writing and the reading of his texts shares much with the problematic relation between improvisation and documentation already encountered. Just as the recording of improvised music is always in danger of supplanting the performative event with a permanent work that, through repeated listening, is quickly drained of the contingency that accompanied the originary working of the work, so too the text, the book, the oeuvre inevitably assumes a solidity and authority that can obscure and ultimately destroy the unpredictable dynamic of thinking. Obviously, in the case of a writer such as Heidegger it is not a question of being present at the live event so to speak but, rather, of developing an awareness of the performative dimension of his thinking in spite of its fixity on the page. It is for this reason, perhaps, that Heidegger places such an emphasis on "listening" and "hearkening," not in response to the call of the text—an empathic model of improvisation quite alien to his method of progressing—but to the silence of Being that the text (and its elucidation) both preserve and destroy. He describes this as follows in relation to his work on Hölderlin's poetry:

> Perhaps every elucidation . . . is like a snowfall on the bell. Whatever an elucidation can or cannot do, this is always true of it: in order that what has been composed purely into a poem may stand forth a little clearer, the elucidating speech must each time shatter itself and what it has attempted to do. For the sake of preserving what has been put into the poem, the elucidation of the poem must strive to make itself superfluous. The last, but also the most difficult step of every interpretation, consists in its disappearing, along with its elucidations, before the pure presence of the poem.[16]

In light of the above Adorno is clearly not always a good reader of Heidegger. His understanding of the latter's ontology as a "jargon of authenticity," a slur directed against the fixing of language in obfuscating formulas, is completely, and one might almost say wantonly, deaf to the silent work of the text, which is engaged precisely in the *unfixing* of language. For all of its apparent exclusivity—another hallmark of jargon—the admittedly idiosyncratic method Heidegger adopts in his writing is always rooted in "everydayness," *giving* again and again what is already *there*. If one takes, for example, Heidegger's famous description of truth as unconcealment, this is not jargon; the intention is not to fix truth to a new and unfamiliar formula but, on the contrary, to become engaged *in* this unconcealment, thus rendering the description itself part of truth's work. Jargon freezes over the substance of thinking, entrapping it in a complexity that is as distracting as it is unproductive. Heidegger's relationship to language is quite different than this, setting everything in motion, stripping away layer after layer of those solidified meanings that have attached themselves to the all too familiar configuration of words and their all too familiar relation to petrified things.

> For language . . . likes to let our speech drift away into the more obvious meanings of words. It is as though man had to make an effort to live properly with language. It is as though such a dwelling were especially prone to succumb to the danger of commonness.[17]

The movement of his thought is of a constant turning, as if holding words (and no word is unworthy of attention) up to the light, a light or an illuminated space (*Lichtung*) created by this turning: *espacement*. An archaeological site of sedimented and forgotten meanings, the word becomes illuminated and itself illuminates by resonating with the dormant sounds of its own past, a fusion or confusion of the senses—of seeing and hearing—characteristically Nietzschean and inherited by Heidegger. Considered as performance, Heidegger, perhaps more than any other philosopher, seems to think on the page, recalling again the orator who "does not think before speaking, nor even while speaking; his speech is his thought." The question is, to what extent is such speaking/thinking improvised?

For Heidegger, Socrates is the "purest thinker" precisely because his speaking *is* his thinking. But contrary to Derrida, who famously sees such a privileging of speaking as an assumption of the presence and closeness of truth, Heidegger's understanding is that the speaking that would draw us, or "call" us, into thinking hearkens to that which, far from being present, withdraws into the enigmatic. For him it is *writing* that is thought-*full*, unless one develops, as he does, a strategy of writing as one speaks, a written speaking/speaking writing that is on occasions not so far removed from the talk-improvisation of performers like David Antin. It is here that the improvisatory dimension of this manner or method of thinking might be detected:

> We are drawing into what withdraws, into the enigmatic and therefore mutable nearness of its appeal. Whenever man is properly drawing that way, he is thinking—even though he may still be far away from what withdraws, even though the withdrawal may remain as veiled as ever. All through his life and into his death, Socrates did nothing else than place himself into this draft, this current, and maintain himself in it. This is why he is the purest thinker of the West. This is why he wrote nothing. For anyone who begins to write out of thoughtfulness must inevitably be like

those people who run to seek refuge from any draft too strong for them.[18]

And yet, Heidegger writes. Indeed, he writes rather a lot, a fact that in light of the above requires him to write differently, something he certainly achieves but which is not always fully understood by his readers: a different writing demands a different reading. Obviously we are not considering a form of thoughtlessness here; clearly there is thought but, and this is the difference, it is no longer conceived as a fullness out of which the writing emerges, but as an action:

> Most *thought-provoking is that we are still not thinking*—not even yet, although the state of the world is becoming constantly more thought-provoking. True, this course of events seems to demand rather that man act without delay, instead of making speeches at conferences and international conventions and never getting beyond proposing ideas on what ought to be, and how it ought to be done. What is lacking, then, is action, not thought.[19]

To act, to think, to speak "without delay," such urgency requires the skills of an improvisor, a performative, intellectual, and rhetorical agility that does not await the arrival of a thought that in all of its fullness can be attached to a methodology that would only then launch a thought process that carries its origin along with it like a lead weight. But then compared to the lightness of foot exhibited and celebrated by Nietzsche, Heidegger's manner of thinking seems labored by comparison, a fact particularly noticeable, ironically, in the latter's four volumes devoted to the work of Nietzsche himself. Indeed, laboring the point is a particular Heideggerian trademark but it is also a peculiarity of his thinking that needs to be understood correctly in that the seemingly endless repetition of words and phrases is not primarily concerned with the clarification of a pregiven thought or body of thought but is rather quite literally the labor of thinking, a work where the working of that work is not hidden behind a self-satisfied thoughtfulness but is played out on the surface of the text. For Heidegger, the fullness of thought comes after and not before thinking.

Ontology, Hermeneutics, Phenomenology

In Heidegger's case, if we can make a more precise attempt to identify the improvisatory dimension of his method, it is the manner in which his thinking takes place within the difference of Being and beings that would seem to be the significant issue. In particular, it is the way in which this difference requires Heidegger to mobilize three different registers of thinking simultaneously—the ontological, the hermeneutical, and the phenomenological—all of which are responsible for the particular and peculiar movement of his texts. Clearly, Heidegger has one big ontological thought—the "forgetting" of Being—but as a thought that contains its own forgetting it is "thought-provoking" rather than thought-full. It is this auto-amnesia that propels the thought of Being out of its unattained ontological ground into the hermeneutical and phenomenological fields that together mobilize the thinking played out across the Heideggerian text.

Phenomenologically, the Husserlian epoché here takes place at the level of sound, where the remembering of Being must begin with the "hearkening" to the being of words, individual words, trivial and overlooked, each illuminated by this particular phenomenological attention. Much of the labor in Heidegger's writing is precisely this refusal to bypass those words that most would ignore as insignificant, merely the vehicles for the articulation of our own thoughtfulness. It is this, the faltering step of the thinker endlessly pausing to take up again and again a word to be turned around and around that creates a productive tension in Heidegger's writing between the ontological ec-stasis of Being and the phenomenological dynamic of being, and it is here that his skill as an improvisor is most evident.

The "forgetting of Being" is not an established fact to be known and bemoaned like the "decline of the West" or the "loss of the Real"; it is an *event* that is itself an integral part of the thinking/action that would remember Being as it withdraws into the concealment that is proper to its nature. In other words, this is an active rather than a passive forgetting very much in the Nietzschean vein. For Heidegger the act of thinking is not the remembering of Being but the remembering that we have forgotten Being and, as such, it is only a beginning, a perpetual origination of the memorial task from within the phenomenological being of everyday words and things. As suggested, it is this difference and the persistent memory of this difference that constitutes the terrain upon which Heidegger's improvisation is enacted.

The phenomenological reduction that strips words and things of their naturalized status, allowing them to flare up and interrupt the dull continuity of their being, only takes on ontological significance to the extent that such illumination can be explicated hermeneutically beyond this, the instant of revelation. It is here, in spite of their radical differences, that, as Paul Ricoeur recognizes, "phenomenology cannot constitute itself without a *hermeneutical presupposition.*"[20] Although the idealism of Husserlian phenomenology might wish to deny this mutual dependence, the onto-logical thrust of the phenomenological dimension of Heidegger's thought propels him into the hermeneutical domain where the real productivity, or what he calls the "productive logic,"[21] of thinking can be made evident. In particular it is the distinction Heidegger makes, in common with all hermeneutists, between the emptiness of "circular reasoning" and the productivity of the hermeneutical circle that opens up and lays the ground for what will here be described as his improvisatory pursuits.[22]

In at least one respect all hermeneutics contains an element of improvisation to the extent that any art of interpretation requires a degree of trial and error in the pursuit of an explication that will bring full understanding of the text. As a method of textual exegesis hermeneutics acknowledges that, while there are always many and competing interpretations possible, the ultimate aim is to so reduce the distance between the text and its interpretation that the difference driving the hermeneutical circle in a sense vanishes into an identity without remainder. At least since the hermeneutical work of Friedrich Schleiermacher in the early nineteenth century, however, grounded as it is in a concept of *misunderstanding* rather than understanding, and *infinite* interpretation rather than finite exegesis,[23] hermeneutics has developed a much more aporetic relationship with the truth. Heidegger's concept of Being as concealment/unconcealment, proximity/distance, calling/withdrawing, and his rejection of empathy reflects this historical and philosophical shift while introducing a certain play into his own hermeneutical strategy—one that has considerable improvisatory force. Interestingly, Schleiermacher already recognized that what might be called the infinitization of hermeneutics demands a more inspirational art of interpretation than was to be found in existing methods of exegesis, one, it should also be added, based upon practical contingencies rather than the rigorous constraints of a given methodology:

> The task is infinite, because in a statement we want to trace a past and a future which stretch into infinity. Consequently, inspiration is as much a part of this art as any other. Inasmuch as a text does not evoke such inspiration, it is insignificant.—The question of how far and in which directions interpretations will be pressed must be decided in each case on practical grounds.[24]

Reminding us that we have been considering philosophy as a practice throughout and promoting thinking as an action, Schleiermacher's rec-

ognition of the practical nature of hermeneutics raises a different set of
questions. Not "What does the text mean?" but "What is the significance of this text?" "Does it inspire me?" "In practical terms, what can
I do with this inspiration?" "Where might it take me?" "How might I
act?" Or to use Ricoeur's language, "What kind of world might open
before me?" Of course, where Schleiermacher differs from Heidegger is
in his assumption or demand that the text must inspire *us* if it is to have
significance, whereas it is a prerequisite of the latter's philosophical trajectory from phenomenology into hermeneutics that it is *us* who must bring
significance to the text through the act of thinking. The more inspired
the thinking, the more significant the text. But it is precisely this acknowledgment of the necessity of inspiration in the production of meaning that arouses the suspicion that the noble art of interpretation is in
danger of being reduced to a vacuous playing with words. Heidegger is
not unaware of this but, instead of raising doubts about the playful dimension of interpretive thinking, such jibes encourage him instead to deepen
the concept of hermeneutical play:

> Is this return [to the origin of the word "call"] a whim, or is it
> to play games? Neither one nor the other. If we may talk here of
> playing games at all, it is not we who play with words; rather,
> the essence of language plays with us . . . for language plays with-
> out speech. . . . Is it playing with words when we attempt to give
> heed to this play of language and to hear what language really
> says when it speaks?[25]

As we have seen, without the giving and re-giving of the *given* (*es gibt*),
the *there* (*il y a*) is destined to remain frozen within its common and everyday there-ness, devoid of the play that would open it to the possibility
of its own Being. In this sense, the hermeneutical opening up of words to
their own possibility does not require the imposition of a pregiven game
plan that would subject language to the forces of play but demands instead a sensitivity and an attentiveness to the play of and within words
themselves. Heavily influenced by Heidegger, Gadamer's well-known discussion of play in *Truth and Method* reiterates this thought while also, if
read in a certain way, offering some insight into Heidegger's mode of proceeding. Speaking of, among other things, the "play on words," Gadamer
continues:

> In each case what is intended is to-and-fro movement that is not
> tied to any goal that would bring it to an end. . . . The word

> "Spiel" [play] originally meant "dance." . . . The movement of playing has no goal that brings it to an end; rather, it renews itself in constant repetition. The movement backward and forward is obviously so central to the definition of play that it makes no difference who or what performs this movement. . . . It is the game that is played—it is irrelevant whether or not there is a subject who plays it. The play is the occurrence of the movement as such:[26]

> The structure of play absorbs the player into itself, and thus frees him from the burden of taking the initiative, which constitutes the actual strain of existence. This is also seen in the spontaneous tendency to repetition that emerges in the player and in the constant self-renewal of play, which affects its form (e.g., the refrain).[27]

The above passages offer some insight into what could be described as the play of Heidegger's hermeneutics, itself to-ing and fro-ing between the phenomenology of being and the ontology of Being, which has already been identified as the terrain upon which the improvisational dimension of his thought can be detected. For anyone who has read Heidegger, Gadamer's description of play will immediately strike a chord, capturing, as it does, the particular manner of progressing typical of the former's philosophical method. As we have tried to establish throughout this book, the freedom associated with improvisation does not *have* to be thought through a model of autonomy that would cut its links with any determining anteriority in the name of a pristine now untarnished by the wear and tear of time. As observed in the aesthetics of Kant, where free play is grounded in the free play of the faculties that must be felt *before* such freedom can be acted upon aesthetically, so Heidegger's playing with words—his core improvisational act—is only conceivable once the play of language itself can be heard and then given again as if for the first time. In Kantian terms we must have a feeling for the play of the imagination and the understanding before we can take pleasure in the aesthetic act—a feeling for play before we can play. Similarly, Heidegger demands that we "hearken" to the play of language before we embark on the task of speaking, writing, and thinking, before, that is, we begin to play with words. Thus, any liberties Heidegger might appear to take with the words he uses and reuses should not be associated with the radical novelty aspired to by some forms of free-improvisation but, rather, with the re-novative practice discussed throughout the last chapter. The words are always already *there* but Heidegger's aim is to *give* them to us again as other than what they are or what they seem—not the radical alterity associated with the Levinasian project to break with Heideggerian Being but the otherness of a language that was and will be different to itself thanks to the play of its own possibility and the playful act of thinking that both hears and resonates along with this exemplary linguistic movement.

On the face of it Gadamer's assertion that play is without a goal would seem to separate his concept from the Heideggerian project, which, after all, is fundamentally committed to the remembering of Being. But if Gadamer's words are weighed carefully it is clear that his real intention is to separate play from "any goal that would *bring it to an end*," which, once again, is an acknowledgment of Schleiermacher's infinitization of hermeneutics. So while it is the unconcealment of Being that draws Heidegger into the play of language, the transposition of this play into a hermeneutical art of interpretation that can only move to and fro from being to Being results in the goal being endlessly obscured by the very act of approaching it. This is the "withdrawing" of Being that Heidegger speaks of, the infinite concealment of truth that demands the infinite "turning" of thinking as it holds words, in all of their "commonness," to the hermeneutical light that both reveals and re-veils at the same time.

As Schleiermacher recognizes, the infinite hermeneutical task must be cut to the size of finite practical aims, which, in Heidegger's case, requires the channeling of linguistic play through specific language games and specific words as they function within them. It is not necessary here to pursue the manner in which Heidegger extracts the most common words from their "everyday" existence and puts them to work in the hermeneutical task of unconcealing Being—such an account can be found in most of the secondary literature. Of interest here is not so much *what* he does with the words or what he makes them say but more the particular sensitivity and skill necessary to identify *when* a particular linguistic move should be made, how long it should be pursued, and when the balance of concealment and unconcealment tips into a deficit and must be abandoned. This is not to suggest for a moment that *what* Heidegger manages to draw out of the most common word or phrase does not demonstrate an extraordinary linguistic virtuosity, one that undoubtedly has an improvisatory dimension. But notwithstanding the undeniable philological and hermeneutical mastery displayed by Heidegger as he begins to open again and again a path from being to Being, it is the incessant blocking of this pathway, the constant interruption of any emerging teleology, that points toward a less visible but more profound form of improvisation. In some ways it is a form of improvisation that can be related back to our earlier consideration of Cartesian method, which, to look at it again, is an extraordinary mechanism for diversion and delay.

Delay and Dis-traction

Descartes' four "rules of method" as laid out in his *Discourse on Method* read like this:

- Be patient and avoid precipitancy.
- Divide any problem into as many parts as is feasible.
- Always begin with the simplest objects that are known and "ascend" to the most complex.
- Completely survey the above material and process to ensure that nothing is left out.[28]

For Descartes it is only those "who walk very slowly" who make progress and not those who "run and go astray."[29] Indeed, Descartes himself acknowledges that it is the "brief duration of [his] life," rather than any ontological barrier, that militates against absolute knowledge. That is to say, it is patience and method—a patient method—that offers the only possibility of attaining truth while being, at the same time, responsible for the infinite prolongation of the thinking process and the withdrawal of truth into the distance that such patience allows to remain uncharted. Heidegger does not suffer this predicament; he accepts it and, indeed, *promotes* it as the proper condition of thinking. However, whatever the similarities there is one major difference that immediately announces itself. Descartes' view is that while the task will certainly be prolonged, the adoption of a proper philosophical method will nevertheless "*straighten* the path to knowledge and truth,"[30] while Heidegger's method of delay both slows the progress along the path of knowledge while it also (and this is the difference) *multiplies* those paths in an ever-expanding network of hermeneutical possibilities.

The familiar analogy of being lost in the woods can illustrate the point: Descartes would advise concentrating on one tree and slowly walking a straight line in that direction and no other,[31] while Heidegger would recommend climbing one tree after another in the hope of catching a glimpse of the goal beyond the woods. Where the former recommends ignoring the trees in order to reach the goal outside of the woods, the latter would remind us that *any* tree has the potential to be a point of reference and, as such, should not only be treated as a means to an end but also as an end in

itself. Indeed, perhaps the goal is not beyond the woods *or* the trees, perhaps there is no need to leave the woods at all, perhaps it is only necessary
to create an illuminated space within it by addressing each tree, branch,
leaf, bud differently: hermeneutically. Perhaps it is in the very nature of
thinking to be lost in this way, which might suggest that this is not something that simply happens by mistake but must be willed, worked at, and
achieved as a philosophical task: errancy.

Regarding this incessant multiplication of reference points, Blanchot
uses the writing of Franz Kafka as an example, illuminating a curious
and unexpected affinity with Heidegger. The suggestion is that in many
respects the following passage fits Heidegger as well as it fits Kafka:

> Kafka often showed that his genius was a prompt, ready one; he
> was capable of reaching the essential in a few swift strokes. But
> more and more he imposed upon himself a minuteness, a slow ap-
> proach, a detailed precision . . . without which a man exiled from
> reality [Heidegger would say Being] is condemned to the errors
> of confusion and the approximations of the imaginary. The more
> one is lost outside, in the strangeness and insecurity of this loss,
> the more one must appeal to the spirit of rigor, scruple, exacti-
> tude. . . . , he who belongs to the depths of the limitless and the
> remote . . . that person is condemned to an excess of measure.[32]

Without wishing to overstate the similarities between Kafka's exile from
reality and Heidegger's exile from Being, the fact remains that the impact
of the latter on the thought of Blanchot helps to make him a very per-
ceptive reader of Kafka, a fact that, in turn, reflects back on the ways in
which we might read Heidegger himself. Indeed, the latter's own "turn"
toward the poetic, with its blurring of the boundaries between philosophy and literature, begins to suggest that thinking is not that which is simply grounded in a thought, attached to its logical conclusion, and then de-
fended in a manner that hides the swiftness of such thoughtfulness behind
the interminable academic formalities of discussion, debate, disputation,
and dialogue. As with Kafka it is the ever-multiplying detours of thinking—the incessant interruption of the desired continuity between K and
Klamm/being and Being—that produces the work, and which can only be
sustained as the working of the work while this mode of distraction remains in force. Dis-traction, the removal of grip, of the necessary bite to
propel thinking toward its singular *têlos*, is the enemy of a thoughtfulness,
which must remain on the straight road to truth, afraid or contemptu-
ous of the drifting and sliding of the more adventurous or distracted. The

importance and significance of the literary or poetic "turn" taken by Heidegger is that it allows a clearer distinction to be made between the determinate logic of a methodology that always carries its têlos within it and the severe but indeterminate rigors of a method that does not. Both allow a degree of improvisation but they are different. Certainly, the utilization of a specific methodology does not preclude the trial and error associated with improvisation any more than does a literary or aesthetic method; it is just that the status and nature of error is different in each case. In many ways a methodology might be understood as the "straight line" that will eventually lead us to our goal by alerting us to the fact that we are always in danger of going astray. But methodologies nevertheless allow the possibility of error and can even encourage risk taking, but such improvisatory prowess, for all of its intellectual virtuosity, is performed secure in the knowledge that such a curvature of thought is always measured against the teleological straightness that the methodology provides.

We live and work within a network of "positions," of "camps," "schools," and "factions," all engaged in the carving up of the "smooth space" of thinking into the striated territories that allow both a sense of belonging as well as a mode of movement within or between such territories. By spawning methodological frameworks designed to guide the perplexed, restrain the thought-full, and provide the necessary foil for any negative improvisatory freedom, such "positions" keep us on the straight and narrow, away from the blindness and confusion of error. Yes, there is trial and error but with the emphasis very much on the trial rather than the error, that is to say a temporary, short-term, strictly limited, and delimited aberration that not only confirms but strengthens the horizons between one position and another and the perceived boundary between truth and error.

Not so method: a method of progressing has no need to attach itself to a "position." Indeed, a "position" already has its têlos secreted within it (that's what makes it a "position"), thus rendering the very notion of progress, so dear to the methodological mind-set, redundant. But turning that on its head, if method can happily do without an identifiable têlos (as it can), surely it too cannot legitimately utilize the notion of progress or progression either? True, unless, that is, one can conceive of a mode of progression that is nontêleological, one where progress in the act or activation of thinking and the production of work actually *depends upon* error and the failure to reach a goal. To be in error is not to be wrong; error is not the contrary of truth but a particular articulation of a *distance* from the truth. To err is to stray from the straight and narrow path, indeed from any path. Erring is drifting, a slipping away, a dis-traction that, while losing sight of the truth, nevertheless continues to "hear" it or "hearken" to it as a distant presence that in actuality requires error in order to maintain and protect this presence. Blanchot describes such erring as "research," an endless "turning" and returning that resists the desire to terminate the "fascination" of error in the rush for a terminal truth. He speaks of an "essential error":

> Error is an obstinacy without perseverance that, far from being a rigorously maintained affirmation, pursues itself by diverting the affirmation toward what has no firmness. Essential error is without relation to the true, which has no power over it. Truth would dispel error, were they to meet. But there is an error of sorts that ruins in advance all power of encounter. To err is probably this: to go outside the space of encounter.[33]

Recalling again Nietzsche's "strong will" that has the strength precisely *not* to will, and remembering too that the "will-to-truth" needs, perhaps, the greatest strength of all to resist its lure, erring does not just happen; it requires a method, a "mode of progressing" that in a sense resembles the production of detours or the creation of diversions and distractions. In this regard it is only by working *away* from the goal that the goal is kept in view, but as the obscured essence concealed by this work. If, for instance, the task is to remember Being or to remember that Being has been forgotten, then this task itself requires a method of forgetting, thus allowing the necessary work of concealment to hold this absent Being in place.

Smooth Space

It is perhaps for this reason that Deleuze, in speaking of the infinite detour and drift of "smooth space," introduces his notions of close-range hearing and short-term memory as part of his own construction of a method of thinking that breaks with the teleological. In fact, and in spite of the overarching question of Being that seems on the face of it to overdetermine his thought, Heidegger's actual method of thinking, the to-ing and fro-ing action on the page, more closely resembles the "smooth" nomadic movement described here by Deleuze:

> A painting is done at close range, even if it is seen from a distance. Similarly, it is said that composers do not hear: they have close-range hearing, whereas listeners hear from a distance. Even

writers write with short-term memory, whereas readers are assumed to be endowed with long-term memory. The first aspect
of the haptic, smooth space of close vision is that its orientations,
landmarks and linkages are in continuous variation; it operates
step by step.[34]

Where this resonates with Heidegger's method of thinking is that, in
spite of his avowed memorial task, the memory of Being is constantly
displaced by the close-up tactility of his relation with language, the turning and re-turning of words in "continuous variation" where each step
becomes a task in itself, a repeated re-origination where everything is
both the same and different, old and new. Although Deleuze is hardly
a Heideggerian, nevertheless the mark of Heidegger's thinking on what
might be described as the militant erraticism of Deleuze is often evident
where, as in the case of his distinction between the smooth and the striated, Being and being are both held together in this infinitely mobile
concatenation of têlos and detour, or, as Deleuze expresses it in his own
vocabulary, the "absolute" and the "local":

> The opposition between the striated and the smooth is not sim-
> ply that of the global and the local. For in one case, the global is
> still relative, whereas in the other the local is already absolute. . . .
> There exists a nomadic absolute, as a local integration moving
> from part to part and constituting smooth space in an infinite
> succession of linkages and changes in direction. It is an absolute
> that is one with becoming itself, with process. It is the absolute
> of passage.[35]

To repeat: Deleuze's nomad is our improvisor, and any concept of improvisation to be created by philosophy must both describe, embody, and
either suffer or celebrate what could be described, on the one hand, as
the existential "tragedy," or, on the other, as the nomadic joy of the improvisor who enacts before our eyes the predicament of preservation and
destruction experienced by all art. Deleuze instances Heidegger's invention of Being and his own invention of the ritornello as philosophical
concepts worthy of note. They are related to each other, to the smooth
and striated, and each in turn to improvisation. That is to say, both the
infinite hermeneutical transition from the phenomenology of the everyday to the ontology of essential Being and what Deleuze describes as
the territorialization of the ritornello[36] are constitutive of a space that
has an essential relation to improvisation in its formation, continuation,

and eventual destruction. Deleuze speaks of improvisation in terms of a world, but again he is not describing a space that is *there* but, on the contrary, one that is only *given* through the territorializing repetition of the ritornello. Strangely, this is one of the very rare occasions where Deleuze mentions improvisation:

> One launches forth, hazards an improvisation. But to improvise is to join with the World, or meld with it. One ventures from home on the thread of a tune. Along sonorous, gestural, motor lines that mark the customary path of a child and graft themselves onto or begin to bud "lines of drift" with different loops, knots, speeds, movements, gestures and sonorities.[37]

It would be difficult to imagine a better description of the improvisatory process than this, but that is not the point—we are not looking for descriptions but for a *concept* of improvisation. Certainly, one is not provided by any of the thinkers that have concerned us here, none of whom would have considered themselves improvisors—so much the pity. Nevertheless, there might be detected an emergent philosophical concept of improvisation rooted in the very practice of thinking itself. As said before, it is not so much *what* the philosopher is able to make his chosen words say so much as *when* a word is taken up and turned in the hand, in the hermeneutical light, and *when* it is necessary to forget it again for the sake of the movement of thought and the task of finding something else to remember. This should act as a reminder that any concept of improvisation worth considering must acknowledge the primary importance of *timing*, the decisive *now* so vigorously promoted by improvisors and yet so often confused with the ecstatic immediacy of "being in the moment," in a quasi-utopian aesthetic community of hyperaware communicators bound together by the common desire for an empathic dialogical fix unavailable elsewhere.

Timing

As already seen with the example of comedy, timing has less to do with introducing something into the moment, a decisive and substantial "call" demanding a "response" (laughter), and more to do with exposing the difference between the *there* and the *given*, something that is achieved by moving within the *there*, step by step from one moment to the next in a series of linkages that are suddenly broken by a detour that defamiliarizes the familiar. Heidegger often progresses in much the same way.

Thinking his way through the there-ness of the "they," the repeated interruption of the "everyday" and its naturalized continuities are intended to give us the opportunity to remember that Being has been forgotten, but not as a singular event demanding a singular response (despair perhaps, rather than laughter), but as the origination and re-origination of a work that at the decisive moment must also be interrupted before the creation of a *work* brings the labor of unconcealment/concealment to an end. These texts demonstrate an infinite agility that might be described as improvisatory in view of the fact that the timing necessary to keep the working of the work working (through the decisive interruption of the formation of a *work*) is not something that can be built into the work as part of its têleological structure. The moment of transition from the phenomenological to the hermeneutical to the ontological and back again, the tragic resolve of the existential subject to will at the decisive moment the next moment as if it would return eternally—these cannot be planned in advance of the work itself. They are, rather, the very essence of the performative principle and can only be determined by the contingency of that performance and the hyperawareness of the thinker, not to the dialogical demands of another subject but to the productive possibilities of the unfolding work that must be preserved up until the inevitable moment of destruction. Only in this way can the end of the improvisation signify another beginning, and the sense of an ending really signify the rhetorician's or ironist's uncanny awareness of the need for a change before the transformative power of art freezes into a *work*.

The current work can now end, not because it has reached a conclusion, a têlos that would return thinking back to the thoughtfulness which, in truth, it has been trying to escape throughout, but because a sense of what an ending might be is only now just beginning to emerge. Also in truth, and already mentioned in passing, this work is itself a work of improvisation throughout, a fact that is not worn as a badge of honor but suffered as a curse. In spite of the fact that most improvisors would have us believe that they have chosen improvisation, often in the face of the very real cultural advantages offered to those who inhabit the "straight" world, in most cases one suspects that the opposite is true: improvisation has chosen *them*: no choice. Certainly the (unintended and unplanned) presence of Heideggerian Being throughout these pages lends this curse a tragic intensity that is something of an embarrassment for the deeply ironic author that began these pages, but, interestingly, this merely demanded a more improvisatory approach to irony itself.

It should be said that the experience of improvising a book on improvisation did not feel very improvisatory at the time—writing half a page a day (max.) is hardly "being in the moment"—but if, as suggested, it is not a question of being "in the moment" but rather of willing the next moment as if it would eternally return as a future past, then the emphasis shifts to the will that can show strength and resolve by *not* willing. But for some improvisors this might sound rather too voluntaristic. It might not be a question of choosing not to will but of *not being able* to will, trapped between one faltering step and another, *not able* to find a link between one close-up, short-term memory and the next. Without a plan or formula such an apparent stalling does not destroy improvisation but, rather, introduces a delay into it that should remind us that, as a method of progressing, one might have to develop a degree of patience regarding the decisive moment to act. The temporality of Samuel Beckett's response to Georges Duthuit exemplifies this delay—improvisation in slow motion.

> D.—One moment. Are you suggesting that the painting of van Velde is inexpressive?
> B.—*(A fortnight later)* Yes.
> D.—You realize the absurdity of what you advance?
> B.—I hope I do.[38]

Clearly, thinking can take time, not in order to get things right (Beckett only hopes he is being absurd), but to ensure that the infinite detour of error and erring remains productive, which, in turn, means that the task of thinking is always outside of itself, outside of the moment, outside of the work. Throughout we have articulated this alterity through the Heideggerian separation of Being and being, for no other reason than that such a mode of thinking comes closest to the concept of improvisation we have been groping for, if not inventing. No doubt (and in all seriousness) improvisors could learn a great deal indeed by reading Heidegger and those who have been influenced by aspects of his thinking—Blanchot, Deleuze, Derrida, Levinas—not in order to root their practices in the dubious ideology of authenticity that has ebbed and flowed in his wake (and here Adorno is right) but, rather, as a way of breaking with the still hegemonic humanism that, by getting entangled in the intentionalities of the subject and the dialogical aesthetics of intersubjectivity, has failed to arrive at a concept of improvisation that could lift it out of the anecdotal.

Derrida the Improvisor

By problematizing such founding principles as freedom and play, and by introducing both an ontological and an ironic consciousness into the above discussion as a way of locating improvisation within the linguistic, rhetorical, and performative structures that are themselves in play at any one time, the real issue has been to arrive at a concept of improvisation that, if nothing else, would allow Derrida himself (as promised much earlier) to recognize his own improvisation. If this is achieved then perhaps the floodgates would open for all of those improvisors out there who are as yet unaware of the improvisatory nature of their own method of progressing. So, to bring these thoughts to a conclusion, here are Derrida's words again:

> It's not easy to improvise, it's the most difficult thing to do. Even when one improvises in front of a camera or a microphone, one ventriloquizes or leaves another to speak in one's place. The schemas and languages that are already there, there are already a great number of prescriptions that are prescribed in our memory and our culture. All the names are already preprogrammed. It's already the names that inhibit our ability to ever really improvise. One can't say whatever one wants; one is obliged, more or less, to reproduce the stereotypical discourse. And so I believe in improvisation, and I fight for improvisation, but with the belief that it is impossible. But there, where there is improvisation, I am not able to see myself, I am blind to myself. And it is what I will see, no, I won't see it, it is for others to see. The one who has improvised here, no I won't ever see him.[39]

Is improvisation "the most difficult thing to do"? The widespread fear of improvisation might lead one to think so and, as already noted, a great many of the books and manuals on improvisation are devoted, at least in part, to fear management and strategic guidance, but Derrida's problem is a different one. He is not afraid to improvise; he simply doubts its possibility. He wants to improvise, he *does* improvise, but at the same time there is a certain fraudulence that seems (perhaps surprisingly) to unsettle him, a sense in which improvisation requires a pure presence within a language and its performance that is unachievable within the "differancial" absence that he has devoted so much time to. Improvisation, for Derrida, requires an absolute self-presence that can only be articulated spontaneously in a language that allows the improvisor to speak for himself or herself and not for or through an-other—no ventriloquizing. But, of course, it is precisely the "prescriptions" of language that get in the way. Elsewhere he expands upon this failure:

What is important here is the improvisation—contrived like all so-called free association—well anyway, what is called improvisation. It is never absolute, it never has the purity of what one thinks one can require of a forced improvisation: the surprise of the person interrogated, the absolutely spontaneous, instantaneous, almost simultaneous response. A network of apparatuses and relays—and first of all language . . . —has to interrupt the impromptu, put it beside itself, set it aside from itself. A battery of anticipatory and delaying devices, of slowing-down procedures are already in place as one opens one's mouth . . . in order to protect from improvised exposition.[40]

So, one has to, one fails to improvise.[41]

Unlike Boulez and Berio, Derrida seems to think that it is cultural memory, the prescriptions of "preprogrammed" "names," that "inhibits our ability to improvise"; but is this true? Certainly he is right, "one can't say whatever one wants," but why is it necessary to tie improvisation to such a questionable notion of self-expression and linguistic/aesthetic singularity? The task of the improvisor is not to speak but to improvise; as we have tried to emphasize throughout, improvisation has little or nothing to do with communication and more to do with ensuring that the channels of communication are kept open and alive. Derrida has things the wrong way round: it is not the "battery of anticipatory and delaying devices" that will "protect" us from improvisation but, rather, improvisation that can and should protect us from *them*. In fact, what Derrida sees as the "impossibility" of improvisation brings us much closer to its essential nature once stripped of the humanistic and expressionistic cultural garb that clings to it. To recognize, as he does, that "where there is improvisation, I am not able to see myself" is not the end of improvisation but a crucial moment in the invention of a concept of improvisation that would, if nothing else, liberate it from the foibles and idiosyncrasies of individual practitioners and their self-legitimating discourses.

Standing or sitting in front of the microphone or camera, bemoaning the fact that he can't improvise or doesn't "particularly like improvising, except in very favourable conditions,"[42] Derrida, perhaps disingenuously, loses sight of the extraordinary vein of improvisation that runs from Nietzsche through Heidegger into his own writing. In each case it is not a question of speaking from out of a pure spontaneity but, rather, of putting that "beside itself," setting it aside in order for the task of listening and thinking to commence. As with Heidegger's "hearkening," Derrida's strategy of reading is to allow writing to speak for itself, in all of its richness, playfulness, contingency, and, on occasion, anarchy. To lose oneself—one's self—in this incessant and dis-tracted movement, where everything that is *there* (in Derrida's case the familiar texts of a philosophical tradition) can forever be *given* again and afresh, this is not the death of improvisation but its true beginning. A beginning that the improvisor is, by placing him or herself *outside* of the moment, responsible for beginning again, and again . . . eternally.

Notes

CHAPTER ONE

The chapter epigraphs are from Johnstone, *Impro: Improvisation and the Theatre*, 116; and Benjamin, "On the Concept of History," 392.

1. Sorrell, "Improvisation," 776.

2. For example, *Scrapheap Challenge* in the United Kingdom and *Junkyard Wars* in the United States.

3. Adorno, *Philosophy of Modern Music*, 33.

4. Ibid., 36–37.

5. Luhmann, *Art as a Social System*, 32.

6. Heidegger, "The Origin of the Work of Art," 52.

7. Ibid., 17.

8. Hegel, *Aesthetics, Vol. 1*, 31. Or as the improvisor Eddie Prevost (perhaps with less philosophical perspicacity) expresses it: "Improvisation is both an act and art of self-definition. . . . A free improvisation is a vehicle for self-expression. Self-definition and assertion of self are only possible in contrast to other selves. Other models of 'self' may need to be reviewed. Collective improvisation is a medium for this examination." See Prevost, *No Sound Is Innocent*, 67–71.

9. Heidegger, "The Origin of the Work of Art," 66.

10. Ibid., 67.

11. Ibid., 68.

12. Ibid., 67.

13. Heidegger, *Being and Time*, 162–63.

> This phenomenon, which is none too happily
> designated as "*empathy*," is then supposed to

provide the first ontological bridge from one's own subject, which is given proximally as alone, to the other subject, which is proximally quite closed off. . . . Of course it is indisputable that a lively mutual acquaintanceship on the basis of Being-with often depends upon how far one's own Dasein has understood itself at the time, but this means that it depends only upon how far one's essential Being with Others has made itself transparent and has not disguised itself. And that is possible only if Dasein, as Being-in-the-world, already is with Others. "Empathy" does not first constitute Being-with; only on the basis of Being-with does "empathy" become possible: it gets its motivation from *the unsociability* of the dominant modes of Being-with. (162, last emphasis mine)

14. Heidegger, "The Origin of the Work of Art," 68.
15. Benjamin, "On the Concept of History," 392.
16. Johnstone, *Impro: Improvisation and the Theatre,* 116.
17. Benjamin, "The Paris of the Second Empire in Baudelaire," 48.

CHAPTER TWO
The chapter epigraph is from Smith, "Improvisation as a Form of Cultural Creation."
1. Anthony Braxton, quoted in Dean, *New Structures in Jazz and Improvised Music since 1960,* 133.
2. See, for example, Monson, "Oh Freedom: George Russell, John Coltrane, and Modal Jazz," which begins as follows: "Improvisation has often been taken as a metaphor for freedom both musical and social, especially in jazz. The image of improvisation as freedom became especially pronounced in the jazz world of the 1960s when the free jazz of Ornette Coleman, Cecil Taylor, Albert Ayler, and others catalyzed aesthetic and political debates within the jazz community and music industry. The political contexts of the civil rights movement in the U.S. and the independence movements on the African continent surely informed the accelerated conflation of musical and political freedom" (149).
3. Berlin, *Two Concepts of Liberty,* 56.
4. Ibid., 16.
5. Ibid., 12.
6. Ibid., 16.
7. Dean, *New Structures in Jazz and Improvised Music since 1960,* 133.
8. Marcuse, *Eros and Civilisation,* 136.
9. Kant, *Critique of Judgement,* 58.
10. Quoted in Toop, *Haunted Weather,* 187.
11. Toop, "Communality or Virtual Sculpture."
12. For an extended discussion of this, see my "Means without End."
13. Bernstein, *The Fate of Art,* chap. 1.
14. Kant, *Critique of Judgement,* 27–28.
15. Ibid., 82–83.

16. Foster, "Taken by Surprise," 7.

17. Bernstein, *The Fate of Art*, 60–61.

18. Ibid., 95.

19. Ibid., 124.

20. Kant, *Critique of Judgement*, 181, quoted in Bernstein, *The Fate of Art*, 94.

21. Bernstein, *The Fate of Art*, 95.

22. Ibid.

23. Ibid., 63.

24. Ibid., 65.

25. Caygill, "Benjamin, Heidegger and the Destruction of Tradition," 21.

26. Ibid., 17.

27. Ibid., 20.

28. Ibid., 29.

29. Ricoeur, *Time and Narrative, Vol. 1*, 33.

30. Heidegger, *Kant and the Problem of Metaphysics*, 105.

31. This is part of an unpublished passage quoted in the film *Derrida*, directed by Kirby Dick and Amy Ziering Kofman (Jane Doe Films, 2002).

32. Prevost, *No Sound Is Innocent*, 60 (emphases added).

33. Bailey, *Improvisation*, 35.

34. Foster, "Taken by Surprise," 4.

35. Richter, "Notes," 1047.

36. Johnstone, *Impro for Storytellers*, 34–36.

37. Kant, *Critique of Judgement*, 152.

38. Ibid., 153.

39. Ibid., 152–53.

40. Ibid., 153.

41. Bailey, *Improvisation*, 83.

42. Johnstone, *Impro for Storytellers*, 130.

43. Heidegger, *Being and Time*, 157ff.

44. Johnstone, *Impro for Storytellers*, 19.

45. Johnstone, *Impro: Improvisation and the Theatre*, 13 (emphasis added).

46. Kant, *Critique of Judgement*, 84 (emphasis added).

47. Ibid., 140 (emphasis added).

48. Ibid., 137.

49. Caygill, "Benjamin, Heidegger, and the Destruction of Tradition," 20.

50. Kierkegaard, *Training in Christianity*, 152–53.

51. See Bryson, *Vision and Painting*.

52. Haring, "Untitled Statement (1984)," 370.

53. Kant, *Critique of Judgement*, 137:

> Hence it is that a youthful poet refuses to allow himself to be dissuaded from the conviction that his poem is beautiful, either by the judgement of the public or his friends. And even if he lends them an ear, he does so, not because he has now come to a different judgement, but because, though the whole public, at least as far as his work is concerned, should have a false

taste, he still, in his desire for recognition, finds good reason to accommodate himself to the popular error (against his own judgement). It is *only in aftertime*, when his judgement has been sharpened by exercise, that of his own free will and accord he deserts his former judgements.

54. Albright and Gere, *Taken by Surprise*, xv.

55. Johnstone, *Impro: Improvisation and the Theatre*, 11.

56. Levinas, "Reality and Its Shadow," 4.

57. Watson, *Derek Bailey and the Story of Free Improvisation*, 220.

58. Quoted in ibid., 221.

59. Hill, "Stepping, Stealing, Sharing, and Daring," 90 (first and last emphases added).

60. Blanchot, *The Infinite Conversation*, 108.

61. Rosenzweig, *The Star of Redemption*, 309.

62. See Schiller, *On the Aesthetic Education of Man*.

63. Rosenzweig, *Star of Redemption*, 309.

64. Ibid., 81.

65. Ibid., 150.

66. Ibid., 190.

67. Ibid., 148.

68. Ibid., 77.

69. Ibid.

70. Watson, *Derek Bailey and the Story of Free Improvisation*, 289.

71. Ibid., 294.

72. Johnstone, *Impro for Storytellers*, 89.

73. Ibid., 94.

74. Ibid., 66–67.

75. Ibid., 339.

76. Ibid., 340.

77. Ibid., 23.

78. Benjamin, *Origin of German Tragic Drama*, 45.

79. Caygill, *Walter Benjamin*, 58.

80. Benjamin, *Origin of German Tragic Drama*, 45.

81. Heidegger, "The Origin of the Work of Art," 76.

82. Clarke, "Improvisation, Cognition and Education," 799.

83. Ibid., 800.

84. Johnstone, *Impro: Improvisation and the Theatre*, 45.

85. Prevost, *No Sound Is Innocent*, 67.

86. Johnstone, *Impro: Improvisation and the Theatre*, 37.

87. Prevost, *No Sound Is Innocent*, 67.

88. Heidegger, *Being and Time*, 162.

89. Ibid. (emphases added).

90. Caygill, "Benjamin, Heidegger, and the Destruction of Tradition," 20.

91. Stewart Lee, review of *Bruise with Derek Bailey* (CD), *Sunday Times*, April 23, 2006, Arts and Entertainment section.

92. Luhmann, *Art as a Social System*, 309.
93. Kierkegaard, *Fear and Trembling*, 118.
94. De Man, *Blindness and Insight*, 178–79.
95. Caygill, "Benjamin, Heidegger, and the Destruction of Tradition," 17.

CHAPTER THREE

The chapter epigraphs are from Tara Duggan, "Improvisation Saves the Day for Pasta Dish," *San Francisco Chronicle*, July 28, 2004, http://www.sfgate.com/cgi-bin/article.cgi?f=/c/a/2004/07/28/FDGMF7SVEJ1.DTL&hw=improvisation&sn =001&sc=1000; and Seed, *The Top Hundred Pasta Sauces*.

On the subject of religion, consider the following from the Catholics United for Faith Web site: "The catechist must reject improvisation as 'equally danger-ous' and the cause of 'confusion' and the 'destruction of unity.' " http://www.cuf .org/faithfacts. A warning for all pasta-loving Catholic improvisors!

1. Johnstone, *Impro for Storytellers*, 25.
2. See http://ideasinfood.typepad.com/ideas_in_food/the_art_of_improvisation/, where the influence of Patricia Ryan Madson's book *Improv Wisdom* (itself heavily indebted to Keith Johnstone) is acknowledged and cited with enthusiasm.
3. Quoted in Wollheim, "A Bed of Leaves."
4. Adorno, *Prisms*, 31.
5. Ibid., 32.
6. Ibid., 20.
7. See Althusser, "Ideology and Ideological State Apparatus."
8. Adorno, "On Popular Music," 445 (emphasis added).
9. Cage, *For the Birds*, 36.
10. Adorno, "Farewell to Jazz," 498.
11. Adorno, *Philosophy of Modern Music*, 154–55.
12. Ibid., 75–77.
13. Adorno, *In Search of Wagner*, 32–33.
14. Ibid., 31.
15. Nietzsche, *The Gay Science*, 324.
16. Boulez, *Conversations with Célestin Deliège*, 115.
17. Bailey, *Improvisation*, 100.
18. Boulez, *Conversations with Célestin Deliège*, 114.
19. Berio, *Two Interviews*, 83.
20. Boulez, *Conversations with Célestin Deliège*, 114.
21. Adorno, *Prisms*, 130.
22. Ibid., 128.
23. Ibid., 123.
24. Adorno, *Aesthetic Theory*, 163.
25. Ibid., 163–64.
26. Benjamin, "On the Mimetic Faculty," 721.
27. Ibid.
28. Ibid., 720 (translation modified).
29. Adorno, *Aesthetic Theory*, 80.

30. Jay, "Mimesis and Mimetology," 32.

31. Adorno, *Aesthetic Theory*, 455.

32. Benjamin, "What Is the Epic Theatre? (II)," 304.

33. Derrida, *Writing and Difference*, 237.

34. Adorno, *Aesthetic Theory*, 118–19.

35. Ibid., 42. Also: "The phenomenon of fireworks can be viewed as a proto-type of art. Since it is evanescent, and since it is made for simple entertainment, it has only received scant attention by aesthetics" (120).

36. Artaud, "The Theatre of Cruelty," 83–84.

37. Ibid., 85.

38. Quoted in Stein, *Richard Wagner and the Synthesis of the Arts*, 167.

39. Adorno, *Aesthetic Theory*, 163.

40. Artaud, *Collected Works, Vol. 4*, 87.

41. Ibid., 182.

42. Benjamin, *Selected Writings, Vol. 4*, 307.

43. Brecht, *Mother Courage and Her Children*, 144.

44. Benjamin, *Selected Writings, Vol. 4*, 307.

45. Derrida, *Points . . .* , 49.

46. Boulez, *Conversations*, 115.

47. Johnstone, *Impro: Improvisation and the Theatre*, 87.

48. Schlegel, "Critical Fragment, No. 108," 43.

49. Benjamin, "On the Mimetic Faculty," 720–21.

50. Gadamer, *Truth and Method*, 103–110.

51. http://www.ayeconference.com/wiki/scribble.cgi?read=InnovationAnd Improvisation.

52. Ibid. Contribution by Steve Smith.

53. Schlegel, "Ideas, No. 69," 56.

54. De Man, *Blindness and Insight*, 178–79.

55. Schlegel, "Athenäum Fragment, No. 116," 31–32.

56. Bailey, *Improvisation*, 115.

57. Ibid., 114.

58. Ibid., 115.

59. See Adorno, "Difficulties," 658.

60. Martin Davidson, "A New Musical Dictionary," http://www.emanemdisc .com/addenda/newmudic.html.

61. Marks, "Against Improvisation," 135.

62. Luhmann, *Art as a Social System*, 69–70.

63. Marks, "Against Improvisation," 135.

64. Foster, "Taken by Surprise," 4.

65. Ibid.66.67.68.

CHAPTER FOUR

The chapter epigraphs are from Nietzsche, "The Uses and Disadvantages of History for Life," 76; and Heidegger, *Nietzsche, Vols. 1 and 2*, 2:135 (Heidegger's emphasis).

1. Heidegger, "Letter on Humanism," 214.

2. Levinas, *Ethics and Infinity*, 48–49.

3. Heidegger, *Being and Time*, 343.

4. Ibid., 164.

5. Heidegger, "On the Essence of Truth," 136 (first and third emphases mine).

6. Heidegger, *Being and Time*, 320.

7. Ibid., 320–21.

8. Ibid., 206.

9. Rosenzweig, *The Star of Redemption*, 309.

10. Heidegger, *Being and Time*, 318 (Heidegger's emphasis).

11. Ibid., 320 (Heidegger's emphases).

12. Nietzsche, *Thus Spoke Zarathustra*, 286.

13. Kierkegaard, *The Concept of Dread*, 55.

14. Baudelaire, "Of the Essence of Laughter," 148.

15. Ibid., 161.

16. Ibid., 148.

17. Adorno and Horkheimer, *Dialectic of Enlightenment*, 141.

18. Levinas, *Ethics and Infinity*, 48–49.

19. Ibid., 52.

20. Levinas, *Difficult Freedom*, 292.

21. Visker, *Truth and Singularity*, 267: "There can be no question about it, the *il y a* is ethicized, functionalized for and within ethics. Its nonsense has become the carrier of a Sense that comes before all opposition of sense and nonsense."

22. Levinas, "The Old and the New," 133.

23. Ibid., 134.

24. Heidegger, *Nietzsche, Vol. 2* (1984); see, for example, 164.

25. Heidegger, *Kant and the Problem of Metaphysics*, 105.

26. Nietzsche, *Untimely Meditations*, 76.

27. Heidegger, *Nietzsche, Vol. 2*, 135–36 (Heidegger's emphasis).

28. Deleuze, *Difference and Repetition*, 54.

29. Ibid., 41.

30. Heidegger, *Nietzsche, Vol. 2*, 202.

31. Deleuze, *Difference and Repetition*, 222.

32. Kierkegaard, *Repetition*, 49.

33. See, for example, Nietzsche, *Twilight of the Idols*, 511.

34. Safranski, *Nietzsche*, 21. Just for reference, "Lust was placed two rungs lower."

35. Derrida, *The Ear of the Other*.

36. See Kant, *Critique of Judgement*, 168: "*Genius* is the innate mental aptitude *through which* nature gives the rule to art."

37. Ibid.

38. Ibid., 170–71.

39. Nietzsche, *Untimely Meditations*, 63: "[W]e have observed the animal, which is quite unhistorical, and dwells within a horizon reduced almost to a point, and yet lives in a certain degree of happiness."

40. Bailey, *Improvisation*, 18.

41. *Derrida*, directed by Kirby Dick and Amy Ziering Kofman (Jane Doe Films, 2002).

CONCLUSION

The chapter epigraph is from *Derrida* (Jane Doe Films, 2002).

1. Deleuze, *Two Regimes of Madness*, 313.
2. Ibid., 377.
3. Ibid., 381.
4. Ibid., 380.
5. Ibid.
6. Bailey, *Improvisation*, x.
7. Blanchot, *The Infinite Conversation*, 8.
8. Ibid., 4. Other "dissidents" include Blaise Pascal, Benedict de Spinoza, Kierkegaard, Nietzsche (and, needless to say, Blanchot himself).
9. Ibid., 3–4.
10. Descartes, "Discourse on Method," 8–9 (my emphasis).
11. Kant, *Critique of Judgement*, 182.
12. Deleuze, "Nomad Thought," 142.
13. Merleau-Ponty, *Phenomenology of Perception*, 180 (emphases added).
14. Ibid., 178.
15. Safranski, *Martin Heidegger*, 100.
16. Heidegger, *Elucidations of Holderlin's Poetry*, 222.
17. Heidegger, "What Calls for Thinking?" 365.
18. Ibid., 358.
19. Ibid., 346 (Heidegger's emphasis).
20. Paul Ricoeur, *Hermeneutics and the Human Sciences*, 101 (Ricoeur's emphasis).
21. Heidegger, *Being and Time*, 30.
22. Ibid., 27–31.
23. Schleiermacher, "Foundations," 82–83.
24. Ibid., 83.
25. Heidegger, "What Calls for Thinking?" 365.
26. Gadamer, *Truth and Method*, 103.
27. Ibid., 105.
28. Descartes, "Discourse on Method," 20.
29. Ibid., 7.
30. Ibid. (emphasis added).
31. Ibid., 25: "In this I would imitate travellers lost in a wood; they must not wander about now turning to this side, now to that, and still less must they stop in one place; they must keep walking as straight as they can in one direction, and not change course for slight reasons."
32. Blanchot, *The Space of Literature*, 82.
33. Ibid., 27.
34. Deleuze, *A Thousand Plateaus*, 494.
35. Ibid.

36. Ibid., 311.
37. Ibid., 311–12.
38. Beckett, "Three Dialogues," 143.
39. *Derrida* (Jane Doe Films, 2002).
40. Derrida, *Points . . .* , 49.
41. Ibid., 51.
42. Ibid., 197.

Bibliography

Adorno, Theodor. *Aesthetic Theory*. Translated by C. Lenhardt. London: Routledge and Kegan Paul, 1984.

———. "Difficulties." Translated by Susan Gillespie. In *Essays on Music*, edited by Richard Leppert. Berkeley: University of California Press, 2002.

———. "Farewell to Jazz." Translated by Susan Gillespie. In *Essays on Music*, edited by Richard Leppert. Berkeley: University of California Press, 2002.

———. *In Search of Wagner*. Translated by Rodney Livingstone. London: Verso, 1991.

———. "On Popular Music." In *Essays on Music*, edited by Richard Leppert. Berkeley: University of California Press, 2002.

———. *Philosophy of Modern Music*. Translated by Anne Mitchell and Wesley Bloomster. London: Sheed and Ward, 1973.

———. *Prisms*. Translated by Samuel and Shierry Weber. London: Neville Spearman, 1967.

Adorno, Theodor, and Max Horkheimer. *Dialectic of Enlightenment*. Translated by John Cumming. New York: Herder and Herder, 1972.

Albright, Ann Cooper, and David Gere, eds. *Taken by Surprise: A Dance Improvisation Reader*. Middletown, Conn.: Wesleyan University Press, 2003.

Althusser, Louis. "Ideology and Ideological State Apparatus." In *Lenin and Philosophy*, translated by Ben Brewster. New York: NYU Press, 2002.

Artaud, Antonin. *Collected Works, Vol. 4*, translated by Victor Corti. London: Calder and Boyers, 1974.

———. "The Theatre of Cruelty." In *Collected Works, Vol. 4*, translated by Victor Corti. London: Calder and Boyers, 1974.

Bailey, Derek. *Improvisation: Its Nature and Practice in Music*. London: British Library Sound Archive, 1992.

Baudelaire, Charles. "Of the Essence of Laughter, and Generally of the Comic in the Plastic Arts." In *Baudelaire: Selected Writings on Art and Artists*, translated by P. E. Charvet. Harmondsworth, U.K.: Penguin Books, 1972.

Beckett, Samuel. "Three Dialogues." In *Disjecta*: *Miscellaneous Writings and a Dramatic Fragment*. London: John Calder, 1983.

Benjamin, Walter. "On the Concept of History." Translated by Harry Zohn. In *Walter Benjamin: Selected Writings, Vol. 4*, edited by Howard Eiland and Michael W. Jennings. Cambridge: Harvard University Press, 2003.

———. "On the Mimetic Faculty." Translated by Edmund Jephcott. In *Walter Benjamin: Selected Writings, Vol. 2*, edited by Michael W. Jennings, Howard Eiland, and Gary Smith. Cambridge: Harvard University Press, 1999.

———. *The Origin of German Tragic Drama*. Translated by John Osborne. London: Verso, 1985.

———. "The Paris of the Second Empire in Baudelaire." Translated by Harry Zohn. In *Walter Benjamin: Selected Writings, Vol. 4*, edited by Howard Eiland and Michael W. Jennings. Cambridge: Harvard University Press, 2003.

———. *Walter Benjamin: Selected Writings, Vol. 2*. Translated by Rodney Livingstone and others. Edited by Michael W. Jennings, Howard Eiland, and Gary Smith. Cambridge: Harvard University Press, 1999.

———. *Walter Benjamin: Selected Writings, Vol. 4*. Translated by Edmund Jephcott and others. Edited by Howard Eiland and Michael W. Jennings. Cambridge: Harvard University Press, 2003.

———. "What Is the Epic Theatre? (II)." Translated by Harry Zohn. In *Walter Benjamin: Selected Writings, Vol. 4*, edited by Howard Eiland and Michael W. Jennings. Cambridge: Harvard University Press, 2003.

Berio, Luciano. *Two Interviews: with Rossana Dalmonte and Bálint András Varga*. Translated by David Osmond-Smith. New York: Marion Boyers, 1985.

Berlin, Isaiah. *Two Concepts of Liberty*. Oxford: Clarendon Press, 1958.

Bernstein, J. M. *The Fate of Art: Aesthetic Alienation from Kant to Derrida and Adorno*. Cambridge: Polity Press, 1992.

Blanchot, Maurice. *The Infinite Conversation*. Translated by Susan Hanson. Minneapolis: University of Minnesota Press, 1993.

———. *The Space of Literature*. Translated by Ann Smock. Lincoln: University of Nebraska Press, 1982.

Boulez, Pierre. *Conversations with Célestin Deliège*. London: Eulenburg Books, 1976.

Brecht, Bertolt. *Mother Courage and Her Children*. Translated by John Willett. London: Methuen, 1980.

Bryson, Norman. *Vision and Painting: The Logic of the Gaze*. London: Macmillan, 1983.

Cage, John. *For the Birds*. Boston: Marion Boyers, 1981.

Caygill, Howard. "Benjamin, Heidegger, and the Destruction of Tradition." In *Walter Benjamin's Philosophy: Destruction and Experience*, edited by Andrew Benjamin and Peter Osborne. London: Routledge, 1994.

———. *Walter Benjamin: The Colour of Experience*. London: Routledge, 1998.

Clarke, Eric F. "Improvisation, Cognition and Education." In *Companion to Contemporary Musical Thought, Vol. 2*, edited by John Paynter, Tim Howell, Richard Orton, and Peter Seymour. London: Routledge, 1992.

Dean, Roger T. *New Structures in Jazz and Improvised Music since 1960*. Milton Keynes: Open University Press, 1992.

Deleuze, Gilles. *Difference and Repetition*. Translated by Paul Patton. London: Athlone Press, 1994.

———. "Nomad Thought." In *The New Nietzsche: Contemporary Styles of Interpretation*, edited by David Allison. Cambridge: MIT Press, 1985.

———. *A Thousand Plateaus*. Translated by Brian Massumi. London: Athlone Press, 1987.

———. *Two Regimes of Madness: Texts and Interviews 1975–1995*. Translated by Ames Hodges and Mike Taormina. Cambridge: Semiotext(e), MIT Press, 2006.

De Man, Paul. *Blindness and Insight: Essays in the Rhetoric of Contemporary Criticism*. Minneapolis: University of Minnesota Press, 1983.

Derrida, Jacques. *The Ear of the Other*. Translated by Peggy Kamuf. Lincoln: University of Nebraska Press, 1988.

———. *Points . . . : Interviews, 1974–1994*. Translated by Peggy Kamuf and Elizabeth Weber. Stanford: Stanford University Press, 1995.

———. *Writing and Difference*. Translated by Alan Bass. London: Routledge and Kegan Paul, 1978.

Descartes, René. "Discourse on Method." In *Philosophical Writings*, translated by E. Anscombe and P. T. Geach. London: Nelson, 1970.

Foster, Susan Leigh. "Taken by Surprise: Improvisation in Dance and Mind." In *Taken by Surprise: A Dance Improvisation Reader*, edited by Ann Cooper Albright and David Gere. Middletown, Conn.: Wesleyan University Press, 2003.

Gadamer, Hans-Georg. *Truth and Method*. 2d rev. ed. Translated by Joel Weinsheimer and Donald G. Marshall. London: Sheed and Ward, 1989.

Haring, Keith. "Untitled Statement (1984)." In *Theories and Documents of Contemporary Art: A Sourcebook of Artists' Writings*, edited by Kristine Stiles and Peter Selz. Berkeley: University of California Press: 1996.

Hegel, G. W. F. *Aesthetics, Vol. 1*. Translated by T. M. Knox. Oxford: Oxford University Press, 1975.

Heidegger, Martin. *Being and Time*. Translated by John Macquarrie and Edward Robinson. Oxford: Basil Blackwell, 1962.

———. *Elucidations of Holderlin's Poetry*. Translated by Keith Hoeller. New York: Humanity Books, 2000.

———. *Kant and the Problem of Metaphysics*. Translated by Richard Taft. Indianapolis: Indiana University Press, 1990.

————. "Letter on Humanism." Translated by Frank Capuzzi. In *Martin Heidegger: Basic Writings*, edited by David Farrell Krell. New York: Harper and Row, 1977.

————. *Nietzsche, Vols. 1 and 2.* Translated by David Farrell Krell. San Francisco: Harper Collins, 1991.

————. "On the Essence of Truth." Translated by John Sallis. In *Martin Heidegger: Basic Writings*, edited by David Farrell Krell. New York: Harper and Row, 1977.

————. "The Origin of the Work of Art." In *Poetry, Language, Thought*, translated by Albert Hofstadter. New York: Harper and Row, 1971.

————. "What Calls for Thinking?" Translated by Fred Wieck and J. Glenn Gray. In *Martin Heidegger: Basic Writings*, edited by David Farrell Krell. New York: Harper and Row, 1977.

Hill, Constance Valis. "Stepping, Stealing, Sharing, and Daring: Improvisation and the Tap Dance Challenge." In *Taken by Surprise: A Dance Improvisation Reader*, edited by Ann Cooper Albright and David Gere. Middletown: Wesleyan University Press, 2003.

Jay, Martin. "Mimesis and Mimetology: Adorno and Lacoue-Labarthe." In *The Semblance of Subjectivity: Essays in Adorno's Aesthetic Theory*, edited by Tom Huhn and Lambert Zuidervaart. Cambridge: MIT Press, 1997.

Johnstone, Keith. *Impro for Storytellers.* New York: Routledge, 1999.

————. *Impro: Improvisation and the Theatre.* London: Faber and Faber, 1979.

Kant, Immanuel. *The Critique of Judgement.* Translated by James Creed Meredith. Oxford: Clarendon Press, 1952.

Kierkegaard, Søren. *The Concept of Dread.* Translated by Walter Lowrie. Princeton: Princeton University Press, 1946.

————. *Fear and Trembling.* Translated by Howard and Edna Hong. Princeton: Princeton University Press, 1983.

————. *Repetition.* Translated by Howard and Edna Hong. Princeton: Princeton University Press, 1983.

————. *Training in Christianity.* Translated by Walter Lowrie. Princeton: Princeton University Press, 1941.

Levinas, Emmanuel. *Difficult Freedom: Essays on Judaism.* Translated by Sean Hand. London: Athlone Press, 1990.

————. *Ethics and Infinity: Conversations with Philippe Nemo.* Translated by Richard Cohen. Pittsburgh, Pa.: Duquesne University Press, 1985.

————. "The Old and the New." In *Time and the Other*, translated by Richard Cohen. Pittsburgh, Pa.: Duquesne University Press, 1987.

————. "Reality and Its Shadow." In *Collected Philosophical Papers*, translated by Alphonso Lingis. Dordrecht: Martinus Nijhoff Publishers, 1987.

Luhmann, Niklas. *Art as a Social System.* Translated by Eva Knodt. Stanford: Stanford University Press, 2000.

Mane, Erica de. *Pasta Improvvisata: How to Improvise in Classic Italian Style.* New York: Scribner's, 1999.

Marcuse, Herbert. *Eros and Civilisation.* London: Sphere Books, 1969.

Marks, Victoria. "Against Improvisation: A Postmodernist Makes the Case for Choreography." In *Taken by Surprise: A Dance Improvisation Reader*, edited by Ann Cooper Albright and David Gere. Middletown, Conn.: Wesleyan University Press, 2003.

Merleau-Ponty, Maurice. *Phenomenology of Perception*. Translated by Colin Smith. London: Routledge, 1962.

Monson, Ingrid. "Oh Freedom: George Russell, John Coltrane, and Modal Jazz." In *In the Course of Performance: Studies in the World of Musical Improvisation*, edited by Bruno Nettl and Melinda Russell. Chicago: University of Chicago Press, 1998.

Nietzsche, Friedrich. *The Future of Our Educational Institutions*. Translated by J. M. Kennedy. Edinburgh: T. N. Foulis, 1909.

———. *The Gay Science*. Translated by Walter Kaufmann. New York: Vintage, 1974.

———. "The Uses and Disadvantages of History for Life." In *Untimely Meditations*, translated by R. J. Hollingdale. Cambridge: Cambridge University Press, 1983.

———. *Thus Spoke Zarathustra*. In *The Portable Nietzsche*, translated by Walter Kaufmann. New York: Viking Press, 1954.

———. *Twilight of the Idols*. In *The Portable Nietzsche*, translated by Walter Kaufmann. New York: Princeton University Press, 1954.

Peters, Gary. "Means without End: Production, Reception, and Teaching in Kant's Aesthetics." *Journal of Aesthetic Education* 38, no. 1 (Spring 2004).

Prevost, Eddie. *No Sound Is Innocent*. Harlow: Copula, 1995.

Richter, Gerhard. "Notes." In *Art in Theory: 1900–1990*, edited by Charles Harrison and Paul Wood. Oxford: Blackwell, 1992.

Ricoeur, Paul. *Hermeneutics and the Human Sciences*. Translated by John Thompson. Cambridge: Cambridge University Press, 1981.

———. *Time and Narrative, Vol. 1*. Translated by Kathleen McLaughlin and David Pellauer. Chicago: University of Chicago Press, 1984.

Rosenzweig, Franz. *The Star of Redemption*. Translated by William Hallo. New York: Holt, Rinehart and Winston, 1971.

Safranski, Rudiger. *Martin Heidegger: Between Good and Evil*. Translated by Oswald Osers. Cambridge: Harvard University Press, 1999.

———. *Nietzsche: A Philosophical Biography*. Translated by Shelley Frisch. London: Granta Books, 2002.

Schiller, Friedrich. *On the Aesthetic Education of Man*. Translated by Elizabeth Wilkinson and L. A. Willoughby. Oxford: Oxford University Press, 1982.

Schlegel, Friedrich. "Athenäum Fragment, No. 116." In *Lucinde and the Fragments*, translated by Peter Firchow. Minneapolis: University of Minnesota Press, 1971.

———. "Critical Fragment, No. 108." In *German Aesthetic and Literary Criticism: The Romantic Ironists and Goethe*, edited by Kathleen Wheeler. Cambridge: Cambridge University Press, 1984.

———. "Ideas, No. 69." In *German Aesthetic and Literary Criticism*, edited by Kathleen Wheeler. Cambridge: Cambridge University Press, 1984.

Schleiermacher, Friedrich. "Foundations: General Theory and Art of Interpretation." Translated by J. Duke and J. Forstman. In *The Hermeneutics Reader*, edited by Kurt Mueller-Vollmer. Oxford: Basil Blackwell, 1985.

Smith, LaDonna. "Improvisation as a Form of Cultural Creation." *The Improvisor: The International Journal on Free Improvisation*, http://www.the-improvisor.com/ladprop1.html.

———. "Improvisation as Prayer . . ." http://www.the-improvisor.com/web%20ARTICLES/Improvisation_as_Prayer.htm.

Sorrell, Neil. "Improvisation." In *Companion to Contemporary Musical Thought, Vol. 2*, edited by John Paynter, Tim Howell, Richard Orton, and Peter Seymour. London: Routledge, 1992.

Stein, Jack M. *Richard Wagner and the Synthesis of the Arts*. Westport: Greenwood Press, 1973.

Toop, David. "Communality or Virtual Sculpture." Paper presented at a conference on "The Place of Improvisation and the Improvisation of Place," University of the West of England, July 2005.

———. *Haunted Weather: Music, Silence and Memory*. London: Serpent's Tail, 2004.

Vaihinger, Hans. *The Philosophy of "As If": A System of the Theoretical, Practical and Religious Fictions of Mankind*. London: Routledge, 1984.

Visker, Rudi. *Truth and Singularity: Taking Foucault into Phenomenology*. Dordrecht: Kluwer Academic, 1999.

Watson, Ben. *Derek Bailey and the Story of Free Improvisation*. London: Verso, 2004.

Wheeler, Kathleen, ed. *German Aesthetic and Literary Criticism: The Romantic Ironists and Goethe*. Cambridge: Cambridge University Press, 1984.

Wollheim, Richard. "A Bed of Leaves." *London Review of Books* 25, no. 23 (2003).

Index